PARADOXES OF EUROPEAN FOREIGN POLICY

Paradoxes of European Foreign Policy

Edited by

Jan Zielonka
*European University Institute,
Florence, Italy*

KLUWER LAW INTERNATIONAL
THE HAGUE / LONDON / BOSTON

A C.I.P Catalogue record for this book is available from the Library of Congress.

ISBN 90-411-0571-9

Published by Kluwer Law International,
P.O. Box 85889, 2508 CN The Hague, The Netherlands

Sold and distributed in North, Central and South America
by Kluwer Law International,
675 Massachusetts Avenue, Cambridge, MA 02139, USA

In all other countries, sold and distributed
by Kluwer Law International, Distribution Centre
P.O. Box 322, 3300 AH Dordrecht, The Netherlands

Kluwer Law International incorporates the publishing programmes of
Graham & Trotman Ltd, Kluwer Law and Taxation Publishers,
and Martinus Nijhoff Publishers.

Printed on acid-free paper

All Rights Reserved
© 1998 Kluwer Law International
No part of the material protected by this copyright notice may be reproduced or
utilized in any form or by any means, electronic or mechanical,
including photocopying, recording, or by any information storage and
retrieval system, without written permission from
the copyright owner.

Printed and bound in Great Britain by
CPI Antony Rowe, Chippenham and Eastbourne

Table of Contents

List of Abbreviations   vii

Preface
Yves Mény   ix

Introduction
Constraints, Opportunities and Choices in European Foreign Policy
Jan Zielonka   1

Chapter I
The European Union: A New Type of International Actor
Richard Rosecrance   15

Chapter II
A Foreign Policy in Search of a Polity
Jean-Marie Guéhenno   25

Chapter III
Convergence, Divergence and Dialectics: National Foreign Policies and the CFSP
Christopher Hill   35

Chapter IV
Identifying Institutional Paradoxes of CFSP
Reinhardt Rummel and Jörg Wiedemann   53

Chapter V
The Instruments of European Union Foreign Policy
Karen Elizabeth Smith   67

Chapter VI
The European Union's Performance in World Politics: How Should We Measure Success?
Knud Erik Jørgenson   87

Chapter VII
Defining the European Security Policy
Guido Lenz   103

Chapter VIII
Balancing Europe's Eastern and Southern Dimensions
Esther Barbé   117

Chapter IX
Policies without Strategy: the EU's Record in Eastern Europe
Jan Zielonka 131

Chapter X
From European Union to Atlantic Union
Charles A. Kupchan 147

List of Contributors 165

Index 167

List of Abbreviations

APEC	Asia-Pacific Economic Cooperation
ASEAN	Association of South East Asian Nations
AU	Atlantic Union
CCP	Common Commercial Policy
CFSP	common foreign and security policy
CJTF	Combined Joint Task Forces
COREPER	Committee of Permanent Representatives
CSCE	Conference on Security and Cooperation in Europe
CSCM	Conference on Security and Cooperation in the Mediterranean
EAC	European Atomic Community
EBRD	European Bank of Reconstruction and Development
EC	European Community
ECU	European Currency Unit
EFTA	European Free Trade Area
EMU	European Monetary Union
EP	European Parliament
EPC	European Political Cooperation
EU	European Union
FAWEU	Forces Answerable to the WEU
FYROM	Former Yugoslav Republic of Macedonia
G7	Group of Seven
GATT	General Agreement on Tariffs and Trade
GDP	gross domestic product
GNP	gross national product
GRIT	graduated reduction of international tensions
GSP	Generalised System of Preferences
IGC	Intergovernmental Organisation
IGO	Intergovernmental organisation
ILO	International Labour Organisation
MFN	Most Favoured Nation
NACC	North Atlantic Cooperation Council
NAFTA	North American Free Trade Agreement
NATO	North Atlantic Treaty Organisation
NGO	Non-governmental organisation
NIS	Newly Independent States
OECD	Organization of Economic Cooperation and Development
OSCE	Organisation for Security and Cooperation in Europe

PfP	Partnership for Peace
PHARE	Pologne et Hongrie Assistance à la Restructuration Económique
TACIS	Technical Assistance to the Commonwealth of Independent States
TAFTA	Trans-Atlantic Free Trade Area
TEU	Treaty of the European Union
UN	United Nations
UNSC	United Nations Security Council
WEU	Western European Union
WTO	World Trade Organisation

Preface

Jan Zielonka, the editor of this collective volume, is right in having characterised European foreign policy as paradoxical. If identity is defined negatively as well as positively it is indeed surprising that the Member States of the European Union should attempt to build up some kind of foreign policy while they do not yet constitute a full-fledged polity. The paradox starts with the basic fact that the European Union considers the rest of the world to be foreign, while at the same time, each Member State continues to view the other members of the Union – and to some extent to relate to them – as foreign countries as well. The new is not yet born and the old is still alive. The Union's delegations abroad are not yet real embassies and the Member States' embassies still represent national interests in other countries. European foreign policy, its ambiguities and weaknesses but also its hopes and expectations, is one of the many contradictions that Europe must continue to face for many years to come. Confusion and hesitation are and will be an expected outcome of any European policy. In a way, it is a structural feature and perhaps a necessary device that will help the Union shift from 12 or 15 national foreign policies into one; to make national and domestic what had previously been considered foreign; to share with others what was considered to be the most exclusive domain of the nation state.

Thanks to the initiative of Jan Zielonka and the support of the Jean Monnet Chair funded by the European Union, the Robert Schuman Centre has benefited from the contributions of several of the most distinguished scholars, observers, and actors in this field. A special series of seminars took place at the European University Institute in Fall 1996, with the aim of producing a book and putting into place the elements of a stimulating debate. In the course of 1997, several of these lectures were revised and updated, taking into account the Draft Treaty of Amsterdam. Two additional chapters were also commissioned. The chapters benefited from the splendid editing of Nida Gelazis who is a Research Associate of the Robert Schuman Centre. Since its creation in 1993, it has been the goal and ambition of the Robert Schuman Centre to contribute to thought and discussion about the most acute problems that Europe currently faces. Many programmes and research projects have been set up through the establishment of Joint Chairs with the Departments of the European University Institute and cooperation with institutions and individuals from all over the world, dealing with questions such as European institutions, enlargement, environment, welfare policies, deregulation, and monetary policy to name a few. More than 200 Working Papers have been produced during the first four years, and this book is just one of a series of books that the Robert Schuman Centre has published or is about to publish covering various fields and disciplines.

Both Jan Zielonka and I hope to contribute to a better knowledge and understanding of the nascent European policy which – perhaps with too much 'hardiesse' – tries to define what is foreign before being able to fully constitute itself as a domestic entity. Setting up a European foreign policy is not only ambitious and challenging: indeed it means building up Europe itself.

Yves Mény
Director of the Robert Schuman Centre

INTRODUCTION

Constraints, Opportunities and Choices in European Foreign Policy*

Jan Zielonka

The European Union is a strange sort of international actor and its foreign policy is full of paradoxes. Is the Union a superpower in the making or a foreign policy failure? Is it in the process of embracing or brushing off its newly-democratic neighbours? Is it a partner or a rival of the United States? Are the Union's policy objectives different from those of its Member States and does it have the means to meet these objectives? The end of the Cold War and the tightening of economic interdependence have hastened Europe's need to define its world role, but the Union is a master when it comes to avoiding making choices.

The draft Treaty of Amsterdam is the most recent example. The Treaty was supposed to create a foreign policy structure that would allow Europe to act efficiently when faced with conflicts such as the one in the Balkans. The Treaty was intended to restructure EU institutions in preparation for eastward enlargement. It was supposed to create a diplomatic – if not military – machinery in proportion to its ever-increasing economic might. However, these high expectations have come to naught. The Union chose not to choose. The draft treaty of Amsterdam failed to clarify the Union's basic aims and functions and it only added to the ambiguity of its institutional arrangements concerning foreign and security policy. Consider Art. J.7 of the draft Treaty of Amsterdam, concerning foreign and security policy: 'The common foreign and security policy shall include all questions relating to the security of the Union, including the progressive framing of a common defence policy ... which might lead to a common defence, should the European Council so decide.'

Disguise, ambiguity, and a general unwillingness to make bold choices have been permanent features of European foreign policy from the start. Although the 1957 Treaty of Rome was formally about economic integration and intra-European interests, it nevertheless provided a *de facto* international role for the EC by creating a common trade policy and envisaging association agreements between the EC and third countries. The European Political Cooperation project, launched in 1970, was initially only about foreign policy 'consultation,' but it gradually and more or less silently moved to policy 'coordination,' and even 'common policies.' To support these policies the Union began using trade, aid, and even sanctions as foreign policy means, although again, the use of these means was not envisaged from the start but emerged after a long and protracted bargaining process. Though the strategy behind the Union's policies remained ambiguous, their reach was expanding to Eastern

Europe, South Africa, and the Middle East. When the Soviet empire begun to crumble the Union seemed compelled to assume a greater international role in Europe. The 1992 Maastricht Treaty proudly proclaimed the creation of a 'Common Foreign and Security Policy' (CFSP), but the Treaty stopped short of creating a workable foreign policy decision-making system. The Treaty also failed to equip the Union with military instruments of action. Soon afterwards, the weakness of the CFSP arrangement was exposed in the Balkans, where the Union failed to live up to its initially ambitious aims. The Intergovernmental Conference leading to the draft Amsterdam Treaty was supposed to enhance the Union's capacity for making and implementing decisions, but, as this book shows in more detail, the improvements adopted in the long and laborious process of negotiations were small and cosmetic. Moreover, we do not really know what the Union's principal foreign policy objectives are: who are its true friends and enemies? and where are its borders likely to be within a few years time?

Conflicting national interests within the Union are often seen as a major factor behind the Union's reluctance or inability to make major choices. But does one know what these choices ought to be? What kind of Europe would best serve its citizens and the world community? Should one endorse Jean Monnet's vision of a 'United States of Europe'? Does the old model of a territorial state still apply? Is the vision of a European military superpower still attractive? Or should Europe become a 'civilian power' or a new type of 'condominium'? Can a civilian power effectively manage to cope in an uncivilised world? And can a new type of condominium ever be made democratic? This book attempts to address these kinds of questions by providing a comprehensive re-examination of the EU's role in the new context of world politics. The book will try to identify and explain Europe's peculiarities and paradoxes. It will show that these paradoxes create enormous opportunities and constraints for the Union; they shape the Union's institutional set-up and influence its basic political choices.

THE NATURE OF EUROPEAN FOREIGN POLICY

The first chapter argues that the contents of European policies is of lesser importance than the Union's peculiar nature which allows it to re-shape the traditional pattern of international relations. Rather than inducing a balance of power reaction against itself, the Union is acting as a magnet attracting would-be competitors and drawing them into the web of economic and political cooperative frames. 'Europe's attainment is normative rather than empirical' – is the basic message.

This initial assertion of Richard Rosecrance is not necessarily shared by the other authors of this volume: 'The European Union's Common Foreign and Security policy (CFSP) is a misnomer ... . CFSP is an acronym without empirical context.' But then Rosecrance develops arguments that are endorsed by most of the successive chapters: the Union is an exclusive international club – which is its most attractive feature. The fact that its power rests on economic rather than political (let alone military) assets allows it to reverse the balance of power logic and get away from the historical legacy of war and conquest.

The point is not only about the primacy of economic fitness over territorial acquisition or military strength. The point is, Rosecrance argues, that economic and political unity produce different external effects. The former attracts other actors because they want to participate in and benefit from the growing market. The latter invites opposition, if not violent reaction from other actors because they fear that the accumulated political and military strength might be used against them.

The Union not only relies on economic power factors, says Rosecrance, it also uses them in a different way than military factors have traditionally been used. Rewards and incentives rather than threats and punishments are usually applied by Brussels, an issue also elaborated upon later in Karen Smith's chapter. The ultimate reward is, of course, EU membership, which explains why the Union was particularly effective in coercing 'good' behaviour from several Eastern European countries hoping to join the exclusive European club of secure and rich nations. But one should also keep in mind that the EU is the largest donor of development assistance and humanitarian aid – endowing it with powerful leverage vis-à-vis the Third World. Moreover, with nearly 380 million consumers, making it the largest market in the world, and a combined GNP higher than that of the United States, the Union is also able to shape behaviour of other industrial powers such as Japan, China, Canada, Russia, and the US itself. In fact, Rosecrance believes that the Union, Japan, and the United States may soon be brought into one economic group that will effectively shape the rules governing economic behaviour which no one will be able to ignore. Stability of the international system will basically rest on the existence of various overlapping clubs such as NATO, the World Trade Organization, and the EU, the latter being the most central actor on the old continent.

Students of International Relations theory will observe that Rosecrance starts with a basic 'realist' assumption: the power structure of the world system is crucial. But then he develops arguments that throw realism on its head: economics reverses the logic of the power game; international balancing efforts have largely proved unsuccessful; and international institutions do matter – in fact they matter a lot. In the second chapter, Jean Marie Guéhenno parts with realist assumptions from the start. His message is that the EU's difficulties result from a crisis of a democratic body politic, not from the persistent silence of national interests. And he adds: 'the weakness of the European polity is no proof of the strength of national polities.'

According to Guéhenno, EU leaders should not aim at creating a European power but at creating a European polity. They should try to redefine the role of power in world affairs aiming at a greater interdependence and democracy.

The 'realist' notion of interest, either national or European, comes under fire by Guéhenno. He shows that interests are neither given nor eternal, but instead undergo a constant evolution in response to internal and external pressures. He points out, for instance, that post-war Franco-German history suggests that there are only permanent allies on the continent rather than permanent interests as Palmerston and Kissinger have argued. And if interests are not permanent in European nation states, they are even more ephemeral in the case of the European Union. One should not assume therefore that pre-existing European interests will be searched for and discovered by Brussels. Nor should Brussels attempt to produce a definition of European interests on its own, because according to Guéhenno, European interests cannot emerge in the absence of a European polity. And thus the proper order for a successful European construction should be: polity first, definition of European interests second, and the creation of a European foreign policy based on these interests only third. What the Union tried in the recent years is to reverse this sequence, but as we know, says Guéhenno, it has ended in failure.

But how can a European polity consisting of a variety of national cultures, religions, and historical myths be created? How can the necessary feeling of belonging to an entity (with ever-moving borders and universal Western ambitions) be stimulated? How can the people of Europe treat the Union's policies as truly theirs if they are made by Euro-bureaucrats and 'technicians'? Guéhenno's answers are as original as his analysis. Institutional improvements he finds useful, but insufficient. Europeans, he argues, must decide how different they want to be from the rest of the world. Instead of trying to define European interests they should try to define the European territory. They should be able to invest in civil society rather than trying to improve the formal structure of democracy. They should begin an open foreign policy debate directly with the people rather than confining it to professional politicians. In short, they should be constantly seeking a European polity.

The reasoning of Rosecrance and Guéhenno represents a drastic departure from the foreign policy agenda of the last 50 years. Christopher Hill's chapter brings us back to the traditional agenda focusing on individual states in Europe and their distinct foreign policies. But Hill does not endorse traditional pessimism about the conflict-ridden nature of power politics in Europe which prevents any meaningful cooperation in the sensitive field of 'high politics.' Hill's message is more balanced and points to a complex dialectical process involving both divergence and convergence of national foreign policies. While he does not pretend to deny continuous if not increasing pressure fragmenting political forces in Europe, he points to the existence of 'solidaristic' forces encouraging multi-lateralism and bringing diverse national foreign policies together. The relationship between European nation states and the Union is not a zero-sum game, he argues, and one should try to draw a balance-sheet between elements of convergence and divergence:

> 'Any assumption of a 'victory' for the forces of either solidarism or fragmentation would be to make a crass teleological error. We cannot know where the European foreign policy system is heading, and the notion of a 'destination' is mere anthropomorphism. What is clear, however, is the interplay which takes place between the national and the collective, and indeed between a range of actors that stretches much further than the EU and its Member-States.'

The interplay between the national and collective is reflected in the Union's foreign policy-making system that Hill attempts to scrutinise in more detail. He uses the analogy of 'multi-level governance' to indicate that the policy-making system involves multiple actors and operates on various levels. Hill sees this multi-level system as a natural response to an ever more complex international environment, but the system does not have a built-in mechanism for ensuring unified action. The dialectic process of convergence and divergence is again at play. On the one hand, a sense of collective European responsibility for international affairs is firmly established. On the other hand, national policies still have important functions and outsiders know how to exploit differences between them. On the one hand, the multi-level government or diplomacy produces uncertainty, delay, and confusion, but on the other hand, it is flexible, powerful, and prevents extremism. On the one hand, the system is able to involve other governmental and non-governmental actors that are crucial for enhancing international problem-solving capacity. On the other hand, the system lacks sound coordination, let alone enforcing mechanisms to produce the intended results.

Hill believes that these 'dialectics of the multiple relationships' are able to produce some wider understanding of the choices with which Europe is confronted. As he puts it: 'A multi-level, multi-actor system cannot go unobserved; it is a form of pluralism writ large which cannot but increase transparency and participation.' He also asserts that the system is sufficiently elastic to incorporate, rather than exclude, separate national policies. He contends that the system is able to work effectively alongside other IGOs, such as WEU, OSCE, and NATO. The system is not simply at the mercy of national and institutional rivalries because the CFSP, despite all its drawbacks, continues to shape national and institutional perceptions, choices, and behaviour.

Hill's conclusions are not fully shared by Reinhardt Rummel and Jörg Wiedemann. Rummel and Wiedemann also recognise the dialectic interaction between communitarian and intergovernmental forces shaping the institutional design of Europe's foreign policies – which is the topic of their chapter. In their view this dialectic, or as they put it 'dichotomy,' produces structure that is contradictory rather than complementary. They contend that the result is ineffectiveness or even complete standstill, in contrast to the increased understanding and flexibility that Hill predicts. The multi-level and multi-actor system indeed exists, but according to the two authors, it fails to generate the solidarity detected by Hill. Like Rosecrance, Rummel and Wiedemann believe that the Common Foreign and Security Policy (CFSP) is basically a misnomer: 'it is neither common, nor foreign, nor dealing with security, nor can be called a policy.' In their view, the CFSP has neither the means nor the capability to produce foreign policy decisions, let alone to implement them.

The three-pillar institutional structure of the European Union comes under fire partly because it artificially separates external and internal sectors of public life, and partly because it generates institutional squabbling between the Council, the Commission, and the European Parliament. Moreover, according to Rummel and Wiedemann the existing intra-institutional set-up discourages rather than encourages cooperation between the EU and other institutions such as NATO, WEU, or UN. This is especially deplorable in view of the fact that the EU is heavily dependent on such cooperation because it 'lacks the authority and the adequate instruments for implementing some of its own decisions.' Finally, the authors argue that the CFSP institutional arrangement encourages conflict rather than unity among individual EU Member States. Not only can individual Member States veto any collective decision, but the arrangement does not recognise the linkage between the capacity of individual Member States to influence decisions and their capacity to implement these decisions. Some countries pressing for more communitarian action in the foreign and security field are even legally constrained from carrying out these actions, not to mention the scarcity of diplomatic and military means that are at their disposal.

Karen Smith's chapter on instruments of European foreign policy acknowledges the existence of institutional 'hurdles' preventing the Union from using its instruments effectively. Like Rummel and Wiedemann, she points to the 'consistency problem' caused by the pillar structure separating different areas of foreign policy. The unclear division of competences between the EU and the Member States represents another serious hurdle, according to the author. But Smith contests the widely-held view that the Union has too few instruments at its disposal and that it needs to acquire military instruments if it wants to become a full-fledged international actor. In her view, the Union has proved to be quite effective in using its diplomatic and economic leverage vis-à-vis other states, especially when applied according to the principle of conditionality. And Smith points out that since the late 1980s conditionality (the use of [primary] economic instruments to encourage democratic reforms and respect for human rights) has become an integral aspect of the EU's foreign relations.

That said, the Union uses instruments in a peculiar manner: it prefers to use persuasion and rewards over threats and punishments. Although conditionality is increasing, Smith argues, the emphasis is still on positive measures. Smith does not find the European predisposition to use 'carrots' less effective than the American preference for 'sticks' – one only needs to look at the Western record in such countries as Iran or Cuba. But she does not find that the EU policy of 'carrots' is guided solely by the utility criterion. It is the need to reach a compromise among the many EU Member States that often prevents the adoption of strong negative measures. Smith also notices that, regardless of all the beneficial aspects of the policy like fostering dialogue and interdependence, a preference for rewards rather than punishments may sometimes imply the policy of complicity and appeasement.

Although Smith endorses the use of 'sticks' in certain situations, she does not think that the Union needs to acquire, let alone apply, military sticks. Military instruments are not 'the panacea they appear to be,' she argues, and the abandonment of the 'civilian power' image may not bring the advantages currently anticipated. The Union is a unique type of community that had renounced the use of force among its members and it should now encourage others to do the same. In her view, the civilian power may well be effective, providing the Member States are willing to use it. 'If they agree on common 'civilian' foreign policies, there are policy instruments available to implement them,' she concludes.

Examining Europe's Performance

Knud Eric Jørgensen tries to assess various conflicting arguments about the Union's performance in world politics. He points out that those praising or cursing the EU's performance hardly ever use precise criteria of success and failure. From where should our standard of measurement come? – he asks – from the actors involved in the political process or from outside observers? Judging the Union according to its declared aims and objectives can well be wrong, he argues, because those aims are usually in flux. Moreover, the Union is often after several different aims simultaneously. For instance, preserving peace and unity in Western Europe is as important for the Union as protecting it from external shocks. Would a bolder policy in the Balkans enhance or damage the EU unity? Nor is it advisable to measure the EU's policy outcomes against imagined absolute standards, he argues. There are things that even the most powerful international actors fail to do.

Comparison with other actors might seem to be the proper method by which to proceed, but Jørgensen disagrees. He asks: Who are the relevant actors for comparison and what is comparable? He then examines various efforts to compare the Union's performance with the performance by such diverse actors as the Council of Europe, the United States, OSCE and NATO. The result is predictable: most cited comparisons have been found to be misguided. Yet, Jørgensen is not suggesting that everything is relative. Instead, he urges us to recognise the existence of 'multiple realities' in European affairs. Like Hill, he urges us to recognise the parallel existence of conflicting trends in Europe and to abandon a one-dimensional perspective on the Union in search of a more dynamic if not dialectic one. He does not indicate what a dynamic perspective implies in practice, but insists that we need to accept 'the 'messy' state of European foreign affairs in which we find an erosion of the domestic-foreign policy divide and where the boundary of the European Union remains blurred.'

This messy state of European affairs is scrutinised in more detail by Guido Lenzi's chapter. 'These are again times when events tend to unfold faster than the human ability to foresee and steer them,' he acknowledges, ' Things just happen, out of benign neglect at best.' But according to Lenzi, we are not in a state of confusion and despair. European nations are aware that the challenges before them cannot be dealt with single-handedly by any one of them and that they cannot continue to sublet their own security to the United States. They also know that they need to face two kinds of challenges: globalisation pressure from the top, and the pressure of domestic politics from the bottom. Moreover, many antagonistic trouble spots and national 'stiffnesses' have re-emerged from under the Cold War glacier, adding another kind of challenge.

How can the EU deal with this explosive mixture of new and old challenges? Should it revive the old Wilsonian dream of a new international order or search for a new European directoire? Lenzi provides us with a set of straight-forward answers to these questions. First, he does not believe that any grand design is available for Europe, and therefore the Union should search for managers rather than designers to cope with the complex transition from, as he put it: 'the Cold War situation of 'no war, no peace' to a scenario where both war and peace can coexist.' Second, the Union must accept complex international realities: hard cores and variable speeds and geometries are already at play, regardless of institutional arrangements. The Union should now try to coherently interconnect these processes. Third, efficiency should not be the only concern of the Union: consensus, legitimacy, and credibility are equally important. In Lenzi's view pan-European security cannot be bestowed or imposed from above: it must be built from the bottom up. Fourth, Europe is 'overendowed' with political declarations and institutions – 'the whole spaghetti-junction' of them. They must not be rebuilt, but made more complementary and coherent. Fifth, the Union is particularly well suited for the 'enlarged security' tasks. The issue of a 'European security space' must urgently be addressed. The 'demand for Europe' is not only about participation in a 'brave new world,' but also about 'reintegration after years of forced partition.'

Esther Barbé is also concerned with the European security space, but she argues that this space includes not only postcommunist Eastern Europe, but also the Mediterranean. She shows how countries such as Italy, Greece, France, and especially Spain are working hard to maintain a balance between the Union's Southern and Eastern flanks. This balancing is borne out of the hard bargaining process between 'Southern' and 'Northern' EU Member States over the degree of the Union's political, and especially economic, commitment to Eastern Europe and the Mediterranean. This leads Barbé to conclude that the disappearance of the Iron Curtain has produced not only centripetal forces deepening the European construction process, but also centrifugal forces driving the process of sub-regionalisation and creating 'spheres of influence' among EU Member States. Geography again is shaping the Union's politics, 'mental maps' are being reconstructed, and countries are taking greater care of their own immediate neighbourhood. Moreover, Barbé argues that the renationalisation process (converting European policy into policing each country's sphere of influence) is also evolving. In her view two cases illustrate this process: the German policy favouring recognition of Slovenia and Croatia, and the Spanish policy of linking European construction to Mediterranean stability.

However, balancing the Southern and Eastern dimension of the Union has its clear limits, the author argues. The EU can adjust the imbalance through development aid to Eastern Europe and Mediterranean. It can also develop a 'parallel program' for institutional involvement in both regions. For instance, proposals for creating a PHARE Plan for the Mediterranean Europe or organising a Mediterranean Partnership for Peace have already been tabled. But the nature of the Union's relations with both regions is fundamentally different, according to Barbé. The relationship between the Union and Central and Eastern European countries is based on mutual confidence: these countries have psychologically agreed to be a part of a pluralistic community of security formed by the Union. They also share an European identity in cultural and political terms. The EU-Mediterranean relationship, on the other hand, resembles more the old 'defence-detente' philosophy. The EU knows that its own security is interlinked with the volatile security situation in the Maghreb and the Middle East. However, the prospect of expanding the security community envisaged by Karl Deutsch is probably realistic in Eastern Europe, but not in the Mediterranean countries in North Africa or the Middle East.

But, are the Union's policies towards Eastern Europe about building the kind of security community envisaged by Deutsch? Are not these policies merely about economic gains, trade, and investment? Does the Union know what its aims in Eastern Europe really are and which means should be used to achieve these aims? Is Western Europe helping Eastern Europe or is it merely helping itself? I deal with these questions in my own chapter.

The chapter finds EU's policies towards Eastern Europe generous, timely, and comprehensive, but argues that most of these policies emerged by default rather than by design. The Union invested enormous financial and political capital in Eastern Europe, but this investment lacked a clearly-defined strategic purpose. This is because of three major deficiencies of the Union's policy towards the region. First, the Union never specified the vision of Europe for which it is striving. Second, policies towards Eastern Europe have been dominated by the Union's internal agenda rather than broader strategic considerations. Third, the Union failed to reform its own institutional structure along the required strategic predicament.

I argue, in line with other authors in this book, that a complex 'postmodern' and post-Soviet international environment is partly responsible for the Union's faults. However, the weakness of the Union's Ostpolitik is also rooted in the peculiar nature of the Union as an international actor. The Union always has had some serious problems in defining the aims and means of its policy because it was faced with persistent differences between EU Member States concerning the nature and scope of integration. Likewise, it always had to accommodate the divergent national interests of Member States. Ambiguity and vagueness of successive arrangements and policies helped achieve the necessary consensus among and across Member States, but it also prevented the Union from acquiring even a minimum degree of strategic purpose. The damaging implications of this fact are evident when we examine the European Ostpolitik.

In the final chapter, Charles Kupchan also deals with strategic dilemmas confronting the Union, but the prime focus of his essay is the future of transatlantic relations. In his view the success of the West has become its undoing: North America and Europe risk drifting apart in the absence of a geopolitical imperative. The European Union in particular has embarked on an excessively federalist agenda, which is likely to stir-up internal and external conflicts and distract the Union from the most important tasks in Eastern Europe and over the Atlantic. Kupchan uses the CFSP and EMU projects as examples of such misplaced ambitions which are producing more suspicion and rivalry in Europe than trust and cooperation. The United States is also increasingly preoccupied with the Pacific Rim at the expense of the traditional European links. Its engagement in European affairs is now largely confined to NATO, which has become a weak foundation for 'bridging the Atlantic.' This is because defence policy no longer enjoys a position of primacy among either electorates or their leaders, and because NATO is involved in a very controversial eastward enlargement project of its own.

Kupchan suggests scaling back Western aspirations and focusing on consolidating what already exists – a peaceful, integrated community of democratic nation states. Instead of constructing a federal Europe that omits North America, Europeans should aim at building an Atlantic community of strong national states, integrating economically, and expanding territorially to Eastern Europe. The EU, WEU, and NATO should subsequently merge into a new political body – an Atlantic Union – that would introduce a single market, uphold collective security, and expand political engagements at the transatlantic level. The military component of the Atlantic Union should be downgraded by eliminating NATO's article V, which provides for collective defence. For Kupchan, the Atlantic Union should not be a military alliance but a civic community with all the beneficial effects envisaged by Karen Smith and Richard Rosecrance in their respective views of the EU and other international institutions. Deepening civic engagement and enhancing democracy within the Atlantic Union (via an Atlantic Parliament, for instance), Kupchan sees as especially important. 'By solidifying a transatlantic community at peace' – he concludes – 'an Atlantic Union would do much more for the West and the rest of the world than Monetary Union among Germany and France, and Luxembourg or tank traps on the Poland-Belarus border.'

FROM PARADOX TO PARADOX

The authors contributing to this book represent different schools and traditions within the field of international relations, and it would be virtually impossible for them to reach a hard consensus on the nature of European foreign policy. Yet despite the evident divergence of their views, it is easy to trace common lines in their assumptions and arguments. For instance, the authors would agree that the Union is a new type of actor that can hardly be analysed in state-centric terms. Moreover, traditional uses of terms, such as power, interests, and polities, have seldom been found adequate in analysing European affairs. The Union can neither be analysed in pure inter-governmental terms nor in pure federalist terms. The Union tries to cope with complex 'multiple realities,' to use Jørgensen's terms, in a sophisticated manner that resembles, to use Hill's expression, 'multi-level governance.'

This book's contributors also tend to agree with Rosecrance's assertion that the Union has enormous collective potential based on its structural and normative assets. This does not necessarily mean that what the Union *does* in practice is inconsequential, but it does mean that the unique structural features of the Union allow it to conduct different, more inclusive, and less deterring or balancing types of foreign policy than is the case with traditional international actors.

The Union may well be a new type of international actor with attractive structural features, but the argument that it cannot do without workable institutions and democratic legitimacy appears repeatedly in different chapters of this book. None of the authors endorse the long-standing thesis that more democracy is a recipe for failure of any foreign policy. On the contrary, the views presented here support an EU institutional set-up that is more transparent, more coherent, and simpler. No one argues that expanding the majority voting system would represent a panacea for effective foreign policies, but no sympathy was expressed for the pure inter-governmental decision-making system of the CFSP.

Several authors asked the EU to abandon any defence and security aspirations, and they all seem to endorse the thesis that the use of civilian power to foster dialogue and interdependence is the right way for the Union to proceed. The book also endorses an active if not embracing policy towards Europe's unstable backyards – Eastern Europe in particular but also, although in a different fashion, towards the Middle East and Maghreb. Closer links between Europe and the United States have also been strongly endorsed in this book, even though not all authors would like to see an Atlantic Union replacing NATO, WEU, and EU.

Moreover, the Union that emerges from the successive chapters is indeed pregnant with strange contradictions and paradoxes. The Union aspires to be a powerful international actor without aspiring to becoming a super-state. It aspires to have a strategic impact in Europe and elsewhere, but it side-steps working out any specific strategy. It has ambitions of preventing and managing conflicts, but refrains from acquiring the military means to do so. It embarks on the project of widening its borders, but continues its deepening project, which makes the entrance hurdles for applicant countries ever higher. It wishes to maintain strong transatlantic links, but continues to build up institutions that would make it more independent from, if not more competitive with the US.

Of course, all political actors would like to have the cake and eat it too. But in the EU's case, the problem is not merely about double talk and tactics. The Union is confronted with at least five basic paradoxes that can hardly be resolved without running into other paradoxes. The first paradox is about the gap between the Union's normative power of attraction and its weak empirical power to do things. The Union has an enormous normative appeal because it represents an ever-growing club of rich, peaceful, socially sensitive, and democratic countries. However, despite its enormous 'power of attraction' the Union has serious problems transforming its normative strength into operational capability. The Union is quite ineffective in shaping the international environment in any instrumental fashion. The problem is not so much the lack of adequate instruments, but the inability to set collective goals and set into motion any collective action in pursuit of these goals. In other words, the Union looks like a giant in normative terms, but when it comes to practice it looks like a dwarf.

This is linked to another paradox: the greatest strength of the Union is its unique ability to address the challenges of modernity, but this strength proves to be a weakness when faced with the challenges of pre-modern politics. Unfortunately for the Union, it needs to cope with both types of challenges, and thus what appears to be an asset when operating in the 'zone of peace' proves to be a liability when operating in the 'zone of war and instability' in Eastern Europe, the Balkans, or the Middle East. The Union's most prominent features, such as diffusion of power, primacy of economic instruments, and built-in multi-lateralism, makes the Union particularly well suited for coping with the modern international agenda of cascading interdependence, mass communication, cross-cutting institutions, and multiple cultural identities. However, when confronted with the traditional pre-modern agenda of military competition, national interests, and imperial pride and glory, the Union is practically helpless because it lacks military instruments, concentration of power, and must rely on slow multilateral arrangements. In the domain of power politics traditional state actors seem to fare much better. But the Union is anything but a traditional state actor: it has no proper government, no fixed territory, no army or a traditional diplomatic service – it even lacks a normal legal status. Aspiring to a super-state position would make it better suited for the old-style hegemonic politics of secret pacts, 'ganging-up,' and parochial 'bullying,' but it would also make it less suited for coping with the pressure of globalisation, interdependence, and plurality.

Another paradox emerges from the Union's balancing act between straightforwardness and ambiguity. The Union was always ambiguous and vague about its basic aims and functions because it was the only way to get the integration project off the ground. The ambiguity of successive cooperative arrangements was basically rooted in the persistent differences within Europe concerning the very nature of integration (federalism vs. intergovernmentalism), the functional scope of integration (high politics vs. low politics) and competing national agendas (e.g., French and Spanish 'anti-Americanism' vs British and Dutch 'pro-Americanism'). Because the Union faced a simple choice – 'integration by disguise' or no integration – ambiguity was an effective way to maintain a respectable degree of consensus. However, ambiguity and disguise also have their negative side effects: ambiguity and disguise prevented the Union from acquiring an identity and strategic purpose. It is difficult to say what the Union's policies truly are and who is behind them. In short, ambiguity helps the Union make progress in designing a new order for the continent, but it prevents it from putting this new order into place.

This brings us to the next major paradox: the logic of deepening and widening the Union are both plausible, but they are not in harmony. Deepening of the Union would mean more coherent institutions, more means at the Union's disposal, and a smoother decision-making process. All this could help the Union overcome the strategic and operational deficit that has been criticised in this book. But deepening would also mean that it is more difficult for outsiders to join the Union, it is more difficult for outsiders to maintain traditional links with individual EU Member States, and more difficult for outsiders to get their arguments through to the Union's internal debates. Through deepening, the Union can become more coherent, robust, and strategically purposeful, but it might lose a part of its normative power of attraction prized by this book's authors. Outsiders will be pulled out rather than pulled in, transatlantic and transpacific partners will become rivals, and politics might again resemble the old pattern of balancing and 'ganging-up.'

Our final major paradox concerns the interplay between the Union's external and internal agendas. One of the Union's greatest achievements is that it managed to secure peace and prosperity among its members. Foreign and security problems between Member States have largely been tamed. However, this has hampered rather than enhanced the Union's capacity to export peace and prosperity to regions outside its borders. The Union's policies towards the outside world are too much about maintaining an 'amicable' relationship among the diverse set of EU Member States. Even worse, EU's foreign policies often fall victim to the parochial and sectoral interests of individual Member States. The long-standing EU policy of extending the 'zone of peace' by further enlarging the EU has its obvious attraction, but it also has its limits. After all, extending EU membership to unstable countries in Eastern Europe or the Mediterranean may import insecurity rather than export security. Likewise it could also destabilise the internal market.

The successive chapters of this book examine in more depth these paradoxes and try to give them practical meanings. No single way of coping with them is suggested, but the authors show how the Union is trying to grapple with them by applying a mixture of incentives and disincentives. The authors show how the EU tries to satisfy rising hopes and calm occasional fears. They tell the story of the Union operating in a complex international environment with no clear signposts. They show that the Union indeed faces a paradoxical situation with which it can only cope in a paradoxical manner.

NOTE

* This introduction greatly benefited from thoughtful comments by Christopher Hill and Reinhardt Rummel. I am also indebted to Richard Rosecrance for inspiring the entire project. Special thanks go to Nida Gelazis for editing this and other chapters.

CHAPTER I

The European Union: A New Type of International Actor

Richard Rosecrance

In this chapter I seek to make three fundamental points: (1) that there has not been and probably will not be a common European foreign or defence policy; (2) that Europe nonetheless has unique and unparalleled foreign policy strengths; (3) that these strengths are in the process of helping to reshape the contours of the wider international system.

THE FAILURE OF EU TO DEVELOP A COMMON FOREIGN AND DEFENCE POLICY

The European Union's Common Foreign and Security Policy (CFSP) is a misnomer. Europe does not speak with one voice on either foreign policy or defence problems. CFSP is an acronym without empirical content. As any student of the integration of Europe knows, there remain important foreign policy differences among France, Britain, and Germany, to say nothing of other member countries. The European Commission's view does not accord with national policies. Greece has a uniquely hostile view of Turkey. Germany has an especially friendly view of Croatia. Britain and France disagree about the American role in Europe. When European states reach a tentative accord, as they have done from time to time on the Middle East, it is a least-common-denominator agreement that has little influence on world politics. There is no prospect of a single European foreign policy. It is even more unlikely that there will be a common defence policy with a single finger on the European (in this case British and French) nuclear trigger.

With the end of the Cold War, it is even less probable that a common foreign policy consensus will be forged. There is no major foe to the East which forces European states to concert and reach agreement. The United States is not the substitute enemy which might cause Europe to do so, nor is Japan or China.

EUROPEAN'S CONTINUING ECONOMIC AND POLITICAL PROBLEMS

Other problems continue to reverberate within the European Union. The Maastricht Treaty and the movement toward European Monetary Union have not solved economic problems. As long as unemployment remains high, there will be agitation for welfare solutions that may be beyond the capabilities of either Member States or of the EU to provide. In one sense, the creation of a common currency (the Euro) in 1999 will make these problems harder, not easier to solve. It will demand greater fiscal discipline and monetary stringency (by the European Central Bank) to launch the Euro at a time when Member States will want fiscal leniency. The Stability Pact will keep the pressure on member governments to hold their deficits down. Some outside observers believe that Europe is too narrowly focused on monetary unity – which imposes great fiscal discipline – when it should be solving domestic problems of unemployment through greater economic growth.

FOREIGN POLICY STRENGTHS OF EU: REVERSING THE BALANCE OF POWER

At the same time, if EU does not have a common foreign policy, it has an extremely felicitous influence upon the external world. It represents a magnetic force in world politics, attracting in disparate countries that otherwise might remain apart. Typically, any growing locus of confederal or federal power might have been expected to cause Balance of Power effects directed against it. When such conditions emerge, historians and analysts expect the formation of opposing alliances and the rearmament of excluded powers. Opposition should have been expressed toward the uniting centre. Peripheral parties should have been forced away.

In Europe's case, however, neither of these has occurred. In very surprising fashion, Europe has reversed the Balance of Power and drawn other nations into its web of economic and political associations. Countries want to join or to be linked with Europe, not to oppose it. Peripheral countries have been centripetally attracted to the European centre, not driven away from it.

Some Europeans speculate that the United States is not pleased with European unity and that America is likely to respond negatively to further integration. The United States, it is said, prefers to deal with individuals states, not with the cumbersome European apparatus. Some also claim that the United States is worried that Brussels will emerge as a rival in the Far East, manipulating relationships with China and Japan to the disadvantage of North America. If this were true, NATO would be in ruins, and there would be few trade successes under the auspices of GATT-WTO, both of which depend upon close European-American cooperation. In fact, as Europe draws together, the United States is also drawn closer to Europe in both economic and political terms. The success of EMU and the common currency will require an American response. The Trans-Atlantic Free Trade Area (TAFTA) project is just one such possibility for new relationships.

Historically the reaction to the uniting of Europe is virtually unparalleled. In the 18th and 19th centuries, the joining of British colonies-states into what became the United States of America did not make friends with the French, British-Canadian, or Spanish territories located next to them. As the United States strengthened and territorially moved westward – to achieve its so-called 'manifest destiny' – Balance of Power effects led to war with Canada in 1812 and tension in the 1840s. It produced the war with Mexico in 1846. The centralisation of the Northern states of the Union also caused a reaction in the South. The victory of the high-tariff, anti-slavery Republican Party[1] in 1860 evoked to Southern secession and produced the American Civil War. Nearly half the country wanted to leave the union, a dispute that almost resulted in the break-up of the United States in the Civil War, 1861-1865.

In other cases, Balance of Power effects also emerged in response to the rise of an amalgamating centre. Napoleon's continental system and the Berlin Decrees of 1807 held out the possibility of a single tariff and trading zone for Western Europe. It protected continental industries and allowed them to strengthen themselves against powerful British competitors. This prospective result, however, did not encourage either Russia or Great Britain to join. Instead they acted to oppose the federalising centre directed by the French Emperor, and this in turn led to the final battles of the Napoleonic Wars. In the 20th century, neither the Japanese nor the German trading blocs of the 1930s inspired outsiders to seek to join. Instead, where they could, they opposed the extension of the two different 'co-prosperity spheres,' and the result was the Second World War.

Of course, an alert reader of these last two paragraphs will already have offered a solution to the problems presented. She will claim that Balance of Power effects only emerged against a single decision-making centre, and not in response to economic integration of a more decentralised kind. It was Hitler's or Tojo's prospective autocratic rule of Europe or East Asia that caused a negative response from outsiders, not economic integration, per se. It was Napoleon's imperium that evoked resistance, not his economic policies. In the American context, US military and political expansion in North and Central America generated opposition, not economic unity as such. This reader, continuing the argument, will then assert that since the European Union does not have a single leader or decision-maker, its policies pose no threat to others, and one would not, in those circumstances, expect Balance of Power effects to emerge.

There is unquestionably something in this point of view, but it overlooks important exceptions to its application. As we know, the United States did not oppose European unification after World War II; it surprisingly endorsed and fostered it. The Marshall Plan would only succeed if the trade barriers dividing Europe were lowered or abolished. It would work even better if there were political unity in Europe. Dimly, as Max Beloff tells us, the United States was aware that it was possibly acting to create a third bloc in world politics independent of the other two, but it still proceeded.[2] Later, President Kennedy's 'dumbbell theory' was predicated on a fully independent, integrated, and sovereign Europe. More recently and even more significantly, Soviet policy should have been expected to follow Balance of Power policies against the uniting and increasingly powerful Europe. The USSR should have opposed the reunification of an independent Germany located within the Western alliance, but it did not. It acquiesced in a single decision-making centre for a reunited, strong, and potentially hegemonic Germany, its hated opponent in the Second World War.

In addition, there seems to be no correlation between Europe's integrative quality and the willingness of others to join (or not to oppose) it. Outsiders did not merely want to become members of the Community when it favoured 'enlargement' over 'deepening.' As the integrative quality proposed or achieved was increased, so too was the desire of outsiders to be included. There were no balance of power reactions directed at a Europe which (after the Maastricht Treaty) aimed at a much higher degree of both economic and political union. Outsiders did not balk at a European Court with the power of judicial review, or at monetary union directed by a single Central Bank.

There is nonetheless, something in the view that economic and political unity have different external effects. In economic terms, an established core of centralised and open markets – in trade and finance – draws others in. They want to participate in and benefit from the growing market. Despite what is said about the impact of economic globalisation, there are still propinquity effects. The countries that are near a high income economy benefit more (in terms of per capita income) than those further away.[3] As income grows, others are attracted to join. Hence as the Canadian-American Free Trade Area succeeded, NAFTA became possible. As NAFTA and EU both succeed, a Trans-Atlantic Free Trade Area becomes more feasible and desirable. Centralised wealth leads others to seek to market and finance their goods in the centre. It has centripetal effects in economic terms. This is why the Third World, distant from the centre of the world economy, has benefited so little from participation in it. In financial and market terms the Third World has also had little to offer. It lacks buying power, and this is what attracts capital and goods from other nations.

In politics and international relations a reverse result has been typically observed. Rather than seeking a further centralisation, power seeks to fill a vacuum. It also tends to oppose strong and concentrated strength. The Balance of Power seeks to distribute power centrifugally, to diffuse it more or less evenly throughout the system.

In the European case, the magnetic force of economics has dominated the divisive force of politics. This in itself is tribute to the greater degree of European economic integration than political unity. It may also be a signal that political unity is not needed for the European Union to have a major effect upon international relations, both within Europe and outside it.

EU'S EFFECTS ON THE WORLD-WIDE BALANCE

Thus, we have a reversal of the Balance of Power on the periphery of Europe,[4] with outsiders increasingly drawn in. But let us, for the sake of argument, concede that the integration of the European Union could produce a Balance of Power reaction directed against the enlarging centre. What then would occur?

To evaluate this question historically, one must remember that no aggressor in the past (with the possible exception of Rome) ever possessed as much as one-half of the power in the then civilised world. Napoleon did not achieve an overbalance. Powers on the wings, Russia and Great Britain, had more than enough strength to bring him (as they eventually did) to heel. Wilhelmine Germany did not acquire it. The Triple Entente of Russia, France, and Britain was stronger than the Dual Alliance at the beginning of World War I.[5] When in 1917, the Triple Entente lost Russian support with the beginning of the Revolution, it more than made up for the deficiency by recruiting the United States to the alliance. Even the British Empire at its height (in 1897) had accumulated no more than one quarter of the world's land area and about one seventh of its population. Earlier in the century when England was the first and only industrial nation, London never possessed more than about one quarter of world gross domestic product.[6] Hitler's territorial conquests never even matched the scope enjoyed by the British Empire. And in terms of GDP, Nazi Germany was less strong than Soviet Russia or the United States individually. Japan's alliance did not tip the balance in favour of Hitler. After the war, Stalin ruled the largest country in the world and presided over Eastern Europe; his territorial reach extended into China. Even then, his power did not come close to rivalling that of the United States by itself. Thus in the past (again with the Roman exception) a potential aggressor could always be opposed by 60-75 per cent of world power if the other countries united against him.

In the future, however, this may no longer be the case. Under these novel conditions, even political and military power might begin to attract, rather than to repel others. Suppose we hypothesise that a core of cooperators is formed to include the United States and the European Union, and that Japan is brought into the group (no doubt for economic as well as political reasons.) This core coalition would then constitute about half of world gross domestic product. What then would be the policy of Russia, a nation with a far smaller GDP and small and ineffective armed forces? If for reasons of access to capital, technology, and markets it seeks to join the core group, what will be the impact upon China? There is a point at which the central core accumulates more than 50-60% of world economic and political power. At that point, others need to be associated with the strong central coalition. If China joins, India would also need to participate. Brazil and even Iran would not have viable alternatives. In this way, centralised economic power could have the long term effect of creating centralised political power. And at the centre would be Europe, a new type of international actor.

STABILITY, INTERNATIONAL THEORY, AND EUROPE

In the past, two different methods have been used to create stability in world politics. The first of these stresses deterrence or punishment mechanisms directed at countries which violate established boundaries or customary usages among nations.[7] The second emphasises reward or reinforcement techniques.[8] Kenneth Boulding believed that the threat to punish another actor if it crossed a particular deterrent line in world politics could lead to threat-counterthreat responses and to the gradual escalation of conflict between sides.[9] Michael Howard contended that in Europe, deterrence of the Soviet Union was not enough. The adversary should also be reassured of the pacific intentions of the Western alliance.[10] Where psychological attitudes play a role in the leader's policy, analysts believe that the graduated reduction of international tensions (GRIT), will come to depend upon reciprocal concessions, not just on threat.[11]

It is well known that stability cannot be provided by reinforcement and reward alone. Neville Chamberlain's failure to appease Adolf Hitler makes that point amply clear. The 'norm of reciprocity'[12] probably applies in relations among international leaders. To be successful, however, it cannot be unconditional reciprocity.[13] In particular conditions, specific reciprocity may be required in preference to diffuse reciprocity.[14] Countries are sometimes asked to respond in particular ways to the concessions made by others. In addition, the system needs to apply some form of sanction if violations of accepted codes of behaviour occur.

The question remains, however, how this can be done in a disinterested manner. National punishment of unilateral violations of established frontiers and norms has not been uniformly successful in the past, to say the least. For some observers, it was national attempts to enforce a Balance of Power which led directly to World Wars I and II.[15] International balancing efforts, and the theory of collective security have also been remarkably unsuccessful.[16] National efforts are hard to distinguish from ex parte action, and international efforts are vulnerable to collective goods and free rider problems. Parties on the sidelines are initially tempted to placate the aggressor, not to balance against him.[17] Countries do not generally believe in the collective security maxim: 'peace is indivisible.'

If universal and also national sanctions are ineffective, is there something in between? It is precisely this intermediate realm that is occupied by a variety of more or less exclusive international clubs, headed by the European Union. Such organisations enjoy a legitimacy that universal organisations do not fully possess. In the future, I believe that stability in world politics will increasingly be provided by the existence and operation of overlapping clubs in various regions of the world. Of course, for these to be successful, there must also be a background level of military disincentives to dissuade hostile action. National forces, NATO, and the possibility of UN intervention must remain both as symbol and fact.

The positive task of reshaping international behaviour, however, could then be undertaken by one or more 'clubs' of nations. The nice thing about clubs (as everyone recognises) is that one has to meet the admission requirements to become a member. To succeed, clubs must be exclusive.[18] Everybody cannot join. Some nations do not reside in the appropriate geographic area. Others do not meet economic or political criteria. The American comedian, Groucho Marx, understood this. He was dubious about joining any club that was willing to extend membership to him: for then it would not be exclusive enough!

As we have already seen, nations react unsympathetically when one national actor tells them to change their behaviour. Unilateral conditionality tends to be resisted. But when conditionality is demanded by a multilateral organisation – as the price of membership in a favoured group which provides technology or capital – there is much less resistance.[19] Even a weak Italian Government may be able to pass a 'Europe tax', but it has difficulty cutting spending and adopting new taxes for purely domestic programs. Italians generally recognise that being one of the charter members of the European Monetary Union is a great political prize, and they may be willing to sacrifice to achieve it.

Such mechanisms have little impact, however, unless they can be generalised. It is possible that they will not be. Russia and China may stand aloof from world coalitions or may act to oppose a central group. Russia is likely to be excluded from NATO and from membership in the European Union. China may find difficulties in entering the World Trade Organisation on favourable terms. A dissatisfied group of Russia, China and Iran could emerge in time.[20]

If such a coalition were opposed to economic globalisation, the free flow of capital, enforcement of contracts, and the transfer of technology, however, it would become a self-defeating organisation. The generally recognised lesson of the Soviet experience was that isolation from the world economy was a disaster. After the stage of heavy industrialisation in which Russia did achieve rapid growth rates, the Soviet economy greatly slowed down, largely because it was isolated from new technological developments and sources of foreign capital. It was saddled with inefficient government ownership and control of industry. Closed to the outside world, it succeeded in exporting nothing but raw materials and minerals.

China appears resolved not to follow the Soviet course and allow its own economy to become isolated. The reintegration of Hong Kong, if managed properly, will further open up the Chinese economic system to the rest of the world. China will benefit from joining the WTO and gaining dependable most favoured nation treatment. Russia will also need to participate in international economic clubs to have access to capital supplies on a world-wide basis. Both countries will have to attain new standards of economic transparency to join.

It is therefore somewhat more likely that an 'encompassing coalition' (generated by common economic interests) will be formed and maintained in world politics than that there will be divisions among Great Powers and the creation of new opposing alliance systems. There has not been such an encompassing coalition since the breakdown of the Concert of Europe after 1848. Despite the ratification of the League Covenant and the establishment of the League of Nations Council, that encompassing coalition could not be put back together after 1918. The United States did not join. Britain and France disagreed with each other over the treatment of Germany. Newly Communist Russia went its own isolated and hostile way.

After the Second World War, the Big Five of the United Nations Security Council did not continue to work together, owing to the outbreak of the Cold War. It was not until the 1990s that the division of the world into two hostile and competing camps was overcome. As a result, there is the possibility of creating a new encompassing coalition in world politics for the first time in 150 years.

It still appears, moreover, that Russia and China want to become members of the top club. Prestige and economic access are important to them equally with traditional political goals. Chinese territorial expansion in the South China Sea would jeopardise those objectives, as would the use of force to recapture Taiwan. A Russian attempt to force members of the present Commonwealth of Independent States to rejoin the old Soviet Union would also set back the reintegration of Russia into the world economy and block her membership into the top group of nations.

How can an encompassing coalition of the future be held together? Along with background military deterrence directed against hostile action, there are important positive incentives to improve national behaviour. These can be offered through a consolidation of overlapping clubs. The world cannot simply tell China what to do. But the world can note that the requirements of joining the WTO as a developed country involve much greater economic transparency, together with full convertibility of the national currency. Chinese control of inflation must be much greater than has been achieved in recent years. Nor can nations tell Russia what to do. But the International Monetary Fund does not have to provide loans to a country which cannot collect the bulk of its own taxes. Observers can point out that all present members of the Group of Seven have democratic, stable governments, low inflation, valued currencies, and relatively low government indebtedness relative to GDP. If Russia wants to become a member, it will have to achieve these or similar standards of economic and political performance.

The Centrality of Europe

Europe occupies the pivotal role in the structure of overlapping clubs. The requirements for joining the European Monetary Union are the most arduous admission standards for any international organisation. Thus, in establishing EMU, member nations have created the most exclusive international club. Its standards set the highest benchmark for economic achievement of all countries, not just for those in Europe. They have set the conditions by which the economic success of all other nations and regions will be judged. In this way Europe has become the most economically attractive region in world politics.

What does this mean in practical terms? It does not mean that Europe's economies have solved problems of rigidities in the labour market or that reform of Europe's social programs is not desirable. It does not suggest that the problem of chronic unemployment has been resolved. European technology still lags behind the achievements of American and Japanese technology.

Europe's attainment is normative rather than empirical. Its attractive force is very great, and others will seek to be associated with it. Of course Russia cannot become a full member of the European Union. It cannot even be an Associate Member. But does this rule out the extension of a single European market beyond the Urals? If we speak of developments in the 21st century, the answer cannot be a negative one. Of course, the United States cannot join. But a TAFTA linking Europe and North America cannot be ruled out as the European economy and market become both more exclusive and attractive. Of course, China become a member of the EU. But the standards imposed upon the central members of EMU (the inner core of Europe) may well be the standards that will, directly or indirectly, ultimately come to be imposed upon China. Will China resent the imposition? Perhaps. But it may also come to recognise that such standards are unavoidable if one wants to be a member of the Top Club in world politics.

It is perhaps a paradox to note that the continent which once ruled the world through the physical impositions of imperialism is now coming to set world standards in normative terms. There is perhaps a new form of European symbolic and institutional dominance even though the political form has entirely vanished.

NOTES

[1] Strictly, of course, the Republican Party was not anti-slavery, but it was against the extension of slavery to new territories-states.

[2] See Max Beloff, *The United States and the Unity of Europe* (Washington, D.C.: Brookings Institution, 1963).

[3] This is the reflection of the operation of the 'gravity model' observed in the work of Edward Leamer. See among others, E Leamer, 'U.S. Manufacturing and an Emerging Mexico,' *North American Journal of Economics and Finance* 4:1 (1993): 54-62.

[4] An important distinction has to be made here between the impact of a federalizing EU and the effect of NATO. NATO, a military alliance, may well, at least in principle, evoke Balance of Power effects. Thus, the admission of Poland or even the Baltic countries to EU presents no problems for Russia. Their admission to NATO, however, raises questions and causes opposition in Moscow.

[5] See Paul Kennedy, *The Rise and Fall of the Great Powers: Economic Change and Military Conflict from 1500 to 2000* (New York: Random House, 1987).

[6] See Paul Bairoch, 'Europe's Gross National Product: 1800-1975,' *Journal of European Economic History* 5 (1976).

[7] For a recent reinteraction of this view see Donald Kagan, *On the Origins of War and the Preservation of Peace* (New York: Doubleday, 1995). Ludwig Dehio offers similar views in *The Precarious Balance* (London: Chatto & Windus 1963).

[8] See Kenneth Boulding, *Conflict and Defense: A General Theory* (New York: Harper, 1962), and the critique of deterrence offered by Karl W. Deutsch, *The Analysis of International Relations* (Englewood Cliffs: Prentice Hall, 1978). See also N. Lebow and Janice Stein, 'Deterrence and the Cold War,' *Political Science Quarterly* (Summer, 1995). A further application of this point is provided by Deborah Larson in *Anatomy of Mistrust: US-Soviet Relations during the Cold War* (Ithaca: Cornell University Press, 1997).

[9] See Kenneth Boulding, 'The Weapon as an Element in the Social System' in *The Future of the International Strategic System*, ed. Richard Rosecrance (Chandler: San Francisco, 1972).

[10] See Michael Howard, 'Reassurance and Deterrence: Western Defense in the 1980s' *Foreign Affairs* 61 (Winter, 1982/83).

[11] See particularly, Deborah Larson, *Anatomy of Mistrust*.

[12] See George Homans, *The Human Group* (New York: Harcourt Brace, 1950) and J.K. Chadwick Jones *Social Exchange Theory: Its Structure and Influence in Social Psychology* (London: Academic Press, 1976).

[13] See Alexander George, *Bridging the Gap: Theory and Practice in Foreign Policy* (Washington, D.C.: United States Institute of Peace Press, 1993).

[14] See Stephen Krasner, 'Assymetries in Japanese-American Trade: The Case for Specific Reciprocity' Policy Paper No. 32, Institute of International Studies (University of California, Berkeley.), 1987.

[15] See Richard Rosecrance and Arthur Stein, 'Beyond Realism: the Domestic Bases of Grand Strategy' in *The Domestic Bases of Grand Strategy* eds. R. Rosecrance and A. Stein (Ithaca, NY: Cornell University Press, 1993).

[16] For contrasting views see Inis Claude, *Swords into Ploughshares: The Problems and Progess of International Organization* (New York: Random House, 1971) (and Kupchan and Kupchan article in *IS*. See also R. Rosecrance and C. Low, 'Balancing, Stability, and War: The Mysterious Case of the Napoleonic International System' *International Studies Quarterly*, (December, 1996).

[17] See the work of Paul Schroeder, particularly 'Historical Reality vs Neo-Realist Theory,' *International Security* Summer, 1994.

[18] As the Grand Inquisitor laments in *The Gondoliers*: 'When everybody's somebody, nobody's anybody.'

[19] See Karen Smith's essay in this volume.

[20] See Samuel Huntington *The Clash of Civilizations and the Remaking of World Order* (NY: Simon and Schuster, 1996).

CHAPTER II

A Foreign Policy in Search of a Polity

Jean-Marie Guéhenno

The inability of the European Union to deal effectively with the Yugoslav crisis has had a lasting impact on the image of Europe and on the confidence of Europeans in European institutions. The supporters of Europe usually answer those critics by pointing to the fact that the Yugoslav crisis broke out before effective institutions were in place; for them, it is a crisis that came too early in the history of the European Union. The sceptics are not convinced by this institutional argument, and underline the resilience of national interest which remains, in their view, the only solid foundation for foreign policy. According to them, it is indeed naive to expect institutions to overcome national rivalries, and the absence of breakthroughs during the intergovernmental conference apparently confirms that cautious view: the so-called 'realist school' of international relations seems to be vindicated by the vitality of national identities, and the weakness of the present 'common foreign and security policy' of the European Union. However, the assumptions on which this 'realist' understanding of foreign policy is based deserve a closer examination, and another hypothesis needs to be explored: the present difficulties of the European Union may reflect, not the resilience of its Member States, but a crisis of body politics, a crisis of democracy: the weakness of the European polity is no proof of the strength of national polities.

NATIONAL INTERESTS RECONSIDERED

Most modern European states are the heirs of monarchs and princes, and our understanding of international relations is very much coloured by this historical origin. We have an almost anthropomorphic view of nations, and we often describe them as though they were living people, with a particular character. This may be a remnant of a time when the foreign policy of a nation was a reflection of the character of the prince who ruled it. Indeed, concentration of power is an essential assumption of the realist school of international relations. Nations are expected to act as unified single actors, and democratic thinking has rarely questioned that assumption. The first challenge of democracy was not to build power and to create a polity, but to control power. Power and the willingness to use it have been considered as a given, a starting point, which did not have to be patiently nurtured and developed.

This genealogy of power has very important implications for foreign policy. It has been assumed that princes pursue their own personal interests, and foreign policy has been defined as an extension of this approach; just as princes worked hard to extend their estates and increase their wealth, often at the expense of their neighbours, modern nations are expected to pursue collectively, and maybe with more sophistication, the same aims. This psychological definition of interest has rarely been questioned, and is generally considered to be self-evident.

The concept of 'national interest' transfers to the nation the personal interests of the monarch, and serves a very useful purpose: at once, it legitimises the democratic control of power and the use of that power. The assumption that each nation has a national interest is still the working hypothesis of most analysts, because it seems to have obvious operational value. The hypothesis creates a common analytical ground, on which 'interests' can be assessed and balanced. As a consequence, the objectives of foreign policy can be easily defined as the pursuit of national interests, and the art of diplomacy is the art of accommodating various and often conflicting national interests.

The concept of 'balance of power' is a direct application of that analysis, and can be conceived as the foreign policy equivalent of Adam Smith's invisible hand. Henry Kissinger, in his book *Diplomacy*, rightly notes:

> Intellectually, the concept of balance of power reflected the convictions of all the major political thinkers of the Enlightenment. In their view, the Universe, including the political sphere, operated according to rational principles which balanced each other. Seemingly random acts by reasonable men would, in their totality, tend toward the common good, though the proof of this proposition was elusive in the century of constant conflict that followed the Thirty Years' War.[1]

This realistic, and very Kissingerian, qualification of the beauty of the concept of balance of power reflects the pessimism of an historian whose vision of history parallels his vision of human nature. Diplomacy is the art of postponing problems, of averting disasters, it has no metaphysical ambition of suppressing evil, or even of building institutions that would overcome the solitary pursuit of national interest. Actually, national interests remain the cornerstone of a good understanding of international relations, and the starting point of any diplomatic endeavour. There is a striking similarity between the nineteenth century British definition of foreign policy, as quoted by Kissinger from Palmerston, and the American definition of diplomacy, when Kissinger was in a position to influence, and sometimes shape it. Palmerston, in 1856, said: 'When people ask me for what is called a policy, the only answer is that we mean to do what may seem to be the best, upon each occasion as it arises, making the Interests of Our Country one's guiding principle.' The same Palmerston uttered the famous sentence: 'we have no eternal allies, and no permanent enemies . . . our interests are eternal, and those interests it is our duty to follow'.[2] These British definitions seem to have inspired the foreign policy reports drafted by Kissinger during the Nixon presidency:

> Our objective, in the first instance, is to support our *interests* over the long run with a sound foreign policy. The more that policy is based on a realistic assessment of

our and others' interests, the more effective our role in the world can be . . . our interests must shape our commitments, rather than the other way round'.[3]

The common theme of all these quotations is that there is a pre-existing, underlying interest that has to be uncovered, deciphered, through analytical and diplomatic skill. The good diplomat is like an archaeologist, digging through the foundations of his nation, to reveal that precious hidden beauty, the true national interest. The only real debate is whether one can entertain an optimistic view of the international system and of human nature; in which case, the invisible hand of reason would bring peace and harmony, because all nations would have identified their true national interests, which would not conflict with each other. After World War I, the promoters of the Société des Nations, who (for the most part) did not question the concept of nation, had such expectations and hoped that democracy (understood as the triumph of reason) would lay the foundations for eternal peace between separate national entities. In a more pessimistic vision shared by Kissinger, peace will always remain a very precarious affair, either because human beings are incapable of consistently identifying their rational interests or because there are irreconcilable interests, and diplomats can consider themselves successful when – like their great ancestors of the nineteenth century so admired by Kissinger – they postpone war for almost a century.

The present difficulties of European integration are therefore seen by many Kissingerians as a confirmation that the whole effort was flawed from the beginning, and that the failure of Europeans to develop a true foreign policy is a consequence of a basic mistake: national interests are the foundation of a foreign policy, and any effort to circumvent them is bound to fail. It is important to determine whether they are right. European integration after World War II is an attempt to create an alternative to both Wilsonian idealism and Kissingerian 'realism' by questioning the assumptions on which they are based. Has it succeeded?

EUROPEAN INTERESTS RECONSIDERED

European integration is based on the assumption that national interests can be changed, that they are not permanent or 'eternal,' as Palmerston asserted. Two world wars and three Franco-German conflicts in less than a century have convinced the French and the Germans that there has to be more to European diplomacy than permanent rivalry dictated by geography and history. In the context of the tabula rasa of 1945, several European leaders took what they thought was a realistic look at European history, and found that the 'permanence' of interests and conflicts depended on the time scale chosen, and that what could appear permanent on a scale of two or three centuries had actually changed quite substantially, if one took a longer view. They also took a realistic look at the progress made in destructive capabilities by modern armies and at the shifting position of European nations vis à vis the rest of the world. They realistically concluded that political will, diplomacy, and institutions could have an impact and change the interplay of interests and that it was a matter of self interest – and maybe survival – to change the perception of their interests by

European nations. There was more to diplomacy than analytical skill in making it possible to decipher one's own interest.

By and large, they have been successful, and European integration has substantially changed the perceptions of national interests. Partly through institutions, partly through a process of globalisation that is not specifically European, the economic circumstances of nations have indeed been changing and with them the perception of national interest. The combination of interdependence and transnational contacts weakens purely national perceptions, and it becomes more difficult to consider national interest as the ultima ratio of foreign policy. For instance, when one looks at the way German people and French people now define their 'interests' and how they define their relations, it is obvious that some fundamental changes have occurred.

However, the founders of the European Community did not question the link between foreign policy and interests. They expected European countries to overcome their old rivalries because they would share permanent common interests. A new European interest would replace the old national interests as the basis of foreign policy. Actually, the fundamental assumption that foreign policy is linked to interests remained unquestioned, and the promoters of European integration believed, in a somewhat Marxist way, that growing economic integration would create a common 'European interest' that would lay the foundation for a common foreign and security policy.

This assumption has led to many rather ineffective efforts to draw up lists of common European interests, the first of which was the famous 'Asolo list.' In a very rational manner, European diplomats have been trying to identify those interests that precede policy, and on the basis of which a foreign policy could be built. We assumed that we only had to make visible what was invisible, explicit what was implicit. Today, one has to reckon that this approach has created no momentum, and that the elusive common European interest has yet to produce an effective common foreign policy. If this failure is not the consequence of the resilience of conflicting national interests, we have to ask whether there is a deeper flaw in our assumptions, and if we have misinterpreted the complex links between interests, polity, and foreign policy.

To transform the perception of national interests is not enough to create a European interest, as we have learned from the Yugoslav crisis: while there were different perceptions and sympathies in Germany and France at the beginning of the crisis, perceptions merged as the crisis developed, and at no time was there a clash of national interests. What was actually striking was the absence, on both sides, of any strong national interest. The only strong interest, which was common to the two nations, was to prevent the crisis from jeopardising the quality of Franco-German relations. This is actually the exact opposite of the Palmerstonian view of national interest. One could say that in today's Europe, there are no permanent interests, there are only permanent allies. Such a proposition is quite different from the assumptions of the founders of Europe, and raises new issues.

First, can we assume, as they implicitly did, that there is already a self-evident European polity? This was never the case in the past, and it is even less true after the end of the Cold War. In its first 30 years, the European Community did not have to define its borders, except when it declined to include – temporarily – Britain and –

more durably – Turkey. Borders were imposed by geography (the Atlantic Ocean) on the western side and by history (the iron curtain) on the eastern side. The relevance of the Atlantic divide was always a question, but the answer could be postponed so long as there was a fundamental threat on the eastern side. European integration was about organising and strengthening the democratic exception at the western tip of Eurasia. Resisting the existential threat on the eastern front was the only serious issue of foreign policy. And while there could be differences, and sometimes quite unpleasant bickering between Americans and Europeans, nobody – not even De Gaulle, in spite of the rhetoric – could seriously question US leadership whenever there was a real crisis.

Today's situation is quite different and questions that were always there but could be conveniently forgotten need to be answered. When an American policy maker[4] describes the United States as a 'European power,' Europeans cannot dismiss the statement easily. Europeans can protest by pointing to geography, but they instinctively understand the limit of such an argument in an era when geography is becoming less relevant. They are then led to stress the differences between a supposedly 'European model' and an 'American model,' but this argument also has its limitations. There are notable differences between European countries and while it is true that the share of GNP that is redistributed through public institutions is much higher in Europe than in the United States, both 'models' are in crisis and most Europeans, while rejecting the 'American model,' would agree that their 'model' needs some very substantial reform. Both 'models' need to be adapted, and they might do well to meet halfway. Another fashionable view is that economic competition for wealth has replaced the traditional political competition for space and security. It is indeed true that the interests of Airbus clash with those of Boeing, but competition between companies is not enough to define competition between countries or groups of countries, and in many sectors of the economy, the transnational diffusion of shareholding, research, production, and marketing may well blur the national identities of companies.

Moreover, to assert that the primary purpose of a nation is to promote the wealth of its citizens just postpones the answer to the question of identity, rather than answers it. How does one define the limits of a particular group collectively pursuing greater wealth? The inhabitants of Turkey and Maghreb, countries that have been linked by geography to the history of Europe, pointedly ask the question and would happily join the European Union. But Europeans do not want to consider the prospect. And while it is easy for them to point to differences in wealth that make such a project impractical, or to human rights violations in some of the countries concerned, nobody doubts that the real reason is religion: although there are several millions Muslims within the European Union, Europeans cannot accept the idea that overwhelmingly Muslim countries could join the Union. But Europeans do not care to admit that fact and would probably find no agreement between them if they tried to give a positive definition of Europe as a Christian or Judeo-Christian entity (they would actually be embarrassed because they would still want to exclude Orthodox Russia from that entity).

This raises a major question on the strategy that is expected eventually to produce a common foreign and security policy. If we reject the utilitarian view that political entities are born when a given community becomes aware of the common interests it has to protect or promote, then the expectation that the consolidation of some – very elusive as we have seen – European common interests will be sufficient to create a European political entity is flawed, and some very different assumptions should be made. Political entities are not born because of a functional logic; the real process may actually be the opposite. Instead of being shaped by common interests, political communities create those common interests and perceptions and a political community becomes strong by providing an answer both to functional and identity needs. If there is to be a European foreign policy, it is not enough to overcome the national interests of the Member States. Common European interests are as much political constructs as the national interests they are expected to supersede: national interests were produced by national polities therefore a European foreign policy requires a European polity, which will produce European interests.

How Do Political Communities Emerge?

Today we face a new situation in European history. Europeans have been used to inheriting the community in which they live. They are now expected to form a community of choice and, unlike the United States, this new community has to define its territorial scope. It does not have to identify the interests of a particular territorial community, but rather to identify the territory that will fit particular interests, which themselves must be selected with a view to shaping a particular community. This is a complete reversal of the process through which we usually interpret the shaping of foreign policy and it differs substantially from the American experience. At the time of the Federalist Papers, what was discussed was whether Americans should form a single nation or several, but nobody contested the proposition that the United States was indeed different from 'foreign nations,' i.e., European nations. The outer limits of the American community were considered to be self-evident: even in a continent as free from traditions as the 'new world,' the political problem that confronted Americans was in a way traditional; they did not have to decide how to define their community, but simply how to manage it.

Europeans have no such luxury: they have to collectively decide how specific and different they are from the rest of the world, on what basis they will define that specificity, and for which Europe. These questions present Europeans with some of their oldest and most enduring contradictions: the continent of monotheism prides itself on its universalism, and it is the birthplace of metaphysics; nowhere more than in Europe do we find this ambition to provide an all-encompassing unified answer that would bring us 'Truth.' Intellectually, Europe can have no borders, and that is why Holbrooke's statement that the United States is a European power may trouble the Europeans more than its author intended.

And yet the universalist ambition of Europe has clashed consistently with the reality of religious and political diversity. Religious wars, in which conflicting views of the 'truth' were in conflict, were more bitter and cruel than elsewhere and the plurality of states in Christian Europe is a reminder of the problematic and contingent character of human institutions. The recognition of the distance between Caesar's world and God's is actually an important component of the European tradition, embodied in the multi-secular rivalry between the pope and the emperor. Historically, European integration, promoted by Christian democrats like Adenauer, Schuman, or De Gasperi, can be seen as an ultimate attempt to bridge that gap, and to achieve a secular universalism, but what kind of universalism is it that has to stop at the hypothetical geographic border of Europe? The founding fathers of the European community did not have to answer that question. Nor did the United States, which could reconcile its universalism with the contingent fact of being a particular country by becoming a model.

But today, we have to recognise the great difference between the existing American polity and the yet-to-be-born European polity. History has created very different emotions on either side of the Atlantic. Every nation has to find a balance between two definitions of itself: between its relation to the past and its common memories, and its ambitions for the future and a common project. In the case of the United states, the balance has clearly been tipped toward the future, and the American nation can be defined as a contract with the future: its founding myth is to provide a second chance to all immigrants who have been let down by their own countries. In the case of Europe, the balance is clearly tipped toward the past and the European contract with the future does not match the strength of national memories, even if national memories do not clash with each other any more.

That difference is crucial because there can be no polity without a sense of belonging, without common feelings, or 'fellow feelings' as Adam Smith would have said. The American polity is still self-evident, and the European polity still is not. Does that mean that if interests are not permanent, emotions are? Or that they change more slowly than interests? Has European integration entered a phase in which it has to engineer common emotions in the same way it engineered common interests? Is it the case that, after having provided for the solid foundations of common interests and cleared the deck of conflicting national emotions, politicians who are responsible for the future of Europe can now build the superstructure of common emotions? In France the importance given to the ultimate goal of a common defence sometimes seems to reflect the French national experience of a country that consolidated its identity when the volunteers of a revolutionary army shouted 'Vive la Nation' at Valmy. In that sense, German and French troops parading together on the Champs-Elysees could be seen as a nascent European army that would spur the imaginations of the European people. Likewise, it is interesting to note that in Germany as well as in France, the supporters of EMU now use political rather than economic arguments. The introduction of a common currency is expected to restart the dynamics of Europe, and move the European Union into a new phase of political integration. The strong symbolism of a single currency – an expression of sovereignty for many centuries and a fixture of our daily lives – is supposed to provide the bridge between the Europe of technocrats and the Europe of citizens. Moreover, identification through economic criteria of the group of countries that will participate in the EMU conveniently recreates a core group, and may establish a polity that will not need to define its borders because, instead of inheriting them from history, it will have inherited them from economics. What a relief for Europeans not to have to make a decision on the limits of their polity!

However, the growing reluctance of the people of Europe to follow the path that is prepared for them raises questions about the method that has been chosen. The manipulation of Europeans contradicts the ideal on which European integration is based. Once again, it seems that European integration is expected to result from the decisions of an enlightened elite that knows better, and will create a 'fait accompli' that will change people's perceptions. This very undemocratic approach for achieving European democracy, while apparently bringing us closer to the emergence of a European foreign policy, may actually make it more difficult to achieve this goal. It assumes a pre-existing 'European interest,' and reduces the issue of democracy to an issue of accountability and democratic control.

Democracy and Foreign Policy

However, democracy is not necessary just to control the policy-making process. It is part and parcel of the substance of foreign policy. In the absence of a clearly defined European polity and of self-evident 'European interests' which could be deciphered by an enlightened elite, the policy-making process which would create a European foreign policy becomes an essential component of a European foreign policy, and an integral part of its substance. The process actually creates the polity and the 'interests.' It is only through the tensions and conflicts of a public debate that we can expect to forge first a European polity, then European interests with which European people can identify, and eventually a European foreign policy. Without a Europe-wide public debate on how Europeans want to define their relations with the rest of the world, the support of the Europeans for 'European interests' will remain as weak as the European polity itself, and it will be practically impossible to develop a sustainable European foreign policy, that is to say a European foreign policy that enjoys the support of the European people.

If this analysis is correct, the institutional steps that are now being taken are quite insufficient. A European foreign policy will not be produced by incremental additions to political cooperation, and CFSP as it now exists, stands no chance because it remains a bureaucratic process with little relevance for the majority of the people. That does not mean that the combination of a stronger policy-making unit (which would be capable of structuring the issues rather than just compromising between the various positions) and more majority voting would not be a major improvement. But it is not enough, and the present discussion on the balance to be found between intergovernmental and supranational procedures remains too technical, and cannot create the needed political momentum: it ignores how important the process is in building the democratic consensus without which no sustainable foreign policy can be developed.

At this stage of European integration, it is crucial to enlist the participation of the European people. But this participation is not a matter of propaganda and communication skills; it must be rooted in the democratic process. It has often been argued, especially in Germany, that this goal can be achieved by enlarging the powers of the European Parliament. The point can indeed be made that the credibility of the European Union would be enhanced if its positions were produced not only by precarious diplomatic compromises, which can be undermined by playing on bilateral relations and 'national' interests, but also reflected the constraints of a democratic debate. For instance, in the case of Turkey, it is clear that the European Parliament indeed plays a role that lends some credibility to the requirements of the European Union vis à vis Turkey. However, those nostalgic for a more traditional and less public diplomacy will recall that the European Parliament has often fallen victim to powerful lobbies, or has taken rhetorical and sometimes irresponsible positions that have done little to improve the quality of a virtual European foreign policy.

A greater role for the European Parliament can provide only part of the answer. A parliament can help create a polity, but it is also a reflection of the dynamism and strength of a particular polity. The quality of parliamentary debate is a reflection of the quality and coherence of the civil society for which it is a political expression. Lobbies are not inherently bad if they take part in a vibrant and balanced debate. The problem with today's Europe is that the very uneven development of a European civil society does not create the conditions for a sound parliamentary debate: some issues are taken up by a powerful lobby, while other issues, which may ultimately be of greater importance, do not trigger any debate. And while the relevance of parliamentary debates will grow as the Parliament acquires more power, it may not be enough to consolidate a polity. It has to find the support, not only of professional politicians, but more importantly of a dynamic civil society. In a world characterised by the diffusion of power, it is an illusion to expect a traditional political institution such as a parliament to provide the foundations for a European polity.

Institutions do not by themselves produce a polity. But some initiatives are the responsibility of governments and European institutions. For instance, at a time of high unemployment and growing doubts about the usefulness of compulsory military service, the creation of a European 'peace corps' could help cement new grassroots solidarity and a sense of commitment to Europe. But more will depend on the initiatives of the civil society itself: the development, on a Europe-wide basis, of non-governmental organisations may achieve more in transforming public spirit and eventually contributing to the creation of a European foreign policy than countless diplomatic meetings.

These steps, combined with real institutional reform, should help build the foundations for a European foreign policy. But the European polity, and subsequently the European foreign policy that may eventually emerge, will be quite different from our historical experience. The difficulty to define the western as well as the eastern borders of Europe, the fact that the search for power has historically created division within Europe rather than fostered unity will change the nature of 'European power.' If it means that the Europeans can regain control over decisions that affect their lives, it will be seen as a legitimate democratic goal, and it will find support. But if European power is perceived to be a goal in itself, it will be rejected by the majority of Europeans, who do not want to replace their old nationalism with a new 'euro-nationalism' that they consider to be as dangerous as older nation-based nationalisms. A European foreign policy will indeed reflect the emergence of a European power. But that power will be sustainable only if it attempts to redefine the role of power in international relations, and aim at European interdependence rather than European independence. At the time of the Renaissance, Italian cities invented the modern model of national interest and international relations which still inspires contemporary diplomacy. Europe will keep up with its best traditions if it can now invent the new paradigm that will fit our transnational world.

NOTES

[1] Henry Kissinger, *Diplomacy* (New York: Simon & Schuster, 1994): 21.
[2] ibid., 95-96.
[3] ibid., 711-712.
[4] Richard Holbrooke, *Foreign Affairs*, March/April (1995).

CHAPTER III

Convergence, Divergence and Dialectics: National Foreign Policies and the CFSP

Christopher Hill

The story of the interplay between national foreign policies and the EU's foreign policy is replete with paradox: has European Political Cooperation (EPC) and the Common Foreign and Security Policy (CFSP) 'rescued' the foreign policy of the national state, as Allen has suggested?[1] Have not the various national policies displayed tendencies of convergence as well as divergence? Is not the very idea of a 'common' European foreign policy still dependent on the existence of separate national policies and a tacit division of labour between them? Of course paradox, ambiguity, and complexity have always been what makes politics and all other human activity compulsory viewing, and their ubiquity here should draw us towards the subject of European foreign policy, not away from it. This chapter will explore the paradoxes of convergence and divergence by developing one of the editor's initial explanatory hypotheses, that of the 'logic of diversity,' and by then moving to a closer examination of what constitutes the 'European foreign policy-making process,' in which both states and European institutions are now so deeply embedded. It will then develop into an argument about the dialectics of this process in which the established elements of both solidarity and fragmentation help define each other.[2]

THE LOGIC OF DIVERSITY

The idea of the 'logic of diversity,' which Jan Zielonka has brought sharply back into focus, derives from the work of Stanley Hoffmann, and in this writer's view it is one of the most profitable ways of approaching Europe's multilayered international relations.[3] Drawing on Rousseau, Hoffmann argued that 'the present [international] system profoundly conserves the diversity of nation-states despite all its revolutionary features'.[4] After the break up of the Soviet empire and the stalling of the Maastricht project this judgement seems more rather than less relevant. Yet this is not a model which merely replicates the stale insights of realism and neo-realism: change is taking place in Europe which goes well beyond a rearrangement of coalitions or patterns of power. As Hoffmann pointed out in the 1990s, looking back, the relationship between the nation state and the European Union (EU) is not zero-sum; the EU has become 'a singular construction' at the same time as it has helped the restoration of the nation state. What is more, the EU 'is now a necessary and permanent part of the European political landscape, and thus a subtle, if often shaky, actor in international affairs.'[5]

When this observation is brought down to the level of daily practice, it means that, on the one hand, 'Europe' does act in various issue areas, such as trade policy, central America, or the CSCE.[6] Moreover Europeans also act variously as individuals, groups, and nations, and are sometimes taken by outsiders to be representative of Europe as a whole. Yet, on the other hand, as this book has pointed out from the outset, there are many things that are not and cannot be done at any level, while the aspirations to a collective foreign policy remain largely unmet. Moreover, the fact that this failure to progress has now registered in the consciousness of elites across Europe means that the 'renationalisation' of foreign policy, or the reassertion of the nation state as an international actor, is freely discussed. Traditional national foreign policies, even German and Italian, are now arguably moving back into the space that the CFSP has proved unable to occupy through an insufficient socialisation of its units into a common mentality and definition of interests.

If this apparent reversal of history seems to go too far, then it should be remembered that the logic of diversity does not imply the return of some seventeenth century sense of triumphant statism.[7] Rather, it refers to the way in which common pressures are exerted on differing 'national situations', to use Hoffman's words again.[8] Different histories mean divergent identities, widely differing political systems (even within the confines of liberal democracy), differing patterns of relationships with the wider world, and differing capabilities at all levels. These contrasts – which need not cause problems or conflicts, but which will inhibit integration – certainly make common action in foreign and defence policy problematical, not least because of the premium put on unity and decisiveness in this area of public policy more than any other. In that perpetual contest between homogeneity and difference, between lumping and splitting, which comes as close as any other to defining politics, European foreign policy-making is stuck with a full measure of 'difference.'

Through this lens of what might be termed 'historical realism,' then, a mass of data can be observed which suggests that if the EU states are not actually 'going back to the future,' they are certainly not rapidly converging on a common foreign policy. Some states are particularly insistent on their independence; some cases are particularly liable to produce a splintering of European reactions. Taking the states first, there is a clear continuum of degrees of socialisation. At one end are the states that welcome the discipline and protection of the CFSP and therefore rarely cause it embarrassment. Here we find the Benelux countries, with the Netherlands now much less worried about balancing European with Atlanticist or ex-colonial loyalties than ever before. Their foreign policies are on a convergence trajectory, such that the realist writer Alfred Pijpers observed recently that 'it is fully realised in The Hague that a unilateral Dutch foreign policy does not make much sense any more, and that the success or failure of national initiatives is to a large extent determined by the limits and possibilities of a common European foreign policy.'[9]

In the middle of the continuum, with some naturally leaning more to one end than the other, we find the majority of EU states generally supportive of CFSP, not anxious to break ranks for the sake of it, but still with distinctive concerns that limit convergence. Spain and Portugal, for example, are enthusiastic neophytes of integration but have concerns in the Mediterranean and the southern hemisphere which make them hesitate before backing the extension of the Community method into foreign policy. Likewise the neutral states, Austria, Finland, Ireland, and Sweden, seek to balance their undoubted desire for shelter under the umbrella of common European positions against their reluctance to be drawn into new defence commitments through a developing EU-WEU relationship. Also broadly cooperative but not always reliable are the two big states, Germany and Italy, which have paradoxically discovered through their founding membership of EPC the confidence to assert themselves more. They still subscribe to the goal of a single European foreign policy, but in practice they have both shown more rather than less willingness to step out of line – whether over Slovenia, Croatia, and Albania in the Balkans, or Iran and China further afield.

At the 'uncooperative' end of the continuum stand the usual culprits: Britain, France, Denmark, and Greece. The two former are Security Council members and militarily powerful states that consequently regard themselves as having special responsibilities that cannot be fettered by *communautaire* procedures. Over the last ten years they have gone their own way (rarely in harness) on major problems such as South Africa, the Gulf, Bosnia, and Algeria. Denmark and Greece are also concerned for their independence, but for rather different reasons. Greece is integrationist in principle, but has not always agreed with the majority view on issues like Macedonia and Cyprus, just as it opted out from common positions on the USSR in the early 1980s. Denmark is less concerned about the substance of foreign policy, but very concerned with issues of principle: it will not relinquish sovereignty in the CFSP, partly for historical reasons and partly out of a generalised opposition to the federal tendency within the EU. Of course even these recalcitrants show no desire to break up the CFSP. Indeed Britain has been broadly positive towards what has been done within it, and France is traditionally in favour of Europe developing as a 'third force' (now presumably a second) in wider international relations. Divergence, in other words, exists within limits and coordination is accepted as an obligation and unquestioned benefit.

Could things, indeed, be any different, now that EPC/CFSP has been in existence for 27 years (the same time-span that separated Gavrilo Princip's shots in Sarajevo from Japanese bombs in Pearl Harbour)? There is an *acquis politique* that new members of the EU have to accept, and all Member States without exception would now find the idea of an EU without a international political presence almost literally inconceivable. This is how far things have come; despite the many setbacks, there is an embedded multilateralism about the EU's foreign policies (sic) in the 1990s.[10]

The multilateralism, however, is intergovernmental, the cooperation is intermittent and the presence is sometimes ineffectual. The limits set by the logic of diversity on European actorness are just as firm as those set by the acquis politique on unilateralism. Are there any reasons to suppose that convergence can continue in foreign policy, and that the famous *saut qualitatif* towards singularity might still be within reach?

The Logic of Convergence

From a theoretical perspective there are four ways in which a positive answer might be given to this question:

Rational calculations might lead Member States in due course to conclude that the advantages of the politics of scale outweigh the temptations of selfishness – in other words, the temptation of chasing Rousseau's rabbit is finally overshadowed by the attractions of the stag hunt, although whether it is because the stag has become more desirable or simply easier to catch is not clear.[11] The economistic, not to say globalist, approach to international relations would expect this to be an inevitable product of the inability of individual units to survive in an integrated marketplace, while the rational strategist would see the advent of regional powers as the logical consequence of nuclear weapons and the exponential growth in the cost of hi-tech armaments. There would, however, be two caveats even for exponents of this view. First, solidarity does not necessarily mean convergence if it is achieved on the basis of calculated self interest, and it follows that a coalition could fall apart through loss of common purpose or under the impact of some disruptive event, if a sense of common identity has not also been forged. Second, the increase in the pace and breadth of EU enlargement throws into doubt part of the logic behind the politics of scale, namely that more automatically means stronger. It is only too plausible that an EU made up of 21 states in the year 2001 (as the Commission recommended in July 1997) will find it even more difficult than it does now to produce a consistently unified and resilient foreign policy.[12]

External demands and perceptions could gradually force the European tower of Babel to quieten down and to speak with a single, comprehensible voice. This is a version of Schmitter's externalisation hypothesis, or even of Josef Joffe's American pacifier.[13] The need to deal with powerful or problematic countries such as the United States or Israel has to some extent already imposed discipline and caution on the European group while the experience of the common commercial policy and the GATT rounds seems to provide obvious lessons for the CFSP. Insofar as more and more regional groupings are seeking bloc to bloc relations with the EU, and key states like Japan or South Africa see it as a partner in the way that they do not look to individual European states or the United States, this set of pressures for solidarity is likely to increase.

The evolution of the international system could push and pull the EU into greater actorness in politics as well as commercial policy. This would be partly a function of the bloc to bloc relations referred to above and partly the result of deeper forces, of which the EU as the first and biggest of all regional blocs is itself the main manifestation. A Waltzian emphasis on the security dilemma produced by the international system for its component parts might well lead one to suppose, particularly in the more fluid and unpredictable one-superpower world, that the EU will be forced to acquire the ability to defend itself and to protect its interests abroad. Security and defence policy will then drive foreign policy, rather than vice versa as is often supposed, by compelling states to create the political process necessary to make decisions on defence. This is essentially the view of those who predict that the United States will not be willing to underwrite the security of another nascent superpower forever, or that the development of new threats to an enlarged and more vulnerable Union will require the capacity to meet them at a military level. On this view, halfway between realism and determinism, the mechanism of the balance of power will lead the EU to its manifest destiny as a great power.

A convergence of values leading to a redefinition of national interests according to a genuine sense of collective identity could be occurring, and might even be near that unknowable point of no return, fostered by common experiences, by common procedures over nearly three decades, and by an increasing sense of the Other(s) – 'we' Europeans are not Americans, Turks, Russians, Moroccans, or whoever else turns up to pose the embarrassing boundary problem.[14] If a sense of common and distinctive civilisation does underpin the European Union, then the question of its precise borders will matter less than the mores and principles which are thought to need preserving and to which by definition no other group would be so committed (this of course begs the question of 'Western' or transatlantic values). If Paul Valéry's remark is true, that 'wherever the names of Caesar, of Gaius, of Trajan and Virgil, wherever the names of Moses, of Saint Paul ... Aristotle, Plato and Euclid have a simultaneous meaning and authority, there Europe is,' then Europe has a secular religion cementing it together.[15] This does not mean – despite 'the triumph of the west' – that the spirit of a crusade is abroad. It is simply that the differences between the nation states in the EU may gradually once again come to seem less important than the things that unite them. This version of neo-mediaevalism (far more than any 'clash of civilisations') could create the conditions for a single foreign policy towards the rest of the world; the EU as a modern version of the Holy Roman Empire – which, as Voltaire pointed out, was itself never holy nor Roman nor even an empire.

Each of these four possible paths for the future convergence of European foreign policies is feasible. Together they might be thought to constitute a powerful case for progression. The key factor, as has often been pointed out from various points of view – realist, rationalist, and constructivist – is whether or not national decision makers are significantly reconceptualising their notions of interest and identity in European terms.[16] 'Interest and identity' are advisedly coupled here; ever since Rosenau's classic critique we have been alerted to ask not just what is the (national) interest at stake, but 'whose interest is the national?'.[17] The identity of the agent therefore helps to define interests, while conversely the pre-existing interests, or stakes in a problem, of a collective entity like a state help to structure its identity. We only need to think of an example like Greece and Cyprus to see the truth of this. Equally, it is important to remember that even if elite decision makers may be shifting their intellectual and emotional boundaries, this does not necessarily mean that they represent their whole societies in so doing. The cold water poured on the Maastricht Treaty by public reaction is a case in point.

In Search of a Balance Sheet

A balance sheet can be drawn up of the elements of convergence and divergence to be found simultaneously in the present system of European foreign policy making.[18] Clearly a mono-causal approach to explaining CFSP outputs is not adequate, and no trend can be definitively identified. Nonetheless, stepping back from the hurly-burly of current affairs makes it possible to place the CFSP in a longer historical perspective, and this may provide some clues to its future.

A freeze frame of the current situation, even if inherently ambiguous, would be interpreted by most people as presenting a negative image of European foreign policy. Far from marking progress, it would seem to show that the motor of foreign policy integration has cut out, leaving the potential ship of state becalmed just as it reaches the open sea. Yet looking back over the 35 years since the first serious effort was made to produce European diplomatic coordination in the Fouchet plans, we can see that we have been here before. There have been many setbacks and periods of stagnation in the journey from Luxembourg to Amsterdam through Copenhagen, London, Stuttgart, Milan, and Maastricht. There is no teleology about this journey, and the present difficulties may turn out to be more than a temporary setback, or merely another staging-post.

Still, there is no denying that since the start of EPC in 1969 the members of the system have become far more familiar and comfortable with each other's foreign policies than they were before. The exchanges of diplomats between the French, German, and even British diplomatic services and the many other procedural innovations are more a symptom than a cause of better working relationships, but the (admittedly limited) common measures over Salman Rushdie and election monitoring in South Africa would not even have been proposed before. 'Europe' had no Mediterranean strategy in the 1960s, and no way of responding jointly to the Six Day War. The United States had no difficulty in dealing with its embarrassed allies individually during the Vietnam War, despite the mass demonstrations on the streets of European cities. The 1968 crises over Cuba and Czechoslovakia passed without the merest glimpse of European coordination. Today this would not be possible. The EU might turn out to be inept, cowardly, or toothless, but the Europeans would at the least agonise over what to do, and they would certainly issue a collective statement on their position. When they cannot even reach an agreement on a declaration, it is a noteworthy event and causes comment. The expectations are now those of commonality, and even of common action; failures to meet these expectations therefore produce political problems inside and outside the EU.[19] This in itself is a mark of considerable change, and of CFSP's status as the most significant system of foreign policy association yet to evolve.

Alternating phases of hope and disappointment for European foreign policy coordination suggest that this historical status has not filtered down to the level of public debate. What they also disguise, however, is the fact that after years of fitful procedural progress EPC/CFSP has now hit a wall of political resistance. It cannot develop further without the creation of a significant executive to mobilise the foreign policy resources of the Member States, to impose discipline, and to implement policy through a single machinery. Without such changes the best that can be hoped for is the present pattern of fitful cooperation, sustained at best for short periods by Member States' fear of isolation and need for cover. Yet conversely, that very jump into foreign policy supranationalism is unlikely to take place without a prior convergence of attitudes, interests, and policies in other issue areas on the part of the Member States – and such convergence is always a matter of the *longue durée*. Perhaps, as the German government has hoped, the great challenges of enlargement and monetary union (far from reinforcing intergovernmentalism as Thatcher and Major gambled) will galvanise constitutional change and thus prevent a bigger Union from collapsing under its own weight. But in the area of foreign policy at least, it must be more likely that an enlarged EU, characterised by differentiated integration in important areas like money and justice, will simply display a wider range of foreign policy positions without providing the means to reconcile them. Poland, Hungary, and the Czech Republic have hardly been an exemplar of group unity, and they will naturally seek to push common policy in the direction of their own distinctive concerns, just as the last three new entrants to the EU have done.[20]

In a broader sense, it may be argued with justice that historical processes are at work which are leading to the convergence of European societies, and perhaps their states, even if convergence has not yet shown up in foreign policy. The sacred concepts of sovereignty and security mean that even diplomats who are professionally international and who in EPC have created a form of European collegiality cannot push foreign policy to the front of the queue for integration. But beneath and around them, the conditions perhaps are being created which could one day make the constitutional move on foreign policy seem inevitable. The desire for peace and prosperity in Western Europe after the second 'thirty years war' produced an economic community and a Franco-German enmeshment that has resulted in the peoples of fifteen states moving freely around each other's territories, becoming relaxed enough with each other to rule out any question of enmity, and sharing an increasingly similar range of rights and services. What is more, as individual states and the very idea of welfarist governments have weakened, so there has been a tendency to look to the EU as a source of shelter in a harshly competitive world (although the United States is still looked to for physical protection).

This is the kind of convergence that has lead some to argue impatiently that European integration, not least in foreign policy, is lagging badly behind both the objective need and the condition of European society. In this light the problem of the lack of 'consistency' between common economic policies and merely coordinated foreign policies becomes an irritating technical distraction rather than a serious issue. The arrival of shared needs and political values (building on Valéry's common cultural heritage) should mean that the real politics now consists in relations with outsiders who might threaten this solid democratic peace and its materially rich foundations. An awareness of globalisation has only heightened the sense that, stripped bare of colonialist advantages and many of the old American subsidies, Europeans can only now survive by clubbing together and accepting the costs as well as the benefits of homogenisation.

From a sociological point of view therefore, there are arguably pressures for convergence in foreign policies which have already produced EPC and its offspring CFSP, and which can be expected, given time, to push things further. There have already been some remarkable developments – Germany, legitimised by its commitment to European cooperation, is beginning to take on peacekeeping responsibilities; France is finding in EPC a way of letting go of the excesses of Gaullism without losing face, and to some extent also its route back to NATO. But these are not in the nature of things spectacular moves, and can only be seen as significant when judged over decades rather than years.

The same is true of the European stance on the Arab-Israeli issue – hammered out in the late 1970s, held to despite the intermittent hostility of all parties to the dispute, and providing a reference point to which all Member States were eventually glad to hold on. Spain and Greece recognised Israel after entering the EC and accepted EPC's even-handed approach to the extent that Spain, once indelibly pro-Arab, now provides Europe's Special Representative in the Middle East.[21] The Europeans have broadly held together under great pressure from Israel, and to a lesser extent the United States, as they have moved towards a greater degree of identification with the Palestinian cause and a more outspoken frustration with Israeli behaviour in the occupied territories. This is a unity – imperfectly observed to be sure – that has been forged in the most testing of circumstances.

Thus the fact that Europe fails to hold together in crises when it is under the media spotlight is not such a decisive indication of incapacity as it often seems. Europeans are gradually coming to view an increasing number of international problems in the same way, and the degree of divergence between Member State positions has narrowed. If national governments do not always obey the strong language of the Treaty of European Union to 'support the Union's external and security policy actively and unreservedly in a spirit of loyalty and mutual solidarity,' they also do not often display the kind of flagrant disregard for established common positions displayed by French Foreign Minister Cheysson in Jerusalem in 1981, when he announced unilaterally that there would be no European initiative in the Middle East.[22] The shock caused by Germany behaving similarly over the recognition of Croatia and Slovenia in December 1991 was the exception that proved the changing rule, both because it was Germany and because consensus has come to be viewed as too painfully achieved to sacrifice lightly. The well-publicised examples of states going their own way are these days largely in areas where it has not yet been possible to converge on an agreed position (as over Macedonia/FYROM) or in those where the position was ambiguous or lukewarm to begin with (as over sanctions against post-Tienanmen China).[23]

From both the top (the freemasonry of diplomats working on the CFSP circuit) and the bottom (the slow transformations of states and societies towards the kind of convergence which the two superpowers once seemed to display but which was never of the same order), the existing system of separate national foreign policies is being squeezed.[24] There is still plenty of life left in it, nevertheless, and the barriers of defence and sovereignty are far from being mere formalities to be swept away by the next charismatic leader able to grasp the nettle of change. But there is a sense in which form and function may be drifting apart, and it is becoming clearer that the problem is the very existence of the Member States themselves. Social and bureaucratic convergence is posing the questions, but only the states can provide the answers – certainly if it means disestablishing themselves.

THE EMERGING EUROPEAN FOREIGN POLICY-MAKING PROCESS

It is to be hoped that if this 'solution' to an historical problem is to be achieved, it will be done calmly and by Europeans in rational control of their political fate. Unfortunately history has a habit of forcing change through crisis and overwhelming threat, as France found in 1940 and the Soviet Union in 1989. A single European foreign policy (and therefore state) may yet be born out of desperation. At present such circumstances naturally seem remote, even apocalyptical. What is more germane is the ability to cope with a wide range of problems arising out of complex interdependence, usually with both political and economic ramifications. Europe has developed a somewhat ramshackle but surprisingly effective system for coping with these diverse demands, and it is worth providing an outline of its operations, since it is the way in which the elements of divergence and convergence currently co-exist.

In recent years there has been much discussion of 'multi-level governance' in world politics.[25] The EU's foreign policy system is not one of government because there is no consistent and comprehensive pattern of decision making – one can never be sure from where the next decision is going to come. But its policy-making culture (for that is what 'governance' means, if anything) is certainly multi-level and mixed actor in character. This can be interpreted in various ways as an equal and balanced system of mixed jurisdictions, national and Community, as a mishmash of confusing and conflicting competences, or as a system in evolution towards communitarianisation[26].

The process in fact goes well beyond the confines of the EU, to which discussion is usually limited; it includes other intergovermental organisations (IGOs), some third states, and increasingly some non-governmental organisations (NGOs) which have been coopted or forced their way into the network of consultations[27] (see Figure 1). Although we always need to keep clearly in mind what the EU specifically can and cannot do, it makes little sense if we try to explain its successes and failures in international relations without reference to the other actors overlapping its area of activity. NATO, for example, is still pre-eminent in defence policy and is no longer bound by 'out of area' restrictions. Equally, its new off-spring, the North Atlantic Cooperation Council (NACC) and the Partnership for Peace (PfP) have made it a major player in the zones beyond Germany's eastern frontier which are one of the EU's foreign policy priorities. France's move back into a closer relationship with NATO has also made it analytically more difficult to separate out the paths of decision and action in relation to policies towards the old Soviet bloc. Thus the two sets of institutional enlargements, NATO's and the EU's, are politically entangled and sometimes deliberately blurred by all parties to them.[28] What is certainly clear is the fact that the EU's decisions towards eastern Europe are not wholly its own.

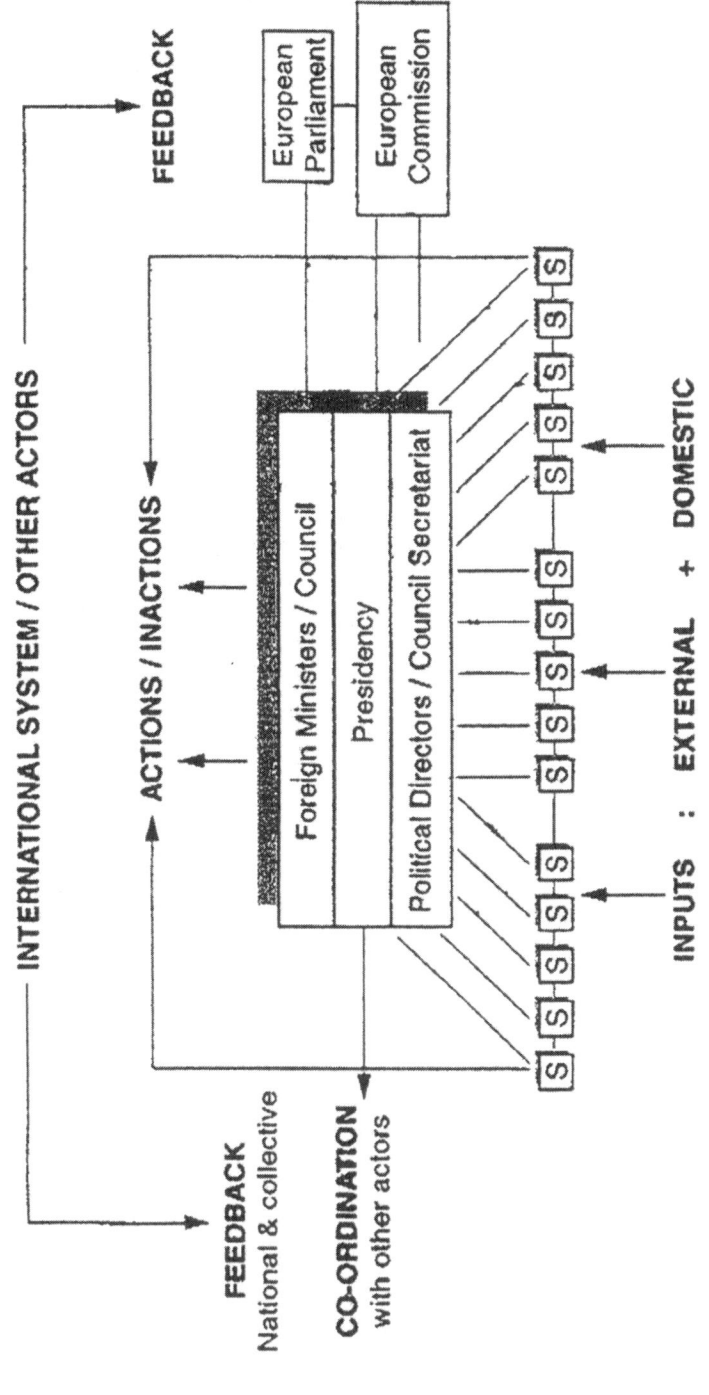

Figure 1 The European Foreign Policy Making Process

This mixed picture is reinforced when we add the ingredient of the WEU. The logical aspirations of many to merge the WEU with the EU have not only not been met by the Treaty of Amsterdam but have not come near to being met. Rather, the deal done on Combined Joint Task Forces (CJTFs) at the June 1996 NATO Berlin Council, has bound the WEU into an even closer relationship with NATO which is theoretically triangular, but in which the EU plays an imprecise role in practice. In the Treaty of Amsterdam there is much talk of the EU 'availing itself' of the WEU, and 'the possibility of the integration of the WEU into the Union, should the European Council so decide,' but a studied vagueness on how the CFSP can issue instructions to an organisation which itself is dependent on NATO for most of its military capability, and which constitutes only two thirds of the EU's membership.[29] Moreover the WEU is still far from being able to create integrated European armed forces, and of the separate states that make it up only France and the United Kingdom are serious military players.

Such mixity of organisations and actors means that it is always difficult to know how to move to agreement – and with whom – during a crisis. The inaction in the Great Lakes crisis of 1996 was partly the result of these uncertainties. Although, when in 1997 it proved impossible to get an EU/WEU peacekeeping force together for Albania, the combination of an Italian initiative, UN legitimacy, and OSCE support produced an alternative that has so far worked better than the cynics predicted. The OSCE, the Nordic Council, and ad hoc arrangements like the Contact Group for Bosnia are other ways in which foreign policy in Europe gets coordinated.

Lurking behind the overlapping institutionalism of course, are other actors that make it even more difficult to know who is shaping 'European' foreign policy. For all its weakness Russia is still a permanent member of the Security Council, and had a place in the Contact Group when Italy did not. Canada is still a member of NATO and of the OSCE. Norway influenced events in the Middle East through the mediation of the Oslo Accords, despite (or perhaps because of) not being in the EU. And the United States is still the most important single influence on the international politics of Europe, despite having withdrawn most of its troops from the continent and despite all the talk in the 1990s of a European Security and Defence Identity. The US affects European society in a myriad of ways. It shares in Europe's policy making through NATO, the OSCE, an inside track of access to the CFSP, the CJTF concept and the G7 of industrialised nations, the UN Security Council, and the various penetrating bilateral relations that it enjoys with all the important European states.[30] The United States, in short, is omnipresent *inside* the common European home and its separate actorness is sometimes difficult to distinguish from that of the Europeans themselves.[31]

The last part of the mixed actor environment from which European foreign policies emerge is relatively new. Non-governmental organisations can no longer wholly be categorised as external influences on formal office holders, pushed to the margins of events by an executive monopoly over external questions. On Third World development questions groups like Oxfam, Médecins sans Frontières, and Christian Aid have become virtual partners of official agencies, and their knowledge of conditions on the ground has made them rather more valuable sources of information than the (increasingly scarce) national diplomats. Not surprisingly their independence from governments can therefore be called into question, and hostage-takings of aid workers are becoming increasingly common. Similarly in Bosnia refugee workers have often had better access to local populations than military or diplomatic representatives, and they have had to confront the same dilemmas about who to help that the Red Cross has suffered with for decades.[32] In the rest of Eastern Europe and the ex-Soviet Union, the various 'know-how' funds of PHARE and TACIS have been created precisely to enable private and public organisations to work in tandem, with the result that some academic groups and private companies have effectively become part of the implementation phase of official policy.

A multi-level system inevitably produces uncertainty, delay and confusion. It also can be flexible, powerful and preventive of extremism. The key question, however, is always whether such a system is in a condition of dynamic transformation towards unified actorness. Even if a clear answer is never going to be possible, we can still address the issue of how much *potential* the system has for self-transformation, and how much of this potential has already been realised.

The matrix out of which any given European foreign policy decision emerges consists of the mixed-actor, multi-level system sketched above, together with the attitudes and perceptions of the political class of the day (meaning both the public and the politicians). The former provides the structure and the latter the agency of the system. But whereas the structure is necessarily slow to change, being under no single actor's formal or practical authority, attitudes and perceptions can be both multifarious and quicksilver in character. They vary between states, within them, and in the same groups over time. But they do not vary randomly. Rather, the processes of social and international change which were discussed in the first part of this chapter, together with the structuring effects of the European institutions themselves, now consolidated over 40 years and including a foreign policy cooperation network most of that time, create a moving platform on which the theatre of politics is played out, inevitably shaped by the character of its stage and set.

The politics of European foreign policy making, therefore, revolves around a dialectic of solidarism/fragmentation where tendencies of each kind are defined and contained by tendencies of the other. The following list of these apparently opposing sets of forces is intended to demonstrate that most elements of the system we now operate display characteristics of both commonality and distinctiveness. We could use the terms centripetal and centrifugal, but this would be too Newtonian a metaphor for a process that has no single centre and no single force acting upon it. Furthermore in human society the way actors think of themselves and their context means a great deal for the way they behave, and the sense of commonality or separateness is central to their identities, morale and purpose.

SOLIDARISTIC FORCES

- Member States now accept that there can be no turning back to the pre-EPC condition. The CFSP, for all its ills, is a permanent and necessary part of their policy environment. Indeed if it did not exist they would probably invent it. CFSP is clearly a significant part of the attraction for potential entrants to the Union, who seek shelter politically within a large bloc as well as to benefit from it economically.

- Even the biggest Members now have a strong sense of the weakness of unilateralism. This does not prevent them from acting unpredictably and in a self-regarding way, but it does mean that they are careful not to bring the CFSP into complete disrepute. There is a *non plus ultra*.

- The smaller Member States now have a heightened sense of collective responsibility for the international system, in particular its European aspect. Neutrality is inevitably attenuated as a result of participating in EPC/CFSP and active involvement, at least in conflict prevention, increases. For some smaller states, like their larger partners, European diplomacy has provided a legitimate way of re-engaging with a wider world, when decolonisation had constituted a form of expulsion. Portugal, Belgium, and the Netherlands are the main cases here.

- Outsiders accept the CFSP process as a working diplomatic caucus. The powerful and the weak, the near abroad and the far distant are all interested in doing business with CFSP. They do not regard it as a busted flush, as the Commonwealth was for so long, or a one-issue association in the way that ASEAN has been. Rather, they see it as a political grouping in the process of becoming whole which may not perform effectively now but may very well do so in the future, and thus needs watching. This is as true of the United States as of Israel, of Iran and of Brazil. The consequent dialogues provide CFSP with status and rationale.

Fragmenting Forces

- National foreign policies still have important functions, such as bilateralism, and the pursuit of particular historical interests. These will at times be perfectly compatible with collective positions (and on a division of labour principle they may actually be desirable), but on others problems over relative gains cannot be avoided.

- Paradoxically, cooperation has given Germany, Italy, and Spain the platform from which to assert national interests more confidently. The criminal and pariah associations of the past had inhibited their behaviour and could only be left behind through involvement in the collective action of a democratic Europe. The new freedom to be treated as 'ordinary countries' which was thereby created does not mean that they wish to leave the safety of the CFSP behind; it is only that they are now less willing to see European foreign policy made by others in their name. Their concern is to shape the substance as well as the procedure of European diplomacy, which will in turn mean occasional clashes with other members – notably Britain and France, who monopolised the leadership of EPC during its first two decades.

- The group of 15 states contains great variety of geography, size, wealth, statehood, and historical roles. This variety provides the EU with a wide range of potential capabilities for foreign policy and also a broad range of different models for foreign policy behaviour. The decision makers and publics of Britain and France are exposed to the perspectives of Austria, Finland, Greece, Spain, and Sweden, as well as to those of their more familiar neighbours and/or alliance partners. There is transformational as well as fissiparous potential here.

- Democratic accountability tends to pull in the same direction as that of national concerns over foreign policy independence. That is, any attempt to exert democratic control over European foreign policy will necessarily be directed at influencing the national government's position in the Council of Ministers, and at forcing change by the threat of a veto or an opt-out. The European Parliament is not yet strong enough in any dimension to be the main focus of agitation. Such actions will, however, expand the knowledge of what the CFSP is about, and are very likely to have transnational effects of emulation or reaction.

- Outsiders have learned how to divide and rule the EU group. Given the mixed-actor system it would be extraordinary if other states needed lessons from game theorists on prisoners' dilemma or stag-hunt strategies as a method for gaining advantage. By the same token, insofar as there is a rational process of calculation at stake, the EU and its Member States will be forced to reassess their own approach to collective action, that is, to the costs and benefits of a given separation of powers.

- Systematic coordination among foreign ministries produces some symptoms of engrenage and collegiality, but bureaucratic politics is also at work. It produces transgovernmental alliances, which do not promote integration but simply cut the cake of European diplomacy in a new way. The Franco-German and Netherlands-Luxembourg 'couples' are the best examples, but Danish and British diplomats have been known to make common cause, and the British and Italian foreign ministries have produced several joint initiatives in recent years. The southern Member States are increasingly caucusing in an attempt to redirect attention from Eastern Europe.[33] It is not completely clear whether these inner groups and shifting alliances help CFSP to function or provide an insurmountable obstacle to its progress.[34]

INTO THE PUBLIC EYE

Any assumption of a 'victory' for the forces of either solidarism or fragmentation would be to make a crass teleological error. We cannot know where the European foreign policy system is heading, and the notion of a 'destination' is mere anthropomorphism. What is clear, however, is the interplay taking place between the national and the collective, and indeed between a range of actors that stretches much further than the EU and its Member States. This has produced a pattern of multi-level diplomacy in which the various elements sometimes compete, sometimes reinforce each other, and sometimes merely coexist. Nested in all this is the CFSP, a focal point despite itself, for unlike the OSCE, NATO, or WEU, the EU is actively trying to bring about accelerated convergence between its members' foreign policies. The continuing strength of national diplomacy is a formidable obstacle to convergence, but it cannot hide the importance and durability of the EPC/CFSP system. It is not simply at the mercy of its members' political rivalries, because in its turn it shapes their perceptions, choices, and behaviour – not least because it is the only way by which Europe can have a high political profile in the global system.

The CFSP has suffered a bad press by pretending that procedural tinkering amounts to a quantum leap forward. But it is sufficiently elastic to incorporate, rather than deny, separate national policies and to work alongside other IGOs like WEU, NATO, and OSCE. The dialectics of these multiple relationships should promote wider understanding of the choices available and the decisions that might be made. A multi-level, multi-actor system after all, cannot go unobserved; it is a form of pluralism writ large which cannot but increase transparency and participation. Technocratic elitism will never go out of its way to encourage public debate, but so far as Europe's many strands of foreign policy are concerned, the day of technocratic elitism may be drawing to a close.

NOTES

[1] David Allen, 'The European rescue of national foreign policy,' in *The Actors in Europe's Foreign Policy*, ed. Christopher Hill (London: Routledge, 1996). This picks up on the ideas of Alan S. Milward, with the assistance of George Brennan and Federico Romero, in *The European Rescue of the Nation-State* (London: Routledge, 1992).

[2] What follows develops, but does not repeat, the author's 'The Actors Involved: National Perspectives,' in *The Foreign Policy of the European Union* eds. Elfriede Regelsberger, Philippe de Schoutheete, and Wolfgang Wessels (Boulder: Lynne Reinner, 1996), and reprinted in adapted form in *Quaderni Forum* 5:1-2 (1996).

[3] Jan Zielonka, *Explaining Euro-paralysis* (London: Macmillan, forthcoming 1998); Stanley Hoffmann, 'Obstinate or Obsolete? France, European Integration and the Fate of the Nation-State,' in ed. Stanley Hoffmann *The European Sisyphus: Essays on Europe 1964-1994* (Boulder: Westview, 1995). Hoffmann's classic essay, first written in 1966 and up-dated in 1973 (the version cited here) still stands as a profound and influential analysis of the historical forces at work in the slow reshaping of Europe. The original can be found in *Daedalus* 95:3 (Summer 1966).

[4] *The European Sisyphus:* Obstinate or Obsolete? (p74).

[5] Ibid: 4-6.

[6] The Conference on Security and Cooperation in Europe. The 'Conference' was transformed in 1995 into an 'Organisation', creating the OSCE.

[7] On the nature of the original principle of *raison d'état*, and its evident remoteness from the philosophy of the modern European state, despite our 'Westphalian' international system, see Adam Watson, *The Evolution of International Society* (London: Routledge, 1992) especially pp182-189, and 195-196. Also see John Vincent, 'Realpolitik,' in *The Community of States*, ed. James Mayall (London: George Allen & Unwin, 1982): 73-84.

[8] 'Obstinate or Obsolete,' see Stanley Hoffman, *The European Sisyphus* (p97).

[9] Alfred Pijpers, 'The Netherlands: the weakening pull of Atlanticism' in *The Actors in Europe's Foreign Policy*, ed. Christopher Hill (p265).

[10] The idea of embeddedness is taken from John Ruggie's notion of 'embedded liberalism.' See his 'International regimes, Transactions and Change: Embedded Liberalism in the Post-War Economic Order,' *International Organisation* 36:2 (1982). Ruggie in turn looked back to Karl Polanyi's *The Great Transformation* (Boston: Beacon Press, 1944), which had distinguished between 'embedded' and 'disembedded' economic interest in multilateralism. Subsequently Ruggie and his colleagues focused our attention back on multilateralism. See *Multilateralism Matters: the Theory and Praxis of an Institutional Form*, ed. John G. Ruggie (New York: Columbia University Press, 1993).

[11] The 'politics of scale' notion was introduced to the study of European foreign policy by Roy Ginsberg, *The Foreign Policy Actions of the European Community: the Politics of Scale* (Boulder: Lynn Reinner, 1989). Rousseau's stag hunt parable is explored in Kenneth Waltz, *Man, the State and War* (New York: Columbia University Press, 1959).

[12] The Commission's view is expressed in 'Agenda 2000,' presented by Jacques Santer to the European Parliament on 16 July 1997.

[13] See Philippe Schmitter, 'Three Neo-Functional Hypotheses about International Integration', *International Organisation* 23:1 (Winter 1969), and Josef Joffe, 'Europe's American Pacifier,' *Foreign Policy* 54 (Spring 1984). Joffe borrowed the term 'pacifier' from Uwe Nerlich.

[14] On Europe's 'others' see Iver B. Neumann and Jennifer Welsh, 'The Other in European Self-Definition: An Addendum to the Literature on International Society,' *Review of International Studies* 17:4 (October 1991). Neumann has continued to produce interesting work on this theme. See his *Russia and the Idea of Europe: A Study in Identity and International Relations* (London: Routledge, 1995), and 'Self and Other in International Relations' in *European Journal of International Relations* 2:2 (June 1996). In this last piece Neumann warns (p168) that '[i]f it is proposed to achieve integration at the price of active othering, that price seems to be too high to pay.'

[15] The quotation is from Valéry's *Regard sur le monde actuel* (Paris: Gallimard, 1945), and is courtesy of Guido Lenzi's 'Reforming the International System: Between Leadership and Power-Sharing,' *The International Spectator* 30:2 (April-June 1965): 69. Also helpful here is Anthony D. Smith, 'National Identity and European Unity', in *The Question of Europe*, eds. Peter Gowan and Perry Anderson (London: Verso, 1997).

[16] For a good summary of the different approaches possible see Karen Elizabeth Smith, 'Explaining Cooperation on an EU Foreign Policy towards Eastern Europe', *Quaderni Forum* 10: 1-2 (1996) especially pp32-41.

[17] James N. Rosenau, 'The National Interest' in his *The Scientific Study of Foreign Policy* (New York: The Free Press, 1971). It was, however, Warner R. Schilling who first broached this kind of question, in his 'The Clarification of Ends – or, Which Interest is the National?,' *World Politics* 8: 4 (1956).

[18] For a balance-sheet of 'what national foreign policies can still do' and 'what national foreign policies cannot do very well' see the author's 'The Actors Involved: National Perspectives,' in *The Foreign Policy of the European Union*, eds. Regelsberger et. al., 1996, op.cit.

[19] Christopher Hill, 'The Capability-Expectations Gap, or Conceptualising Europe's International Role,' *Journal of Common Market Studies* 31:3 (September 1993).

[20] The 57 varieties of differentiated integration produced in the 1980s and early 1990s are discussed by Alexander Stubb, in his 'A Categorization of Differentiated Integration,' *Journal of Common Market Studies* 34: 2 (June 1996). In the IGC, which culminated at Amsterdam in June 1997, the terms 'flexibility' and 'cooperation renforcée' had already overtaken them. On Visegrad et.al., many delicate problems of bilateral relations remain for the countries of eastern Europe. See Monika Wohlfeld (Ed.), *The Effects of Enlargement on Bilateral relations in Central and Eastern Europe* (Paris: WEU Institute for Security Studies, Chaillot Paper no.26, June 1997).

[21] The envoy is Miguel Maratinos, previously Spanish ambassador to Israel. He was appointed by EU foreign ministers in October 1996, apparently at French insistence, immediately after the American envoy, Dennis Ross, flew back to Washington admitting failure. Clearly the aim was to revive the faltering peace process and to raise the EU's profile. See *The Independent* (29 October 1996). But his impact has not lived up to the more extravagant claims, as in 'Europe draw up Middle East conduct code,' *The European* (3-9 April, 1997).

[22] Title V, Article J1.4. The Treaty of Amsterdam adds another injunction to this sentence: 'The Member States shall work together to enhance and develop their mutual political solidarity' (new J1.2). The

Cheysson remark, uttered in the middle of a strenuous effort to implement the previous year's Venice Declaration, can be found in Françoise de La Serre, 'La politique étrangère de la France: New Look ou New Deal,' *Politique Etrangère* (March 1982): 132-133.

[23] On FYROM see Stelios Stavridis, 'The Democratic Control of the CFSP' in *Common Foreign and Security Policy: The Record and Reforms,* ed. Martin Holland (London: Cassell, 1997): 140-144. Holland's case-study of South Africa in the same volume argues that cohesiveness was achieved within a 'designated South African policy' (p181).

[24] Zbigniew Brzezinski and Samuel Huntington, *Political Power: USA/USSR* (New York: Viking Press, 1964).This now virtually forgotten book took the convergence hypothesis, associated with Walt Rostow, seriously, but ultimately declined to support it.

[25] Much of this has arisen from game theoretic work in the United States on the need for various kinds of strategy in international relations, to deal with internal and external demands, as well as the coexistence of anarchy and cooperation. See for example Robert Putnam, 'Diplomacy and Domestic Politics: the Logic of Two-Level Games', *International Organisation* 42:3 (Summer 1988), (reprinted as an Appendix to Peter B. Evans, Harold K. Jacobson and Robert D. Putnam [Eds.] *Double-Edged Diplomacy: International Bargaining and Domestic Politics* [Berkeley: University of California Press, 1993]). Also Robert Axelrod and Robert Keohane, 'Achieving Cooperation under Anarchy: Strategies and Institutions,' in *Neorealism and Neoliberalism: the Contemporary Debate,* ed. David Baldwin (New York: Columbia University Press, 1993).

[26] Simon Bulmer leans towards the first of the three, in his 'Analyzing European Political Cooperation: the Case for Two-Tier Analysis', in *The Future of European Political Cooperation: Essays on Theory and Practice,* ed. Martin Holland (London: Macmillan, 1991). William Wallace prefers the more gloomy view in his *Regional Integration: the West European Experience* (Washington DC: the Brookings Institution, 1994), especially pp72-81. For an example of the progressive school see *CFSP and the Future of the European Union,* an Interim Report of a Working Group of the Bertelsmann Stiftung (Gütersloh: Bertelsmann Stiftung, 1995).

[27] What follows builds upon my earlier attempts to model the system in 'The Foreign Policy of the European Community,' in *Foreign Policy and World Politics,* (8th Ed.), ed. Roy Macridis (New York: Prentice Hall, 1991), and 'The Capability-Expectations Gap,' 1993, *op.cit.*

[28] On the interesting ambiguities of this process, see William Wallace, *Opening the Door: the Enlargement of NATO and the European Union* (London: Centre for European Reform, 1996).

[29] New Article J7 (formerly J.4 of the TEU). Of the 15 EU Member States, ten are full members of the WEU, and five (Austria, Denmark, Finland, Ireland, and Sweden) are Observers. The WEU has three Associate Members and ten Associate Partners from outside the EU's ranks. J7.3 does stipulate that the European Council can set 'guidelines' for the WEU.

[30] On special access to CFSP see Totis Kotsonis, 'A Political Europe in an Atlantic World: A Study in the Development of EPC/CFSP-US Consultation Procedures and a European Political Identity,' PhD. thesis, London School of Economics, 1997.

[31] The work of Michael Smith has always emphasised this transatlantic interdependence and interpenetration. See in particular his *Western Europe and the United States: the Uncertain Alliance,* (London: Allen and Unwin, 1984).

[32] See Jacques Freymond, 'The International Committee of the Red Cross as a Neutral Intermediary,' in *Unofficial Diplomats,* eds. Maureen R. Berman and Joseph E. Johnson (New York: Columbia University Press, 1977).

[33] See Esther Barbé, 'Present and Future of Joint Actions for the Mediterranean Region,' in *Common Foreign and Security Policy: The Record and Reforms,* ed. Martin Holland (London: Cass, 1997).

[34] For a thoroughly dialectical view of the wider issue of European integration and inner groups see Philippe de Schoutheete, 'The European Community and its Sub-Systems,' in *The Dynamics of European Integration,* ed. William Wallace (London: Pinter for the Royal Institute of International Affairs, 1990).

CHAPTER IV

Identifying Institutional Paradoxes of CFSP

Reinhardt Rummel and Jörg Wiedemann

From the European Union's beginning all the way up to the decisions of the Amsterdam Intergovernmental Conference, the process of European integration has been shaped by two competing schools of thought, one aiming to create a communitarian union and the other to establish close intergovernmental cooperation between states. Most of today's achievements in European integration are based on a compromise between, or a parallel use of, these two competing concepts. The dichotomy is clearly reflected in the Union's institutional development and present set-up concerning external relations. Whenever one school was successful in institutionalising new policies, the ideas of the other school were also included. The procedure seems to have led to ineffectiveness – sometimes even to complete standstill. Thus, the combination of the two concepts in one structure is contradictory rather than complementary.

Although many in Europe had hoped for a change after Amsterdam, the basic paradox continues. There are more contradictions – some of which have been reinforced by the decisions of June 1997, others mollified, but by no means abolished. And why should they be? Has not the Union become closer in the last forty years? It seems that paradox is the secret recipe for success. Take Common Foreign and Security Policy (CFSP): if one digs deeper into its structure and functioning, it is neither *common*, nor *foreign*, nor dealing with *security*, nor can be called a *policy*. Yet, most observers and policy makers use the acronym CFSP like a magic formula: it is enough to invoke the name and the EU instantly turns into a major actor – if not a superpower – in world affairs. The paradox is that this mantra effect is even stronger outside Europe than inside. Perceptions are very important in international relations. The EU seems to profit from this fact.

While the EU claims to conduct a common foreign and security policy, it largely lacks the means and capability needed to make decisions and implement them. Theoretically, CFSP can draw support from other EU policies (economic external relations, development policy, humanitarian policy) or from the Western European Union and its connections with NATO. In practice, however, the link with instruments outside of CFSP is not developed to the degree that it would be available whenever needed. Likewise, the EU has not developed a sufficient level of solidarity among its Member States in matters of foreign and security policy. There is also little hope that this will ever change and yet the show goes on. The Amsterdam reform conference solemnly declared to produce 'deepening' as a precondition for 'widening.' It failed at 'deepening' during the June 21 meeting; nevertheless on July 17 the Plan 2000 was launched to widen the Union.

IDENTIFYING INSTITUTIONAL PARADOXES OF THE CFSP

In the first section of this article, we will consider the institutional inconsistencies and contradictions inherent in CFSP and in the larger institutional context within which it operates. In section two, we want to highlight several reasons for these institutional paradoxes, for example the concept of unity: Should unity evolve automatically, or is there a need for coercion? To answer this question we will take a closer look at the aim of CFSP, as viewed from the perspective of the Member States. We will find that the CFSP is viewed as an instrument for achieving national foreign policy goals, which arise from individual Member States' national interests. What is problematic in this context is the fact that national interests and national foreign policy goals are often divergent. Clearly, diverging interests are not a sound basis for unity.

THE EU'S FOREIGN POLICY STRUCTURE:
INSTITUTIONAL RIGIDITY OR WRONG TRACK?

Amsterdam has been another round of trying to fine-tune the operational procedures and the institutional structures of CFSP with the desperate goal of overcoming, or rather transcending, some of its absurdities. Procedural and institutional improvements matter, but they are only marginal efforts as long as the central issue of modernising the content and substance of EU foreign and security policy is not addressed and resolved. Contrary to traditional foreign and defence policy, in the future almost all sectors of public life will have external implications. Therefore, the issues on the external policy agenda will be characterised by these interrelating and overlapping sectors. The present compartmentalised structure of the EU's external relations seems to rigidly ignore the nature of today's international world. Can the EU afford this institutional rigidity or has it chosen the wrong track?

CFSP IN THE PILLAR SYSTEM

The Treaty of the European Union (TEU) stipulates that CFSP is to include 'all areas of foreign and security policy.'[1] The notion of *all areas* certainly comprises major components of the EU's common trade policy, its development policy, its non-proliferation policy, and its humanitarian policies. The definition of CFSP's potential sphere of activity is further extended by Art. J. 4 I TEU, which states that 'all questions related to the security of the European Union' are included in CFSP. If the final aim is to develop a CFSP addressing all questions of foreign and security policy, the current division of labour and power sharing structures within the Union seem inadequate.[2] In a future-oriented foreign and security policy, all external components of the first and the third pillar should be merged into deliberations and decisions within CFSP. There is one provision in the Treaty of Amsterdam that may be interpreted as a step towards modernisation: the strategic questions clause in J.3 (formerly J.8 (1) and (2), first subparagraph) provides heads of state and governments with the theoretical option of broadening the thematic scope of CFSP action.

Nevertheless, the authority of the CFSP foreign ministers remains limited. Despite the fact that they are the masters of the General Council, they still lack the power and the assertiveness to direct their First and Third Pillar counterparts, not to mention WEU defence ministers and the 'European section' of NATO. The consistency of CFSP depends on the institutional links between three structures: CFSP, other EU policies, and the military policies of WEU and NATO. Certainly, the goal cannot be to have the EU foreign ministers dictate policies to their counterparts in the trade and defence departments, but they ought to adopt a comprehensive approach and orchestrate various concerns and instruments in the EU's external relations. But the institutional set-up is not very favourable in this regard – neither in the European Commission, the European Parliament, nor in the Council itself – and Amsterdam did not bring much change in this regard.

THE COMMISSION VS THE COUNCIL – A PROBLEM OF INITIATIVE

Ever since Maastricht the Commission has had the right to make foreign policy initiatives within CFSP. Nevertheless, it has refrained from using the full extent of its competence in Pillar II, fearing that intergovernmental policy directed by Pillar II might contaminate the communitarian Pillar I. This 'contamination problem' was evident in the EU's policy on Rwanda in 1994, when a CFSP common position initiated the (obligatory) action of the European Commission.[3] Likewise, the general decisions on imposing economic sanctions in the cases of the Federal Republic of Yugoslavia, Haiti, and Libya were made within CFSP while the Commission then had to initiate the implementation process by using EC rules of procedure to propose concrete sanctions to the Council.

A series of similar procedures contributed to in-fighting over institutional matters.[4] If the power to decide on communitarian action originates increasingly from deliberations within CFSP, then the function of originally communitarian instruments and actors, such as the Commission and the Parliament, would be gradually reduced to the execution of CFSP policies. The Commission itself could help re-governmentalise the communitarian Pillar I, if it would make full use of its powers in CFSP. Amsterdam has not provided any relief from this dilemma. Instead, since the heads of state and government could not agree on reducing the number of commissioners, the Commission continues to divide the competence for foreign and security policy between five Commissioners, thus undermining its own stance within the institutional texture of the EU.

The European Parliament vs the Council – The Budget Question

If the 'common' in CFSP is to be taken seriously, then all actors should be adequately involved in the policy-making process. One of the most striking paradoxes of CFSP has been the arrangement of its budget. One might assume that EU common action is financed by the EU and, in turn, the availability of EU financial assets should commit Member States to common action. This, however, has not been the case. As the TEU describes, EU funding is a possibility, not a prerequisite, for CFSP action. The incompatibility of aims and powers has created a paradoxical situation under the Maastricht treaty. This has been partly remedied at Amsterdam through an informal understanding between the Council, the Commission, and the Parliament, which at least raises the level of transparency on budgetary matters.

While the European Parliament has the power to control the budget (and thereby gain some influence over Community policy), this power does not apply fully to CFSP. Article 199 TEC states that there are financial assets for CFSP, but it does not stipulate where these assets are to be posted or how much is available. In the past this has led to the use of assets reserved for other purposes. Because CFSP is a reactive policy, it is impossible to propose a CFSP policy agenda and budget for the coming year. This poses a constant problem for allocating sufficient funds to cover CFSP expenses. Amsterdam will not solve this problem by simply stating that the sum spent on emergency measures may not exceed 20% of the total CFSP budget.

Art. 199 TEC contributes to this uncertainty, because it makes a distinction between the administrative and operative costs of CFSP. Administrative costs of CFSP are automatically covered by the Community budget, whereas whether or not to cover operative costs is decided by a unanimous vote in the Council. However, in the absence of a clear definition of 'administrative expenditures' it is left to the Council to decide this matter too, thus giving it the power to circumvent the Community's budgetary decision-making procedure. Moreover, because the Council and the EP had previously agreed not to examine each other's expenditures, the EP's actual power is somewhat limited also in those cases where the normal budget decision making applies. Thus, CFSP is linked to the Community's budget, but not necessarily to the Community's budgetary decision-making procedures.

The Council's Foreign Policy Making

Who is administratively preparing the Council's decisions, and who is advising it on questions of substance? The Maastricht Treaty states that the division of labour between the Political Committee and COREPER is subject to future discussion.[5] It thereby left a very important aspect of CFSP decision making unsettled. The TEU itself suggests that labour is divided between administrative and political work. Art. J. 8 (5) TEU (Art. J.15/Amsterdam) assigned an advisory and controlling function to the Political Committee, indicating that advising the Council on political issues is the main task of the Political Committee. The same article states that Art. 151 TEC is not affected by this provision. This implies that COREPER was meant to extend its preparatory work for the Council to the sphere of CFSP. The provision may seem logical, but in fact it is problematic.

Although COREPER's work was intended to be primarily administrative, much of it actually represents policy shaping, since it prepares Council decisions by reaching consensus between representatives of national foreign ministries and the Commission beforehand. If agreement is reached in COREPER on any given topic, it is no longer subject to Council debate. In effect, this gives COREPER a policy coordination task under Community rules of procedure, including the settling of political issues prior to debate in the Council. The arrangement established by the TEU thus creates competition between both committees, which in turn leads to further complication of CFSP decision making. It may also create competition between different sections of the Member States' foreign ministries, because the Political Directors are represented in the Political Committee, while the Member States 'EU ambassadors' are represented in COREPER. Amsterdam has added another competitor: the 'High Representative', who will have a 'strategy planning and early warning unit'.

CFSP's INTER-ORGANISATIONAL LINKS: WEU, NATO, UN

In order to be effective and credible, CFSP needs more than the backing of other EU policies. Although certain EU policies employ political and economic instruments in solving external problems, the EU lacks the authority and adequate instruments to implement them. Whenever the EU decides to act in these spheres, the relationship between the EU and institutions that possess the necessary authority and instruments, like the WEU, NATO, and UN, becomes important. Viewed in the context of the paradoxical set-up of intra-institutional links, the external inter-institutional links are even more confusing.

Looking at its history, it is hard to find any significant WEU operation. This was particularly astonishing in view of the Yugoslav Crisis. Initially, the US considered this crisis to be a European affair and was not willing to intervene. Since this meant that NATO was stepping aside, it would have been the perfect scenario for using the WEU structure.[6] Despite the availability of the WEU, Britain and France did not assign WEU to command their troops sent to the former Yugoslavia. Like other EU Member States', these troops were conducting operations under the auspices of the UN. This was a result of the Europeans not being unified on the aims of intervention. The Yugoslav crisis demonstrated that CFSP does not have a military arm.

Although CFSP is meant to address all EU security issues, it is designed to address the political issues only. Since the defence ministers did not participate fully in the Maastricht negotiations, the CFSP itself lacks an operational level. This is due to the fact that EPC was given the task of organising European positions and actions in other organisations and institutions. But the aim of CFSP differs fundamentally from that of EPC. CFSP is supposed to be an active EU foreign policy by initiating and determining external action from within the EU framework, eventually leading to the formation of a European defence identity (ESDI). Analysing CFSP actions of the past, one can easily come to the conclusion that CFSP, in practice, essentially is not about planning concrete policy measures, but about reacting to crises. For this purpose, the institutional set-up is entirely insufficient and it is not clear that this will change by setting up the 'strategy planning and early warning unit'.

One major reason for this insufficiency is the lack of a powerful instrument, a 'military arm' of the EU. The EU is not a military organisation and has no troops assigned to it.[7] As a consequence, in order to conduct (military operations or) operations with military assistance, the EU must request assistance from outside its own framework. One possible candidate is the WEU. But the WEU has not been used for such purposes in the past, as was pointed out above. There are two main aspects to be considered when investigating why this has been the case; one relates to the criterion of efficiency, the other to the criterion of commitment.

To understand why the criterion of efficiency is important, one must look at the implications of military action. In order to conduct a successful operation, one needs sufficient numbers of troops, the ability to transport them to the mission area, and reliable intelligence information. Although not lacking in troops, Europe lacks transport capabilities and intelligence information. It also essentially needs a unified command, which the WEU itself cannot provide. In NATO all these insufficiencies are counter-balanced by the integration of American armed forces and American military hardware. Another aspect deserves attention in this context. As was seen during the second Gulf War, in order to accomplish one's goals, it helps to be decisive. American decisiveness, expressed in the will to use force when it is deemed necessary and in the ability to determine the objectives of military action, also accounts for the credibility of American action. In military terms, the decisiveness of American politicians in using military force when it is deemed necessary adds an additional deterrence value to the already well-trained and well-equipped American troops. This aspect seems to pose a major problem for the Europeans. The Yugoslav Crisis demonstrated that Europeans experience difficulties in using military force and to agree on the objectives of a military intervention. Since the Europeans could not agree on the objectives of a military intervention, their combined force could not be used as a deterrent. By contrast, when acting within the NATO framework, European NATO members can count on the assistance of American hardware and, perhaps more importantly, on the political backing of the United States. This makes their own action more credible.[8] In this sense, not even the WEU is able to conduct the limited tasks assigned to it in the Petersburg declaration, without NATO assistance.

The criterion of commitment is important as well, since it may give an account for the backing that Member States actually carrying out the operation will receive. To full WEU Member States, it is unacceptable to give non-full members a say in the decision-making process, because their commitment levels are mirrored by their WEU status.[9] The problems of insufficient linkage between EU and WEU would not occur if there were coherence in the membership policies of all EU Member States. For example, if all Member States were full WEU members as well, the problem of command would not be as pressing as it is today. Likewise, were Sweden, Finland, Austria, and Ireland to become NATO members, there would at least be a real EU group that could speak with one voice.

Under the present conditions the reluctance to ask for WEU assistance is natural. Any attempt to change the current inter-institutional setting by producing some kind of command authority of CFSP over WEU assets, without solving the problem of coherence of membership, is bound to fail. In light of this statement, the assumption that CFSP will benefit from the concept of 'Combined Joint Task Forces' (CJTF) allowing WEU to use NATO structures, may be misleading. Although the concept could turn out to be an effective method for conducting military operations in a European framework, it is not necessarily relevant in a CFSP context. Even if CFSP requests WEU action, there would be no implementation unless the WEU and NATO decided to cooperate. Furthermore, since CJTF does not establish CFSP command authority over WEU troops, the aim, intensity, and duration of WEU operations would be determined outside the EU framework. Thus, the CJTF might eventually bring the WEU closer to NATO than to the EU.

Another aspect, which deserves particular attention, is the notion that those organisations that are capable of implementing EU decisions or requests (NATO and WEU) can only act in accordance with international law. This means that, in case of an emergency, any action taken by NATO or the WEU on behalf of the EU must conform the policy of the UN Security Council (UNSC). This principle also applies to the imposition of EU economic sanctions. The EU's CFSP is weakened, since it does not have a direct say in UNSC decisions. It does not have legal personality, and, is therefore not considered to be subject to international law.[10] To overcome this legal inconvenience, those EU Member States that are also permanent UNSC members are obliged to promote the 'interests of the Union' and common positions, whenever acting within the UNSC.[11] However influential this provision may appear, it is nothing more than a declaration of the fact that the UNSC permanent members, Great Britain and France, are also members of the EU. There are no implications, since real problems cannot arise in practice. This is due to the fact that a common position within CFSP can only be reached if all Member States agree. If they agree, it is unnecessary for Great Britain and France to oppose the position within the UNSC. If, however, GB and France take a different position from that of all other EU Member States, no common position within CFSP has been reached. The 1995 French nuclear testing program provides for a good example. When France ran its nuclear testing program in late 1995, there was no common position on this issue within CFSP. The Council could not decide whether to call on the European Atomic Community (EAC) for action. Also, while some EU Member States supported a resolution in the General Assembly urging France to stop the testing, Great Britain took France's side while other Member States refrained from voting. Even if all other EU Member States would have supported UNSC action against the testing, France and Great Britain (being both permanent UNSC members and in agreement on the subject) would have been able to prevent any binding UN decision contrary to their own interests.

In addition, the EU's internal multiple foreign policy system further complicates matters since it predominates in all EU relations with the UN. However, this paradoxical institutional set-up is necessary since the EU itself can not act within UN bodies, while the Community can. When trying to develop a consistent common policy, the external competences of the EU Council and the European Commission do not coincide with their competences in CFSP decision making. By contrast, the Council and the Commission are only entitled to express their own views within some international organisations, like the UN and the WTO, if they do so as the EC's representatives.[12] Since there is no direct institutional link between the Community's external relations and the Union's CFSP, the outcome of the dual policy process is uncertain.[13]

THE CFSP CONCEPT: DEAD END OR FREEWAY TO AN EVER STRONGER UNION?

The Member States in 1991–92 all accepted the metamorphosis of the European Community. They thereby accepted the transformation of European Political Cooperation (EPC) into CFSP. However, the performance of CFSP in the past suggests that the question regarding the purpose of CFSP has not been clarified. The ultimate aim of CFSP must be to take common action. Nevertheless, in CFSP the requirement of unanimity and the principle of solidarity contradict each other. More importantly, this constellation leads to passivity in some cases because it might prohibit actions in an EU context. Neither the majority nor the minority can use CFSP if there is no common position.

Since each Member State has the right to veto common positions or common actions, any Member State can determine whether or not the others are going to have a common policy within the CFSP sphere of action. This is essentially due to the institutional set-up of CFSP, which leads to permanent confrontation rather than unity. Unlike the EC's communitarian policy process, the EU's CFSP process is not evolutionary by nature. Once the EC has made full use of its 'exclusive competences,'[14] the Member States lack the legal authority to act in the same policy area. Thus, whenever follow-up decisions need to be taken in the same specific policy area, they can only be taken at the Community level. The Member States, having agreed to transfer competences from the national level to the community level, accept this logic of consistency in Community action within the transferred policy areas.

This is not the case with CFSP. The absence of a permanent and clear-cut division of labour between the EU and its Member States, complete with a clear definition of specific policy areas and reserved for an exclusive and consistent common policy, is obvious. Therefore, every follow-up action is subject to another debate about its necessity because the Member States have the option of taking a national decision. In every decision-making process the fundamentally different positions of the integrationists and the intergovernmentalists clash, opening old wounds. For example, the provision for the operational costs of CFSP is designed to give non-integrationist Member States the opportunity to be obstructive. If Community funding of common actions is not possible, the active Member States will have to provide the funding themselves, and apart from being generally opposed to additional expenditures during economic downturns, the active Member States will also face the technical problem of burden-sharing between themselves. Furthermore, whenever the Council decides to draw on Community resources, it re-opens the debate about the EP's role in CFSP.[15] This in turn may lead to the Council's reluctance to use Community assets.

As demonstrated by the lifting of economic sanctions against South Africa and Haiti, the intergovernmentalists have a strong instrument for preventing the majority from acting against intergovernmentalists' interests. Contrary to its intention and meaning, CFSP joint actions can be used to prevent action, rather than initiating it. When institutionalising the EU's use of economic sanctions, the competence for initial decision making was given to the EU Council (CFSP), since it corresponded with EPC practice. Article 228a TEC explicitly empowers the EC Council to take immediate action on economic sanctions whenever the EU Council has decided in favour of a joint action or a common position within the framework of CFSP. It thereby establishes a Community competence to impose sanctions, based on Art. 113 TEC. However, Art. 228a TEC implies that Community Council powers are subordinated in relation to the EU Council powers, vested in the CFSP framework. Since the initial decision to impose economic sanctions has to be taken within the CFSP structure by a unanimous vote, any single Member State can prevent such a decision. Furthermore, the Commission is not necessarily involved in the shaping of the initial CFSP decision but must act within the EC framework.

In the absence of a permanent settlement of institutional provisions, policy makers have institutional objectives per se.[16] This may lead to entirely paradoxical situations. '[Policy makers] may accept particular policy outcomes because of their institutional consequences and may even reject policy outcomes that favour their substantive policy interests because they do not wish to accept the institutional implications.'[17] This situation suggests that some Member States are simply not interested in conducting a Common Foreign and Security Policy. But is this really the case?

NATIONAL INTERESTS AND CFSP

All Member States view CFSP as a potentially useful instrument for achieving their national foreign policy goals.[18] But for some Member States CFSP seems to be the only suitable approach toward having a global foreign policy, while for others, depending on the issue, it is merely an optional approach. Thus, while some Member States may press for EU action, others may try to prevent it. The following lines might highlight what accounts for these different approaches.

From the individual Member States' perspective, EU decision making is national foreign policy making in itself. The Member States' (foreign) ministers meet in the acting decision-making authority of the EU: the general Council. Here they discuss and they may decide on political issues on the basis of national interests. Since EU policy must pay attention to national interests, a 'positive' outcome of the policy process is uninteresting to those ministers whose own nation's interests are not respected sufficiently. And since they have other options, they do not need the EU framework to take action. The fact that Member States' national interests are often divergent has far-reaching implications. An anecdote of the 1994 accession negotiations may be useful to illustrate the argument.

From an EU-centric view point (the so-called Brussels's view point), the 1995 enlargement was beneficial per se, because it would improve the economic situation of the Union as a whole. Although important economic issues had been settled quite satisfactorily before, in the 1992 treaty, establishing the European Economic Area (EEA), enlargement was thought to be even better for the Union: The EU would improve its position in world (economic) politics because its weight automatically increases with every new Member State, for example in GATT/WTO. In the case of Norway, entry would have contributed to an improvement of the EU's internal supply situation (energy; food) and it would have given the EU a stronger stand in the so-called world-wide consumer/producer dialogue on energy-related questions. However, from the individual Member States' perspective, this assessment only partly reflected the heart of the matter. Giving full access to the common market to formerly excluded companies (and in some areas also to states) meant that competition would increase, posing a problem for those Member States whose industries were not very competitive. Thus, Member States negatively affected by the entry of new members were particularly interested in preventing the EU from making concessions. During the 1994 negotiations in-fighting between Spain and Norway on the issue of fishing rights was pronounced. These arguments were transferred to the EU level when Germany pressed Spain to concede to Norwegian conditions for entry. This in turn led to a mini-crisis in Franco-German relations, since the French became concerned about German 'power politics.'[19]

What is most important in this context is the observation that Member States accept the Union's interests only when they do not affect their national interests. Seen from this angle, the Union's foreign policy is the result of a careful balance of the interests between all Member States. Taking the argument to the limit, one can even say that every successful decision made by the EU and the EC is based on such a balance of interests.

This balance of interests is essential, because it creates unity by paying respect to the needs of individual Member States. Furthermore, it is a prerequisite for the solidarity principle. All Member States should show solidarity towards each other. However, in practice, this principle is called on only in situations where an individual Member State's interests clash with the interests of the others. The 'balance' principle legitimises the evocation of the 'solidarity' principle, because all Member States received concrete benefits when the initial decision was made. If a Member State has accepted the initial decision because it was beneficial, it has no right to question it at a later stage. As we will describe in the following section, the TEU in its CFSP title explicitly calls for solidarity, but it does not allow for an adequate balance of interests.

FORMALISED SOLIDARITY – UNITY BY FORCE?

In its declaration no. 27 on voting in the field of CFSP (Maastricht final act), the conference of the representatives of the Member States' governments concluded that in cases where unanimity is required, individual Member States should refrain from dissenting if there is a qualified majority in favour of a common action. The contradictory wording – separating unanimity in vote from consent on an issue – points to what seems to be the key problem with CFSP: Unity. In the TEU, unity is imposed on the Member States by obligating them to act together on a variety of issues.

In this context, the solidarity principle of CFSP is entirely ineffective, because it produces a stand-still in 'policy-production.' On the one hand, it seeks to oblige the single Member States to respect the interests of the majority outside CFSP.[20] On the other, it provides the single Member States with the opportunity to block any majority action within CFSP.[21] This means that any single Member States can determine what is to be 'the common positions or the interest of the union.' On the other hand, the majority may use other frameworks.

Therefore, the solidarity principle of the TEU is also problematic for the minority. There are reasons for some Member States to be more reluctant to communitarise CFSP than others. These reasons are found in the difference of national policies. If all governments would have the same opinions on all policy issues, there would be no debate about majority voting. Since this is not the case, the provision of unanimous voting is a necessity for those Member States that fall into the minority in their policy approach. There are some issues that simply cannot be addressed by the EU, because they are regarded as national issues. In such cases no Member State would ever accept an EU policy contrary to its own aims. The 1995 French nuclear testing program must be seen in this context. France expected solidarity, while some of its CFSP partners were putting pressure on it by acting outside the EU framework. It must be accepted that some issues remain outside the range of EU/CFSP action, although they essentially shape the Union's image in world politics. In this sense, Amsterdam has brought relief to the minority, as it declares the right to block majority decisions, if national interests are at stake.

CONCLUSION

Since CFSP lacks a clear-cut decision-making authority, it cannot enforce all its decisions either through the other pillars or through the Member States. And since the EU lacks legal personality, it has to rely on different actors to implement its decisions outside its own framework. These institutional deficiencies led to an ineffective foreign policy and sometimes even to total passivity. As long as the institutional arrangements remain unsettled, any political issue will automatically be viewed as a means for bargaining over institutional arrangements.

The establishment of a functioning decision-making structure within CFSP, therefore, was the main issue in the debate about the EU's future engagement in world politics. The current structure is ineffective, because it gives every Member State the opportunity to block a decision reached by the rest of the Member States. The use of majority voting instead of unanimity in the decision-making structure, however, is not the cure. This becomes clear when one looks at the capacity of EU Member States. Not all Member States have the capacity to implement a common decision. Thus, giving Member States that are unable to contribute substantially to common actions themselves a say in the decisions on common action is controversial and leads to reluctance towards CFSP from those Member States that bear all the costs. However, a Common Decision would be of very little practical use if the only Member States that could implement it were to refrain from action. This may also explain why the linkage between the Union and those organisations capable of implementing the EU's decisions is insufficient. Since not all EU Member States are full WEU or NATO members, they themselves do not show the same level of commitment as full members of all three organisations.

Reluctance of some Member States to act within CFSP also arises from the way CFSP defines solidarity between the Member States. During the 1994 enlargement negotiations, for example, Spain expected solidarity from its EU partners on the fishing issue, while Germany pressed for solidarity on the overall issue of enlargement. By contrast, in 1995, when Canada accused a Spanish trawler of illegal fishing activities, Spain was backed by its EU partners. When France ran its nuclear testing program in 1995, it expected solidarity from its EU partners. Instead, its partners put pressure on France. These incidents show that solidarity depends on the interests at stake. If the national interests of all Member States can be met sufficiently, solidarity on that issue will automatically appear because there also is unity. If not, a lack of solidarity is inevitable.

The only way to improve this situation is to define the issues that can be resolved by the Union as a whole. To achieve this, a binding, concrete, and specific agenda for CFSP action finally must be shaped. The first step would be to establish a centre for analysis and coordination of Member States' positions on all the issues facing the EU in the near future. This would imply that the EU also finds a way to reach a balance of interests on all specific issues. The next step would be to pre-plan common action regarding these issues. It should be left to the Member States to determine which organisational framework they want to use for the implementation of a common decision. A balance of interests must be reached here as well. If every Member State is satisfied with the outcome, the final step would be a formal 'communitarisation' precluding unilateral Member State action, in contrast with common action. Thus, to make the EU's CFSP work, it is essential to focus on substance first. Only then will the Member States agree on the procedural aspects. If influence could be more carefully balanced with commitment and capabilities of each Member State, CFSP might just turn out to be beneficial for all Member States. The EU may then be able to put CFSP to work.

NOTES

[1] See Art. J. 1 I TEU.

[2] For example, in today's world, development policy must be regarded as an essential part of foreign policy. Furthermore, the case of Algeria proves that deficiencies in the development of third world states may even have a direct impact on EU security. The Maastricht Conference in 1992 paid attention to this fact and dedicated a whole title in the EU's treaty framework to development. However, development policy was not included in the Treaty of the European Union (TEU) itself as an objective of common interest. Instead, the legal basis for a 'common development policy' can be found in Title XVII (Art. 130u-y) of the Treaty of the European Community (TEC). What should actually be called the EU's development policy is described here as the EC's 'development cooperation.' This set up reflects the differing integration

objectives of the EU Member States. On the one hand, decisions regarding 'development cooperation' can be made by a qualified majority – thus, the 'willing' can act. On the other hand, 'development cooperation' is restricted in its contents, as it is merely 'complementary' to the development policies of the Member States. Hence, individual Member States cannot be forced to change their own policies.

[3] See Horst-Günter Krenzler and Henning C. Schneider, 'The Question of Consistency,' in *Foreign Policy of the European Union. From EPC to CFSP and Beyond,* eds. Elfriede Regelsberger, Philippe de Schoutheete de Tervarent, and Wolfgang Wessels (Boulder and London: Lynne Rienner Publishers, 1997): 145.

[4] See Elfriede Regelsberger and Wolfgang Wessels, 'The CFSP Institutions and Procedures: A Third Way for the Second Pillar,' *European Foreign Affairs Review* 1:1 (1996): 40.

[5] See the Declaration regarding practical details of CFSP in the Maastricht Conference's final act.

[6] The WEU was declared the military arm of CFSP and the 'bridge' between the EU and NATO. One was also thinking of the WEU as having a kind of deputy role, in case NATO itself was not willing to act. This is reflected in the Combined Joint Task Forces (CJTF) concept, which allows for the use of NATO structures by the WEU.

[7] Theoretically, this could be changed by transforming Pillar II into a regional defence organisation with additional tasks and assigning Member States' troops to it. The WEU would become an integrated part of CFSP and WEU action would be under CFSP command. This would give the EU command authority vis à vis its Member States and would lead to the creation of strictly European defence forces. However, the problem military integration poses is evident in the reluctance of WEU Member States to integrate their organisation into the EU structure. This situation is not likely to change.

[8] The current debate on American contributions to DFOR underlines this aspect.

[9] In his report on 'The WEU's role in the organisation of European security after the decisions taken by the European Union in Amsterdam and by NATO in Madrid' the rapporteur, Mr. Blaauw, notes that participation of non-full members 'has opened up a gap between the law and reality that continues to widen.' Mr. Blaauw calls for the conclusion of an agreement that would place a 'real commitment' on such members. See *Atlantic News,* 5 November 1997, p. 2.

[10] In its 'Addendum to the Dublin II general outline for a draft revision of the Treaties,' the Dutch presidency included the proposal for a draft version of a 'New Article A in the TEU.' This new article states that '[t]he Union shall replace and succeeds to the European Community, the European Coal and Steel Community and the European Atomic Energy Community,' and that '[t]he Union shall have legal personality.' Moreover, '[i]n international relations, the Union shall enjoy legal capacity to the extent necessary for the exercise of its functions and the fulfilment of its purposes.' While giving legal personality to the EU would ensure that the Union can implement some of its own (CFSP) decisions, merging the existing legal personalities of the three Communities and that of the Union into a single legal entity could ensure consistency in the Union's foreign policy. See 'Addendum to the Dublin II general outline for a draft revision of the Treaties,' CONF/2500/96 ADD. 1 (March 20 1997). Amsterdam did not establish legal personality.

[11] See Art. J.5 IV TEU.

[12] Due to the 'exclusive' competence (see footnote 14) of the EC in the area of trade and tariffs, the Member States themselves can not act on their own. This has led to the working arrangement between the Council (and thus the Member States) and the Commission regarding trade policy. The Council gives a mandate to the Commission to negotiate trade agreements with third countries, and within international organisations, but the Council itself has the decision-making authority. Within GATT and now the WTO, however, the EC may not ratify the agreements. This has to be done by the Member States at the national level.

[13] For example, while the decision to contribute to the Korean Peninsula Energy Development Organization (KEDO) was taken by a common position under CFSP, the Community was to finance the contribution, and the EACommunity was to become a member of KEDO. This division of labour seems to make sense, because it reflects the respective competences of the actors involved. Nevertheless, if the EAC becomes a member of KEDO, it will be difficult to monitor the process through the CFSP structure.

[14] The EC possesses 'exclusive' competences vis à vis its Member States in the area of Common trade and tariffs. Its mere existence prohibits any unilateral Member State action. The EU possesses 'competing' competences as well, which constitute the most common form of legal relationship between the EC and its

Member States. In this case, the Member States can act unilaterally as long the EC has not made use of its own competence. Note, however, that they may not act in contradiction to already established EC policies.

[15] See Elfriede Regelsberger and Wolfgang Wessels, op. cit., p. 41.

[16] See Helen Wallace, 'The Institutions of the EU: Experience and Experiments,' in *Policy-making in the European Union*, eds. Helen Wallace and William Wallace (Oxford: Oxford University Press, 1996): 38.

[17] idem. One should carefully avoid generalising this thesis, because it seems unlikely that Member States will act in this way, if crucial policy interests are at stake.

[18] See Elfriede Regelsberger, 'The Institutional Set-up and Functioning of EPC/CFSP,' in *Foreign Policy of the European Union. From EPC to CFSP and Beyond*, eds. Elfriede Regelsberger, Philippe de Schoutheete de Tervarent, and Wolfgang Wessels (Boulder and London: Lynne Rienner Publishers, 1997), p.74. Christopher Hill points out, in his contribution to this volume, that most Member States even have the option of instrumentalising other organisations. Once they have decided to act on an issue, like the integration of Eastern European states, they can choose the institutional framework.

[19] The dispute was settled in Ioannina, where Spain obtained better access to British territorial waters and was allowed to enter the common fisheries policy regime earlier than originally intended.

[20] For example, Art. J. 5 IV TEU obliges those Member States, who are also permanent members of the UN Security Council, to promote the interests of the EU within the UNSC. Also, Art. J. 1 IV TEU demands that Member States refrain from taking unilateral action which is designed to contradict the Union's interests.

[21] This is due to the rule of unanimity-decisions on common positions and common actions, expressed in Art. J. 8 II TEU.

CHAPTER V

The Instruments of European Union Foreign Policy*

Karen E. Smith

To the extent that it acted in international relations, the European Community (and European Political Cooperation) was frequently described as a 'civilian power', because it lacked military instruments and relied on economic and diplomatic means to try to influence other actors. Paradoxically, just as it seemed that civilian power would be privileged with the end of the Cold War, the Member States began to discuss establishing a common defence policy. The Maastricht Treaty contained provisions for using the Western European Union (WEU) as the defence arm of the European Union's new Common Foreign and Security Policy (CFSP).[1] The issue of a common defence policy was further discussed at the 1996-1997 Intergovernmental Conference, and while the Member States did not agree on proposals for an EU-WEU merger, the 1997 Amsterdam Treaty does provide for closer EU-WEU links.[2] The widespread perception is that the European Union will be unable to act effectively in international affairs unless it can use military instruments. European Commissioner Hans van den Broek has argued: 'To be credible, the Union needs power behind its diplomacy and power to act if diplomacy fails.'[3]

This chapter will analyse the EU's foreign policy tools, taking into account developments in the Amsterdam Treaty. The first section will examine the extent to which the EU can use four general types of policy instruments: propaganda, diplomatic, economic and military. Does it have instruments associated with traditional foreign policy? While the EU has at its disposal several traditional foreign policy instruments, it also lacks several, most notably of the military type. However, the EU can also wield *sui generis* instruments which states cannot use.

Section two will consider the ways in which the EU utilises its instruments to try to influence other actors. The EU tends not to use them coercively, but prefers instead to use them to foster dialogue and interdependence. This is for a variety of reasons, ranging from the exigencies of compromise among the Member States (which can hinder the taking of strong negative measures) to a more profound aversion to using coercion.

The final section will take up the question of whether the EU needs to acquire military instruments to exercise greater influence in international affairs and fulfil its foreign policy ambitions. Expectations about what the EU can do have been running ahead of capabilities[4]: a re-evaluation of the EU's aims could lead to a better appreciation of its strengths and of the merits of civilian power. Military instruments are not the panacea they appear to be, and the abandonment of the civilian power image may not bring the advantages that are currently anticipated.

POLICY INSTRUMENTS CLASSIFIED

Foreign policy instruments are those means used by policy-makers in their attempts to get other international actors to do what they would not otherwise do.[5] David Baldwin has specified four types of instruments used in national foreign policy:
- propaganda, or the deliberate manipulation of verbal symbols;
- diplomacy, or the reliance on negotiation;
- economic, or resources which have a reasonable semblance of a market price in terms of money; and
- military, or the reliance on violence, weapons, or force.[6]

The following four sub-sections will discuss the extent to which the EU has or has used policy instruments of these four general types, and thus the extent to which it can be compared to a traditional state actor. Of course, even where the EU does possess instruments, it must overcome two 'hurdles.'

The first is the familiar problem of 'consistency'. There are essentially two different frameworks (pillars, in Maastricht Treaty parlance) for making foreign policy decisions: the European Community for foreign economic policy, and the intergovernmental CFSP procedures for 'political' decisions.[7] Granted, the dividing line between the two frameworks can be fuzzy: an increasing number of 'global approaches' have been devised, which combine instruments from both frameworks.[8] Furthermore, the Commission can make CFSP proposals (which it could not do under the old European Political Cooperation framework), CFSP actions can be funded by the EC budget, and there has been some EC-CFSP institutional synthesis.[9] Nonetheless, the formal separation between the two pillars remains, as does the need to ensure that policies agreed upon, and the instruments used in both are, at the very least, consistent with each other.

A second hurdle is that of the division of competences between the EU and the Member States. Some of the instruments (mainly economic) discussed below are formally EC instruments. But the Member States use many other instruments separately, although they may choose to coordinate their use (as in the case of diplomatic sanctions). Other instruments (such as regional political dialogue) have been developed in the context of the Community, EPC, or Union, and it may be inconceivable to use them outside of that framework, but they are not under its exclusive jurisdiction. That Member States still control many instruments means that decisions to use those instruments collectively are made case by case (and often by unanimous vote), and can thus be inconsistent.[10]

It should be noted here that although the CFSP contains provisions on taking common positions and joint actions, these are not instruments per se. They are better seen as mechanisms for making decisions to use foreign policy instruments.[11] Decisions to use diplomatic instruments tend to be either common positions or joint actions (as discussed below).

Propaganda Instruments

Propaganda differs from diplomatic instruments in that it is used to influence foreign publics, rather than governments.[12] The Union lacks the machinery (external information programs, control of media) needed to produce propaganda, although the Commission produces information on the EU, directed to both Member State and foreign audiences. The EU issues CFSP declarations, but these are primarily directed at governments (though press statements are also released). Deliberately manipulating words would be difficult to do, since declarations are not only often the result of careful compromise among the Member States, but can be interpreted differently by them when they communicate with other states.

It is also a matter of foreign policy style. Sensationalisation and the manipulation of stereotypes, typical propaganda techniques, are absent in EU foreign policy. It seems improbable that the EU would be accused, as the US recently has been, of 'rhetorical overkill.'[13]

Diplomatic Instruments

The EU, as set up under the Maastricht Treaty, does not have 'legal personality'; only the Community and/or the Member States can assume legal obligations with outsiders. The Community has the power to reach agreements on relations with other international organizations (articles 229-231 of the EEC Treaty), conclude association agreements with third countries (article 238), and negotiate and conclude agreements on commercial policy (article 113).[14]

The Community has concluded trade, trade and cooperation, or association agreements with most states in the world.[15] Often they include arrangements for regular consultations. Formal channels of communication (on first pillar matters) are also provided by the increasing number of diplomatic missions to the Communities in Brussels, as well as by the Commission's and the Member States' representatives abroad.[16]

The Community's competence to conclude international agreements, however, does not cover areas outside its field of internal action. It did not have exclusive competence over all of the matters covered in the GATT Uruguay Round final agreement, for example, so the Member States also ratified it. Other 'mixed' agreements include the Lomé conventions (governing relations between the EU and 70 African, Caribbean, and Pacific countries) and, frequently, association agreements.[17] The Maastricht Treaty explicitly endorsed the Member States' competence to negotiate in international organisations and to conclude international agreements in the fields of monetary policy, environment, and development cooperation.[18]

On the 'foreign policy' side, there is no single diplomatic service and no permanent spokesperson who conveys positions and policies to the EU public and non-member countries. Instead this task is carried out by the rotating presidency (assisted, if necessary, by the previous and next presidencies and the Commission: the troika system). The Amsterdam Treaty states that the presidency will also be assisted in this task by the Council's Secretary-General, which may provide the Union with more continuity in its international representation.[19]

The Member States have agreed, on occasion, to coordinate their positions in international negotiations, such as the Conference on Security and Cooperation in Europe (CSCE) and the Nuclear Non-proliferation Treaty talks. During negotiations in which both economic and political issues are discussed, agreement on mixed representation (Commission and EPC/CFSP) must be worked out.[20]

Thus, the EU hardly 'speaks with one voice' in international affairs. The division of competences between the Member States and the Union, and between CFSP and the EC is evolving and is still contentious.

Table 1 The EU's Diplomatic Instruments

Démarches
Declarations/Statements
High-level visits
Supporting action by other international organisations
Diplomatic sanctions
Diplomatic recognition
Political dialogue (bilateral and regional)
Offering EU membership
Making peace proposals
Sending special envoys
Sponsoring peace conferences
Sending cease-fire monitors
Administering foreign city
Sending election observers

When the EU does speak and act collectively, it has wielded the diplomatic instruments listed in Table 1. Most of these instruments are used by traditional states, though some are more unusual. Many were used by EPC, at least in its later stage (including pro-active instruments such as sending cease-fire monitors, to Yugoslavia). Since the Maastricht Treaty entered into force, the EU has been relatively more active, for example, deciding on joint actions to send envoys and election observers to non-member countries. For all but one (EU membership), decisions to use these instruments are taken within the CFSP framework.

Although démarches and declarations have been the most frequently used instruments (by EPC and CFSP), neither are mentioned in formal documents such as the London Report, Single European Act, or Maastricht Treaty. Démarches are generally confidential messages to other governments, delivered by the ambassadors of the troika (or just the presidency). They request further information on policies or express concern about developments (often relating to human rights).[21]

EPC declarations (or statements) were used to express concern, condemn, announce punitive measures, express satisfaction, encourage specific diplomatic activities, or announce Community initiatives. CFSP statements are generally used for the same tasks.[22] CFSP common positions are more formal and tend to specify the EU's aims. They have been used to announce punitive measures (sanctions) and EU initiatives.[23]

The EU's positions or concerns can be transmitted 'in person.' The troika or Council president will visit non-member countries to state the EU's position.[24] The Member States have also jointly supported action by international organisations to criticise other states, such as sponsoring UN resolutions.[25]

The Member States have agreed to impose jointly diplomatic sanctions, such as withdrawing ambassadors, expelling military personnel in third country representations, and suspending high-level contacts. Implementation of these measures is necessarily national.[26]

Concerted diplomatic recognition has recently been attempted: the Yugoslav republics were to have been recognised jointly. But Germany unilaterally recognised Slovenia and Croatia in December 1991, and Greece blocked joint recognition of Macedonia, so several Member States went ahead and recognised it in December 1993. Bosnia/Herzegovina, though, was recognised collectively (and by the US as well), in April 1992.

Political dialogue is the key forum in which the EU exercises persuasion (see section II) and is also used as a 'carrot' in and of itself.[27] At the end of 1994, the EU was engaged in 25 political dialogues, including with 8 groups of countries (such as ASEAN, Central America, and the Gulf Cooperation Council).[28] The regional dialogues have been used to encourage regional cooperation, as well as to demonstrate political support.[29] Dialogues with important partners (such as the bilateral dialogue with the US or the multilateral dialogue with the Central and East European associates) involve frequent meetings at several levels. Other dialogues (with India or the Gulf Cooperation Council, for example) take place less frequently, at lower levels, and may involve only the troika or the presidency. Generally, the only basis for the dialogue is an exchange of letters or a joint declaration, but the more recent association and cooperation agreements provide for political dialogue.

Offering EU membership has been used to influence other governments, although it is a very particular kind of instrument. It clearly is limited: membership is only open to European states. The prospect of EU membership for the Central and East European associates is proving to be the EU's most powerful instrument to encourage them to undertake major economic and political reforms, and behave as good neighbours. The prospect of membership has also been extended to Cyprus, partly in the hope that it would relieve the stalemate there.

The Union (and EPC before it) has, on several occasions, tried to help resolve conflicts or potentially dangerous disputes, using a variety of instruments. Some of these are fairly low-key, such as advancing peace proposals or sending envoys to participate in the peace-making process.[30] The EU has also taken more high-profile initiatives, namely in the former Yugoslavia. In 1991 and 1992, EPC attempted to mediate in the Yugoslav crisis. It tried to broker cease-fires, dispatched cease-fire monitors, set up a peace conference, and submitted peace plans.

More unusually, the EU was assigned the task of administering the Bosnian city of Mostar, under the terms of the Washington agreement of February 1994 (which created the Bosnian Federation and ended hostilities between Bosnian Muslims and Croats). The EU's mission was to create the conditions for the reunification of the city, by overcoming the division between Muslims and Croats. The EU's administration lasted from July 1994 to July 1996. An EU administrator was placed in charge, and the EU funded infrastructure repair and development and social services. The WEU supplied a team of policemen who tried to establish a unified police force.[31]

In addition, the EU has tried 'preventive diplomacy' and 'peace building'.[32] Concerned about tensions between the EU's associates (and prospective Member States) in Central and Eastern Europe, the EU sponsored the Pact for Stability. This was a series of conferences and roundtables between May 1994 and March 1995, in which the associates were encouraged to reach agreements between themselves concerning minority rights and border disputes. To try to ensure peaceful transitions to democracy, the EU has sent election observers to Russia, South Africa, Mozambique, the Palestinian Authority, and Bosnia/Herzegovina. All of these instruments were employed through CFSP joint actions.

ECONOMIC INSTRUMENTS

The EU can wield a wide variety of economic instruments, as listed in Table 2. These generally fall under the European Community's jurisdiction. However, there are several economic instruments that are not controlled exclusively by the Community. The Member States can still grant export credits,[33] promote investment, and conclude economic cooperation agreements with third countries, as long as the provisions of their agreements do not violate the Community's Common Commercial Policy (CCP). They can tax and freeze foreign assets. Member states can provide debt relief, which has been, for example, a major part of the West's efforts to assist Eastern Europe.

Table 2   The EU's Economic Instruments

Positive Measures	Negative Measures
Conclusion of trade agreement	Embargo (ban on exports)
Conclusion of trade and cooperation agreement	Boycott (ban on imports)
Conclusion of association agreement	Delaying conclusion of agreements
(all of the above on more or less favourable terms)	Suspending or denouncing agreements
Tariff reduction	Tariff increase
Quota increase	Quota decrease
Granting inclusion in Generalised System of Preferences (GSP)	Withdrawing GSP
Providing aid	Reducing or suspending aid
Extending loans (on more or less favourable terms)	Delaying granting of successive loan tranches

Furthermore, the EU's resources are limited. The Community's budget in general is small, and only a small portion of the budget (5.6 per cent in 1996) is devoted to external action.[34] Nonetheless, the Union can wield quite powerful economic instruments, stemming from its relative economic strength. It is still, for example, one of the world's largest aid donors.[35] Imposing trade embargoes and offering trade concessions do not require budgetary funding (though they may exact other costs), and given that the EU is the world's largest trader, these can be very powerful instruments.

The explicit use of EC economic instruments to support EPC orientations did not begin until the early 1980s, in relation to economic sanctions on third countries. In practice, political considerations 'spilled over' into the Community's external economic relations, without intrusion from EPC – as when it concluded a trade agreement with Romania in 1980 to reward that country's independent foreign policy vis à vis the Soviet bloc. Since the late 1980s, politics and economics have become more explicitly intertwined. Conditionality – or the use of (primarily) economic instruments to encourage democratic reforms and respect for human rights – has become an integral aspect of the EU's foreign relations.

Trade, trade and cooperation, and association agreements have increasingly been used explicitly as foreign policy instruments.[36] The decision to open negotiations with third countries is frequently a political one, but not necessarily one taken first in CFSP.[37] The EU often holds out the promise of such agreements if the country concerned meets certain political and economic conditions. Negotiation and conclusion of an agreement will also reflect political support for the country.[38] The content of agreements (schedule of trade liberalisation, intensity and scope of economic cooperation, and provisions for political dialogue) further reflects EU 'approval'.[39]

Rewards are provided to countries according to the new rules on the Generalised System of Preferences (GSP). Additional preferences will be given to countries that apply ILO conventions on freedom of association and child labour, and International Tropical Timber Organisation standards on forest management.[40]

Aid has been extended or increased for political reasons. The Community/Union has given aid to Eastern Europe and the former Soviet Union to boost the process of political and economic reforms there, and thus help ensure security and stability. The extension of (non-humanitarian) aid is also conditional – dependent on the recipients meeting certain political and economic criteria.[41] EU aid has been given for democratisation and human rights projects,[42] and for regional cooperation initiatives. The Union has extended loans to third countries as well.[43]

As for negative measures, the practice of imposing EC trade sanctions was controversial through the early 1980s, because some Member States objected to the use of Community instruments for overt political purposes. The first time Community sanctions were imposed, following an EPC decision, was against the Soviet Union in 1982, with respect to the imposition of martial law in Poland. It then became practice for a political orientation regarding sanctions to be defined in EPC and implemented through EC instruments.[44]

Economic sanctions could include measures that the Member States then implemented on a national basis, because they fell under national jurisdiction. For example, the 1986 ban on new investments in South Africa was decided in EPC, but implemented, via a loosely-binding Council decision, by each Member State.[45] In the early 1990s, however, services were included in EC regulations based on article 113 (CCP) imposing sanctions on Iraq, Libya, and Serbia/Montenegro (in accordance with UN Security Council resolutions), even though there has been a debate over whether the article includes services.[46]

The Maastricht Treaty codified and extended the procedures for imposing sanctions. Article 228a provides for the interruption of economic relations with third countries, following a common position or joint action adopted (unanimously) to that effect in CFSP. Importantly, article 228a covers all economic relations, not just trade or the provision of services. Furthermore, under article 73g, the Council can take negative measures also with respect to capital movements and payments.[47]

Other negative measures that the EU can take include delaying the signing or conclusion of agreements[48], or even suspending or denouncing agreements. In May 1992, the Council decided that agreements with other CSCE states would contain a clause either permitting the agreement to be suspended if human rights and democratic principles are not respected, or providing for appropriate measures to be taken if the parties fail to meet their obligations, including respect for human rights and democratic principles (the non-execution clause). In May 1995, the Council agreed that all future agreements with third countries would contain the non-execution clause.[49] A state can also be withdrawn from the list of GSP beneficiaries if it practices forced labour, exports goods made by prison labour, fails to control the export or transit of illegal drugs, or fails to comply with international conventions on money laundering.[50]

Economic aid has been cut off or reduced as a result of EPC/CFSP decisions on sanctions, as in the 1995 case of Nigeria. In October 1991, following a military coup in Haiti, the Commission suspended aid (provided under the Lomé IV agreement); the decision was then endorsed in EPC.[51] Aid to Sudan, Zaire, and Malawi has been suspended for human rights violations.[52]

MILITARY INSTRUMENTS

The EU's lack of a military capability is its most conspicuous instrument 'deficit.' Collective defence was, and still is, the domain of NATO, and Member States retain national forces. Denmark, Greece, and neutral Ireland opposed even discussing defence matters in EPC. However, in both EPC and CFSP, the Member States have agreed to impose arms embargoes, although these are implemented nationally.[53] In addition, military personnel have been subject to diplomatic sanctions.

The end of the Cold War put defence on the agenda. The withdrawal of many US forces from Western Europe, the Gulf War, and the Yugoslav crisis seemed to indicate that the Community/EPC needed to provide for its own defence and to back up diplomatic and economic sanctions with military capability. Increasingly, the WEU (little more than a framework for discussing defence issues) was seen as a potential military arm, and this was reflected in the Maastricht Treaty.[54] Under article J.4(2) of the CFSP, the EU can request the WEU to elaborate and implement decisions and actions which have defence implications. Thus far, the WEU has only been involved in one EU joint action, that on Mostar (see above).[55]

Although an EU-WEU merger has been repeatedly proposed, the UK and the neutral Member States in particular oppose it. The Amsterdam Treaty states that close institutional relations are to be fostered with the WEU; if the European Council so decides, the WEU could eventually be integrated into the Union. The EU can avail itself of the WEU to elaborate and implement decisions relating to humanitarian and rescue, peacekeeping, and crisis-management tasks (including peacemaking); all Member States could participate in these tasks, even if they are not full WEU members.[56]

The WEU has been developing its operational capacity. The Combined Joint Task Force (CJTF) framework, launched at the January 1994 NATO summit, is also supposed to help remedy the WEU's weaknesses. WEU forces would be able to use NATO assets (logistics and intelligence) in out-of-area operations. But the US has insisted that it must approve the use of NATO assets, which raises the issue of a potential US veto of the use of military instruments by the EU/WEU.

Given the combined weight of the Member States, the EU must be considered potentially a very influential international actor. It has at its disposal many of the same traditional foreign policy instruments used by states, as well as a few unique ones. In comparison to other international organisations (even the UN), it can certainly wield more foreign policy instruments. But the EU also lacks several instruments, even in economic areas. In addition, the EU's use of the instruments can be hindered because the division of competences between the Community and CFSP, and between the national and European levels, is still contested. The Member States must agree unanimously to use many of the instruments that the EU does have (and frequently they do not). Reaching agreement among the Member States can entail compromising the 'strength' of the measures taken, which could thus reduce the EU's potential influence. Resources are also necessarily limited and choices must be made about where and when to utilise them. How effective the EU will be will depend on context (influence in some situations may simply be difficult to exercise), as well as on how the EU decides to wield its instruments and for what purpose.

HOW DOES THE EU USE ITS INSTRUMENTS?

Providing that agreement can be reached on a common policy or approach, how does the Union use its policy instruments? There are six ways in which an international actor can influence other international actors. It can:

- use persuasion (elicit a favourable response without explicitly holding out the possibility of punishments);
- offer rewards;
- grant rewards;
- threaten punishment;
- inflict non-violent punishment; or
- use force.[57]

Which techniques seem to be preferred by the EU? (We can obviously exclude the use of force, because the Union has yet to use it.) Broadly speaking, there is a preference for using persuasion and 'carrots' (offering/granting rewards) over 'sticks' (threatening or inflicting punishments).[58] Rather than coerce other actors, the EU tries to convince them, using persuasion or rewards, to behave responsibly, cooperate with each other, or democratise and respect human rights.[59]

Extending the promise of an agreement or aid when countries meet certain conditions has become a regular practice. In December 1996, for example, the EU promised to negotiate a cooperation agreement with Cuba if the Cuban authorities make progress towards democracy.[60] Negotiation and conclusion of agreements can then be delayed, if needed. Negotiations on trade and cooperation agreements with Romania and Bulgaria were suspended in 1989 because of concerns about human rights abuses there.

But the EU clearly has difficulties breaking off relations that have already been established.[61] Sanctions have, of course, been imposed on third countries, often in accordance with UN decisions, and the Community/Union has initiated international sanctions (as in Yugoslavia).[62] But unilateral negative measures seem harder to take, especially over the issue of human rights and democracy. The Community has suspended development cooperation (aid) with weak states, such as Sudan and Haiti. With respect to more important third countries, such as Algeria and Indonesia, the EU relies on persuasion or démarches and declarations.

The reluctance to use coercion can make manifest serious inconsistencies in the EU's approach. While CFSP statements condemn the behaviour of a state, trade concessions and aid flows remain unaffected. Aid can even serve as an alternative to negative measures: in June 1996, the Council supported aid to improve the human rights situation in East Timor, but has not imposed negative measures on Indonesia over the issue.[63]

There are several reasons for this reluctance. Commercial interests were part of the reason why the 1986 sanctions against South Africa affected only 3.5 per cent of EC-South African trade,[64] and why sanctions against China have not been reconsidered since 1990.[65] The EU's 'critical dialogue' with Iran left Member States free to import Iranian oil; oil was also not included in the list of sanctions imposed on Nigeria in 1995.

The reluctance to use coercion for primarily commercial reasons is not, of course, limited to the EU. US policy towards China is also heavily influenced by commercial interests. But there are other reasons why the EU hesitates to use coercive measures, which are specific to the Union.

The need to reach a compromise among the Member States can entail backing away from strong negative measures. For example, in 1986, the Member States could only agree to impose diplomatic (rather than economic) sanctions on Syria, but '[t]he Twelve did not come to the rational view that the wider interest required a moderate approach; the moderate approach was all that they could manage in the face of differing national positions.'[66]

Delaying agreements can reflect the interests of one Member State in impeding the development of relations with a third country. This can happen when unanimity is required to proceed with a positive measure. Portugal is blocking the signing of a new EU-ASEAN cooperation agreement in protest of the Indonesian annexation of East Timor. Greece has frequently slowed the development of relations with Turkey, ostensibly over human rights abuses. But such objections have not been enough to prompt the EU to break off relations, which likewise requires unanimity. The EU's 'message' is thus unclear.

There are also more profound objections to the use of coercion. The Community's reaction in 1982 to the Polish crisis differed greatly from that of the United States, and exemplifies its different approach to coercion. The US imposed sanctions on Poland and the Soviet Union. This fit with its general opposition to trade and economic cooperation with the Soviet bloc. The EC, in contrast, reluctantly imposed (rather limited) sanctions against the Soviet Union, under pressure from the US. The Member States considered it more important to maintain trade ties and detente with their eastern neighbours, as a way of stabilising political relations and reducing the military threat in Europe.[67] Jan Zielonka has labelled these two different approaches interdependence and economic containment.[68]

Although conditionality is increasingly used in the EU's foreign relations, the emphasis is still on positive measures. There is some opposition within the EU to applying strict conditionality because it would isolate those states that most needed aid and ties with the EU and generate instability. Integration, dialogue, and trade should be used to engender democracy, economic reforms and 'good behaviour'. Sanctions may only hurt the population, or cause it to rally to the government's support. In addition, the EU cannot exercise influence if it has no ties to the country concerned.

These dilemmas were evident in the debates over the response to the Russian intervention in Chechnya in December 1994. In early 1995, the EU delayed the conclusion of an interim trade agreement with Russia and insisted that Russia accept an international monitoring mission in Chechnya; by June, the EU had decided to proceed with the agreement even though fighting was still raging. The view that Russia should be integrated into Western institutions and cooperation networks prevailed over the view that it should be coerced into stopping the fighting.[69]

The EU's aversion to negative measures has recently led to clashes with the US over relations with Cuba and Iran. The US has banned trade with the two countries; the EU had been engaged in a critical dialogue with Iran, and is promising to expand cooperation with Cuba.[70] Both approaches may actually be indicative of the limits to outsiders' influence on developments within other countries. On the US position towards Iran, one observer has argued, 'Seventeen years of constant pressure have wrought little change. Clinton's confrontational approach may not fare better, given the lack of support by US allies.'[71] A *New York Times* editorial on US policy towards Cuba charged that 'neither Congress nor President Clinton seems inclined to try anything more creative than the isolation strategy that over nearly four decades has failed to budge Fidel Castro from his autocratic ways.'[72] But the EU's critical dialogue with Iran did not succeed in persuading Iran to respect human rights and behave more responsibly in international affairs.[73]

It is not utopian to maintain that fostering interdependence and dialogue could have a positive influence. The EU is well-equipped to pursue such a strategy. But a preference for persuasion and carrots opens it up to charges of complicity and appeasement.[74] Sanctions might be necessary just to express the EU's displeasure with a country's behaviour. Inconsistent use of sticks and carrots may eventually lessen the EU's influence.

Paradoxically, the EU has been busy discussing how to augment its coercive capacity, by wielding military instruments. But simply increasing a potential capacity to use coercion does not mean the EU will be any more willing or able to do so. Nor is it clear that it should do so: military instruments may not be any more effective than the EU's other instruments.

THE END OF CIVILIAN POWER IN EUROPE?

Several observers have argued that civilian power is of limited utility in a world filled with leaders, groups and countries willing to use force to achieve their goals. For Michael Clarke, the Union's potential to encourage peaceful behaviour is limited to the long run, because 'economic interdependence, international institutionalism, and the incentive to join prosperous security communities are difficult to manipulate for the good in short-term crises.'[75]

The Community/EPC experience in Yugoslavia is often cited. It used several diplomatic instruments to try to solve the crisis and then employed the full gamut of negative economic measures against the former Yugoslavia, yet it could not coerce the parties into reaching an agreement.

> Although the possibility of a WEU intervention was discussed, most Member States proved extremely reluctant to make use of military force. This, together with the fact that the WEU's operational capabilities continue to be extremely limited, seriously weakened the Member States' leverage over the warring parties and clearly illustrated the limits of 'civilian power' instruments such as diplomatic negotiations and trade sanctions.[76]

The 1996-1997 Intergovernmental Conference discussed various proposals to develop the EU's ability to respond to crises using armed force. Collective defence will remain NATO's primary responsibility, but the Amsterdam Treaty provides for closer EU-WEU institutional links, and for the possibility that all the Member States could participate in WEU-implemented humanitarian, peacekeeping, and crisis management operations. Even though the Amsterdam Treaty disappointed those who advocated an EU-WEU merger, the EU still seems to be heading towards an expansion of its military capabilities and the issue of a common defence policy remains on the agenda.

There are, however, several reasons to object to this move. It could raise 'jurisdictional' problems with NATO, which is even busier developing its peace-keeping and intervention capabilities.[77] It could also weaken the UN, as Simon Nuttall has noted:

> [I]t will presumably be the aim of members of the Union to support the peace-keeping role of the United Nations. To maintain an independent military peacekeeping force would cast doubt on this aim. And if the primacy of the United Na-

tions' peace-keeping responsibility is recognized, it matters little whether the Community's contribution is made through national or Community contingents.[78]

More importantly, the assumption seems to be that if the EU can use force, its influence will increase: '[t]he Union's foreign policy suffers from its inability to project credible military force.'[79] Yet this assumption is based on an optimistic view of the utility and effectiveness of military force. As Ken Booth has argued:

> In their instinct to 'do something', many people seem to have forgotten the limited utility of foreign forces in complex conflicts whose terrain features forests, mountains, cities and sanctuaries: Vietnam, Afghanistan, Beirut and Belfast. There is a dangerous over-confidence in military force in some quarters, which recent history does not support.[80]

It is by no means clear that military force can help resolve conflicts; there may be little that outsiders can, or should, do. Intervention in internal conflicts (even for humanitarian purposes) is simply not considered legitimate unless sanctioned by the UN. Given this, it would be better to concentrate on improving the UN's ability to intervene.

The EU's concentration on acquiring an intervention capability is also paradoxical in that states in practice have been hesitant to intervene at all in conflicts: witness the discussions over sending soldiers to Albania or Zaire, in 1996-1997. And assigning international forces tasks over and above protecting humanitarian deliveries is controversial.[81]

A civilian EU is to be preferred because 'security' in the post-Cold War world has acquired a much broader connotation than military security: threats to security within and between states arise from a variety of sources, including ethnic disputes, violations of human rights, and economic deprivation. And the EU is very well placed to address the long-term causes of insecurity. Mathias Jopp has argued, 'as many conflicts and tensions are rooted in political, social and economic instabilities, the Union is much better equipped than any other international organisation to address related problems.'[82] As Christopher Hill has written, 'Its comparative advantage is in the long-term effort to change the environments out of which crises tend to spring – so as to inoculate against them.'[83]

The end of the civilian power image would entail giving up far too much for far too little. An EU intervention capability could be seen by outsiders as a step towards the creation of a superpower that uses military instruments to pursue its own interests. Of course, one could argue that based on its past record, the EU would probably not behave as the superpowers did during the Cold War. Nevertheless, it would signal the end of the EU's (potential or actual) contribution to a different kind of international relations, in which civilian instruments are wielded on behalf of a collectivity which had renounced the use of force among its members and encouraged others to do the same.[84]

CONCLUSION

Rather than seeing military force as a panacea, the EU should re-examine the use of the instruments it has already. Removing the divisive issue of a common defence policy from the agenda could make way for such a re-appraisal. The division of competences between the Community and CFSP, and between the Union and the Member States, has been one of the obstacles to using the EU's instruments; overcoming this division, however, requires Member State agreement. Clearly the way in which the EU is represented in international negotiations and organisations could be reformed. The barriers between the pillars could be smoothed. 'Global approaches' combining a variety of instruments, seem to be a promising strategy (in particular because they exploit the Union's strengths) and could be used more often. While employing coercion would still require Member State agreement – a greater capacity for policy analysis and planning (as provided for in the Amsterdam Treaty) could indicate when a stronger negative message should be sent.

More importantly, however, a re-evaluation of the EU's strengths would show that civilian power could be effective, providing the Member States are willing to cooperate on foreign policy issues. If they agree on common 'civilian' foreign policies, there are policy instruments available to implement them.

NOTES

[*] I would like to thank several people who offered helpful comments on early versions of this chapter: Jan Zielonka, Christopher Hill, Richard Rosecrance, Renaud Dehousse, and the participants of the 'Explaining Europaralysis' seminar at the European University Institute.

[1] The Maastricht Treaty entered into force on 1 November 1993. It sets up a European Union consisting of three 'pillars'. The first pillar contains amendments to the three European Communities treaties (the European Coal and Steel Community, or ECSC; the European Economic Community, or EEC; and the European Atomic Energy Community, or Euratom). The CFSP provisions (the second pillar) replaced the framework for European Political Cooperation (EPC) as codified in Title III of the 1987 Single European Act. The third pillar provides for cooperation in justice and home affairs. The Maastricht Treaty renames the EEC as the European Community, but sometimes the term European Community implies all three European Communities, and sometimes it implies the Community **and** the Member States acting within the bounds of EPC. In this chapter, European Community refers to the old EEC; European Union refers to the collectivity (since 1993).

[2] At the time of writing, the Treaty had not yet been ratified, so reference to it is necessarily provisional.

[3] Hans van den Broek, 'Why Europe Needs a Common Foreign and Security Policy', *European Foreign Affairs Review* 1:1 (July 1996): 4.

[4] As Christopher Hill argued in 'The Capability-Expectations Gap, or Conceptualizing Europe's International Role', *Journal of Common Market Studies* 31:2 (September 1993).

[5] David Baldwin, *Economic Statecraft* (Princeton: Princeton University Press, 1985): 8-9.

[6] Ibid: 13-14.

[7] The Amsterdam Treaty maintains the formal division between the two frameworks.

[8] For example, the pre-accession strategy for the Central and East European associates, approved by the Essen European Council in December 1994, mixes aid, economic cooperation, and political dialogue. This was not a CFSP decision. Other global approaches have been articulated first in CFSP (such as the 1994 common position on Rwanda). Under the Amsterdam Treaty, the European Council is to decide on 'common strategies', which could be a way to develop further global approaches.

[9] An enlarged EPC Secretariat was merged into the Council Secretariat, several EPC and Council working groups were combined, and the Council (rather than the ministers of foreign affairs meeting within EPC) is formally acknowledged as the primary decision-making body. The Amsterdam Treaty clarifies the procedure for funding the CFSP (which had been a major point of contention with the European Parliament after Maastricht).

[10] The Maastricht Treaty provided for qualified majority voting (QMV) to implement CFSP joint actions, but this first required a unanimous vote. Under the Amsterdam Treaty, Member States can abstain from CFSP votes. QMV can be used to adopt joint actions and common positions that are part of a common strategy, or to implement joint actions or common positions. But a Member State can oppose the use of QMV, and block decisions.

[11] Recent common positions, for example, announce economic sanctions; recent joint actions include sending election observers to third countries. The Member States are to ensure that their policies conform to common positions and are bound to follow joint actions, a firmer obligation than hitherto recognised. The difference between common positions and joint actions in practice, though, has been obscure. The Amsterdam Treaty states that joint actions address specific situations where operational action by the EU is considered necessary, and common positions define the EU's approach to a particular matter. Both can be used to implement common strategies.

[12] See K.J. Holsti, *International Politics: A Framework for Analysis* (Englewood Cliffs: Prentice-Hall, 1995): ch. 7.

[13] Shahram Chubin, 'US Policy Towards Iran Should Change – But It Probably Won't', *Survival* 38:4 (Winter 1996-1997): 18.

[14] The ECSC and Euratom have similar powers, but only Euratom can conclude association agreements with third parties. D. Lasok and J.W. Bridge, *Law and Institutions of the European Communities* (London: Butterworths, 1991): 60-61. Under the Draft Treaty of Amsterdam, the Council can authorise the presidency to negotiate international agreements which fall within the CFSP framework; the Council would then conclude them unanimously.

[15] Because these agreements provide for trade concessions and economic cooperation, they will be covered under economic instruments – although they could be considered diplomatic instruments since they result from negotiation.

[16] The Commission's own delegations promote and protect the interests of the Communities and the Member States; the presidency's representations in particular present the joint views of the Member States and the Commission where competence is shared. Iain MacLeod, Ian Hendry, and Stephen Hyett, *The External Relations of the European Communities: A Manual of Law and Practice* (Oxford: Clarendon Press, 1996): 215-220.

[17] Robert MacLean, ed., *European Union Law Textbook* (London: HLT Publications, 1995): 195-196. The Amsterdam Treaty states that the Council could decide unanimously that the Community conclude international agreements on services and intellectual property, two areas excluded from the Common Commercial Policy.

[18] Joerg Monar, 'The Foreign Affairs System of the Maastricht Treaty: A Combined Assessment of the CFSP and EC External Relations Elements', in *The Maastricht Treaty on European Union: Legal Complexity and Political Dynamic*, eds. Joerg Monar, Werner Ungerer, and Wolfgang Wessels (Brussels: European Interuniversity Press, 1993): 148.

[19] This was a compromise on a proposal for a 'Mr. or Ms. CFSP', who would play an important role in formulating foreign policy and representing the EU.

[20] The classic case here is the CSCE Helsinki Final Act negotiations (1973-1975): the Commission participated in the talks on East-West economic cooperation, but the Presidency signed the Final Act on behalf of the Community. The CFSP provisions stipulate that the Member States shall coordinate their action in international organisations and at international conferences.

[21] Some seventy démarches on human rights were delivered in 1995. General Secretariat of the Council, 'Annual Memorandum to the European Parliament on the activities of the European Union in the field of human rights, 1995', 19 June 1996.

[22] Over 100 statements are made yearly. See the list of CFSP statements made between November 1993 and March 1995 in Annex X (a), European Union – Council, *Report of the Council on the Functioning of the Treaty on European Union* (Luxembourg: OOPEC, 1995).

²³ In 1995, 12 common positions were adopted, half of which related to sanctions on Serbia/Montenegro.

²⁴ The Council president, Dutch Foreign Minister Hans Van Mierlo, visited Albanian President Sali Berisha in March 1997 to insist that a peaceful solution be found to the crisis there.

²⁵ In March 1997, for example, the EU Member States jointly sponsored a UN Security Council resolution (vetoed by the US) condemning Israel's decision to construct new settlements outside Jerusalem. The Member States regularly jointly propose resolutions on human rights in the context of the UN (Commission on Human Rights, Third Committee of the UN General Assembly).

²⁶ Under EPC, diplomatic sanctions were imposed against Libya and Syria (in 1986) and China (in 1989); under CFSP, diplomatic sanctions have been imposed on Nigeria (in December 1995) and Burma (in October 1996).

²⁷ See Simon Nuttall, *European Political Cooperation* (Oxford: Clarendon Press, 1992): 283-287, for an account of the origins of political dialogue.

²⁸ A list of the dialogues is in *Report of the Council on the Functioning of the Treaty on European Union*, pp. 94-100. The 1981 London Report stated that the Presidency could respond to requests from third countries for contacts, and organise meetings with the troika or in the margins of EPC ministerial meetings. SEA article 30(8) declares that the Member States 'shall organise a political dialogue with third countries and regional groupings whenever they deem it necessary.' The proliferation of dialogues, however, increasingly strains the CFSP machinery, making less intense dialogues a necessity.

²⁹ One example is the San José dialogue with the Central American states, set up in 1985 to try to counterbalance (or mitigate) the US presence in the region. On the regional dialogues, see Elfriede Regelsberger, 'The Dialogue of the EC/Twelve with Other Regional Groups: A New European Identity in the International System?', in *Europe's Global Links: The European Community and Inter-Regional Cooperation*, eds. Geoffrey Edwards and Elfriede Regelsberger (London: Pinter, 1990), and Jörg Monar, 'Political Dialogue with Third Countries and Regional Political Groupings: The Fifteen as an Attractive Interlocutor', in *Foreign Policy of the European Union: From EPC to CFSP and Beyond*, eds. Elfriede Regelsberger, Philippe de Schoutheete de Tervarent, and Wolfgang Wessels (Boulder: Lynne Rienner, 1997).

³⁰ Examples include the 1980 Venice Declaration on the Middle East, and the 1981 proposal for an international conference on Afghanistan. In 1996, the EU appointed special envoys (in joint actions) to the Middle East and to the Great Lakes region in central Africa, to contribute to the peace processes there.

³¹ See Barbara-Christine Ryba, 'La Politique Etrangère et de Sécurité Commune (PESC): Mode d'Emploi et Bilan d'une Année d'Application (fin 1993/1994)', *Revue du Marché Commun et de l'Union Européenne* 384 (January 1995): 28-39; *EU Bulletin* 7/8 (1994): 66. The administration was set up in a series of CFSP joint actions.

³² The Commission, in a highly unusual (and perhaps exceptional) political role, has also mediated a dispute, in 1992-1993, between Slovakia and Hungary over the Gabcikovo dam project on the Danube. See Gabriel Munuera, *Preventing Armed Conflict in Europe: Lessons from Recent Experience*, Chaillot Paper 15/16 (Paris: Western European Union Institute for Security Studies, 1994).

³³ Under article 112 (EEC), the member states are to harmonise their export credit systems, and the ECJ ruled in 1975 that export credits fall under EC competence, but the Member States have resisted 'handing over' this instrument.

³⁴ In 1996, total Community expenditure was over ECU 83.5 billion; this figure represented 1.24 per cent of Community GNP and 2.5 per cent of Member States' public expenditure. The European Development Fund, which provides assistance to 70 developing countries under the Lomé convention, is not included in the Community budget, but is counted in total expenditure. For 1996-2000, the Fund will amount to about ECU 13 billion. The 1996 budget was ECU 81.8 billion; ECU 4.7 billion was devoted to external action. See European Commission, *The Community Budget: The Facts in Figures* (Luxembourg: OOPEC, 1996).

³⁵ Organisation for Economic Cooperation and Development, Development Assistance Committee, 'European Community', *Development Cooperation Review Series* 12 (1996): 7.

³⁶ The difference between the three types of agreements is one of quality, from those that provide a legal framework only for trade to association agreements that set up a much closer relationship. Decisions on which type of agreement will be concluded with a particular country are, at base, political.

³⁷ The prospect of negotiating an agreement may form part of a policy decided in CFSP, however, as in the December 1993 joint action on South Africa (in *Official Journal* OJ L 316 [17 December 1993]).

[38] Or 'third party': in February 1997, the EU signed a trade and cooperation agreement (with provisions for political dialogue) with the Palestinian Authority.

[39] Of course, the Member States' willingness to let in imports also reflects the influence of domestic interests.

[40] Regulation no. 3281/94, in OJ L 348 (31 December 1994). The GSP offers developing countries tariff reductions for their manufactured exports and some agricultural exports to the EU.

[41] Before 1991, the Community often claimed that its aid to developing countries was non-political. In November 1991, the Council introduced human rights as an element in its relations with developing countries. Declaration on Human Rights, Democracy and Development, *EC Bulletin* 11 (1991): 2.3.1.

[42] In 1996, the budget for such projects amounted to ECU 80.2 million, which was only a small part of the external action budget (ECU 4.7 billion).

[43] European Investment Bank loans are provided in the Community's agreements with third states. Euratom and ECSC loans are currently available for Central and East European countries and the EU has given macro-financial support to countries experiencing balance of payments problems.

[44] Simon Nuttall, 'The Institutional Network and the Instruments of Action', in *Toward Political Union: Planning a Common Foreign and Security Policy in the European Community*, ed. Reinhardt Rummel (Baden-Baden: Nomos Verlagsgesellschaft, 1992): 75-77.

[45] Martin Holland, 'Sanctions as an EPC Instrument', in *The Future of European Political Cooperation: Essays on Theory and Practice*, ed. Martin Holland (London: Macmillan, 1991): 189-190. The UK thus felt it could ignore the decision and unilaterally lifted the ban in February 1990.

[46] See MacLeod, Hendry, and Hyett, *The External Relations of the European Communities*: 352-366, and Marc Vaucher, 'L'Evolution Récente de la Pratique des Sanctions Communautaires à l'Encontre des Etats Tiers', *Revue Trimestrielle de Droit Européen* 29:1 (January-March 1993).

[47] A Member State could still take unilateral measures under article 73g, unless the Council decides, by qualified majority vote, that the member state should abolish them. See MacLeod, Hendry, and Hyett, *The External Relations of the European Communities*: 354-356.

[48] Decisions to delay agreements have been taken by the Council, Commission and European Parliament (EP). The EP has used its assent powers under the SEA to delay agreements with third countries because it disapproves of their human rights situations. It has blocked financial protocols or aid agreements with Syria, Israel, and Turkey, for example.

[49] Such provisions were included in the Lomé IV agreement, following the mid-term review in 1995. See the Commission communications: 'On the Inclusion of Respect for Democratic Principles and Human Rights in Agreements between the Community and Third Countries', COM (95) 216 final, 23 May 1995, and 'The European Union and the External Dimension of Human Rights Policy: From Rome to Maastricht and Beyond', COM (95) 567 final (22 November 1995). Without the human rights clause, suspension or denunciation of agreements would have to be justified on other grounds, and in accordance with the provisions of the agreements themselves and international law on treaties. These considerations contributed to the 1991 decision not to denounce the Lomé convention with respect to Haiti (following a coup d'etat) or to impose trade sanctions (which would have violated the Lomé convention). See Pieter Jan Kuyper, 'Trade Sanctions, Security and Human Rights and Commercial Policy', in *The European Community's Commercial Policy after 1992: The Legal Dimension*, ed. Marc Maresceau (Dordrecht: Martinus Nijhoff, 1993): 405-421.

[50] On 24 March 1997, the Council suspended GSP for Burma because of the widespread use of forced labour there.

[51] Vaucher, 'L'Evolution Récente de la Pratique des Sanctions Communautaires': 48-49.

[52] See Demetrios James Marantis, 'Human Rights, Democracy, and Development: The European Community Model', *Harvard Human Rights Journal* 7 (Spring 1994): 23. Some of these decisions were first taken in EPC (Zaire), others were first taken by the Commission (Malawi, Sudan). Commission, 'Rapport sur la mise en oeuvre de la resolution du Conseil et de ses Etats Membres sur les droits de l'homme, la democratie et le developpement du 28 novembre 1991,' SEC (92) 1915 final (21 October 1992).

[53] In EPC, Member States imposed arms embargoes on South Africa and China. Two recent CFSP common positions impose arms embargoes on Sudan (15 March 1994, in OJ L 75 of 17 March 1994) and Afghanistan (17 December 1996, in OJ L 342 of 31 December 1996). While the common position on

Sudan specifies that the Member States are to take the necessary steps to apply the embargo, that on Afghanistan merely states that an arms embargo shall be imposed.

[54] The WEU coordinated its members' naval forces in the Gulf War. In September 1991, the EC foreign ministers asked the WEU to draw up plans to send a peacekeeping force to Yugoslavia, although no action was taken on this. The WEU participated in the monitoring of the embargo against Serbia/Montenegro on the Danube river and in the Adriatic sea.

[55] See Mathias Jopp, 'The Defense Dimension of the European Union: The Role and Performance of the WEU', in *Foreign Policy of the European Union*, eds. Regelsberger, de Schoutheete de Tervarent, and Wessels. In late November 1996, the EU Council requested the WEU to examine how it could contribute to a joint action to enable the delivery of humanitarian aid to eastern Zaire and facilitate the return of Rwandan refugees (in OJ L 312, 2 December 1996). But the potential intervening states then decided not to intervene, as the refugees were returning to Rwanda anyway.

[56] Even the neutral Member States supported this. See the memorandum from Finland and Sweden, 'The IGC and the Security and Defence Dimension: Towards an Enhanced EU Role in Crisis Management', 25 April 1996.

[57] Holsti, *International Politics:*125-126.

[58] The EU may nonetheless resemble more closely Christopher Hill's 'power bloc model' of European foreign policy (according to which the EU uses its economic strength for political purposes) than it does the 'civilian model' (relying primarily on persuasion and negotiation). Christopher Hill, 'European Foreign Policy: Power Bloc, Civilian Model – or Flop?', in *The Evolution of an International Actor: Western Europe's New Assertiveness* ed. Reinhardt Rummel (Boulder: Westview, 1990).

[59] With respect to human rights and democracy, positive, rather than negative, conditionality is clearly emphasised. The November 1991 Declaration on Human Rights, Democracy and Development states that the Community 'will give high priority to a positive approach that stimulates respect for human rights and encourages democracy', but will consider appropriate responses in the event of grave and persistent human rights violations. *EC Bulletin* 11 (1991): 2.3.1.

[60] Common Position on Cuba, in OJ L 322 (12 December 1996).

[61] This even though Member States could escape individual responsibility for breaking off relations. In addition, 'multilateral' conditionality (which can entail applying sanctions) as applied by the EU may be considered more acceptable and legitimate than conditionality applied by a single state. But the new human rights clauses, for example, state that the priority is to keep agreements operational wherever possible.

[62] See Annex IX in *Report of the Council on the Functioning of the Treaty on European Union*, on implementation of UN Security Council resolutions on sanctions and acts based on article 228a. The first time a Community agreement was denounced was on 25 November 1991, when the Council denounced the cooperation agreement with Yugoslavia (part of a sanctions package). Vaucher, 'L'Evolution Récente de la Pratique des Sanctions Communautaires': 45-47.

[63] Common Position on East Timor, in OJ L 168 (6 July 1996). Likewise, the 1977 Community Code of Conduct on South Africa was a set of voluntary guidelines for EC firms with subsidiaries operating in South Africa, providing for higher levels of pay and fringe benefits for black workers. But less than 200,000 workers benefited from the Code and it could be considered a cover for inaction on sanctions. Martin Holland, *The European Union's Common Foreign and Security Policy* (Europa Institute, University of Basel, Working Paper no 3, 1994): 11.

[64] Ibid.

[65] See Steven Weber, 'European Union Conditionality', in *Politics and Institutions in an Integrated Europe*, eds. Barry Eichengreen, Jeffry Frieden, and Jürgen von Hagen (Berlin: Springer, 1995): 208-209. Indeed, in April 1997, several EU Member States refused to support a resolution condemning China in the UN Commission on Human Rights, which had been jointly supported by the Member States every year since 1989. They were more interested in smoothing relations and concluding important commercial deals with the country.

[66] Nuttall, *European Political Cooperation*: 307.

[67] See Beverly Crawford, 'The Roots of European Self-Assertion in East-West Trade', in *The New Europe Asserts Itself: A Changing Role in International Relations*, eds. Beverly Crawford and Peter W. Schulze (Berkeley: University of California, 1990).

[68] Jan Zielonka, 'Introduction: Eastern Europe in Transition', in *After the Revolutions: East-West Trade and Technology Transfer in the 1990s*, eds. Gary K. Bertsch, Heinrich Vogel, and Jan Zielonka (Boulder: Westview, 1991): 2-4. They have also been labelled 'asphyxiation' (blocking economic flows inhibits or halts bad behaviour) and 'oxygen' (economic activity leads to positive political consequences). See Franklin L. Lavin, 'Asphyxiation or Oxygen? The Sanctions Dilemma,' *Foreign Policy* 104 (Fall 1996).

[69] See Andrew Marshall, 'EU Ponders the Russian Riddle', *The Independent* (18 March 1996).

[70] In April 1997, the EU suspended the critical dialogue with Iran, after a German court found that the Iranian regime had ordered the 1992 assassination of four opposition members in Berlin.

[71] Fawaz A. Gerges, 'Washington's Misguided Iran Policy', *Survival* 38:4 (Winter 1996-1997): 10-11.

[72] 'A Frozen Approach to Cuba', *The New York Times* (10 January 1997).

[73] Mouna Naïm, 'La dialogue avec l'Europe n'a pas amélioré la situation des droits de l'homme en Iran', *Le Monde* (10-11 November 1996). The EU did manage to get Iran to promise not to encourage anyone to murder writer Salman Rushdie, but the promise is not in writing and there is still a bounty on Rushdie's head. 'Taking on the Mullahs', *The Economist* (18 January 1997).

[74] A former CIA director criticises the 'Franco-German' approach to 'wink at Tehran's support for terrorism and rationalise, in effect, appeasement of it.' R. James Woolsey, 'Appeasement Will Only Encourage Iran', *Survival* 38:4 (Winter 1996-1997): 19.

[75] Michael Clarke, 'Future Security Threats and Challenges', in *The European Union's Common Foreign and Security Policy: The Challenges of the Future*, eds. Spyros A. Pappas and Sophie Vanhoonacker (Maastricht: European Institute of Public Administration, 1996): 66. Another observer argues: 'Si l'Union souhaite prendre au sérieux son aspiration, inscrite dans le traité sur l'UE, de jouer un rôle significatif sur la scène internationale permettant de prévenir et d'agir, notre conviction est qu'elle n'aura pas d'autre choix que de se doter d'une défense européenne.' See Ryba, 'La Politique Etrangère et de Sécurité Commune (PESC): 28-39; *EU Bulletin* 7/8 (1994): 35.

[76] Spyros A. Pappas and Sophie Vanhoonacker, 'CFSP and 1996: A New Intergovernmental Conference, an Old Debate?', in *The European Union's Common Foreign and Security Policy*, eds. Pappas and Vanhoonacker: 5.

[77] It should be noted that it is not clear where either the EU or NATO will intervene in the future. In conflicts in the former Soviet Union? Given Russia's propensity to act alone there, this does not seem likely. In Africa? This would counter the recent attempts to build African peacekeeping forces and could raise concerns about neo-colonialism. Elsewhere in the world, Latin America and Asia, seems even less likely. Central and Eastern Europe, for the moment at least, fortunately does not appear a likely target for intervention. That leaves the Balkans, but neither the EU nor NATO intervened in Albania (leaving the job of 'humanitarian intervention' to an Italian-led ad hoc force), for example.

[78] Simon J. Nuttall, 'The Foreign and Security Policy Provisions of the Maastricht Treaty: Their Potential for the Future', in *The Maastricht Treaty on European Union*, eds. Monar, Ungerer, and Wessels: 136.

[79] European Commission, 'Reinforcing Political Union and Preparing for Enlargement', COM (96) 90 final (28 February 1996): 13.

[80] Ken Booth, 'Military Intervention: Duty and Prudence', in *Military Intervention in European Conflicts*, ed. Lawrence Freedman (Oxford: Blackwell, 1994): 67.

[81] The mission to Albania is an example: the UN mandate excluded the disarming of the population, even though this is a major security concern.

[82] Mathias Jopp, *The Strategic Implications of European Integration*, Adelphi Paper no. 290 (London: Brassey's, 1994): 67.

[83] Christopher Hill, 'EPC's Performance in Crises', in *Toward Political Union*, ed. Rummel: 149.

[84] François Duchêne argued in favour of a civilian power Community well over 20 years ago. 'The European Community and the Uncertainties of Interdependence', in *A Nation Writ Large? Foreign-Policy Problems before the European Community* eds. Max Kohnstamm and Wolfgang Hager (London: Macmillan, 1973).

CHAPTER VI

The European Union's Performance in World Politics: How Should We Measure Success?

Knud Erik Jørgensen[*]

Notions like 'success', 'failure', and 'progress' have accompanied the EPC/CFSP process since it was launched in the late 1960s, and they are likely to remain a part of the on-going political process.[1] Like its predecessors, the 1996-1997 intergovernmental conference (IGC) resolutions are bound to be discussed in these terms. It is not surprising, then, that studies of Europe's common foreign policy are also scattered with references to international successes and failures. Indeed, academics and other observers have been eager to describe and explain the EC/EU's successes and failures. These explanations may be fair or unfair, appropriate or inappropriate assessments of events, developments, and responses. But how can we distinguish good assessments from poor ones? One approach suggests that analysts identify clear criteria for both success and failure, then make two lists, one for the EU's foreign policy successes and another for its failures – and subsequently write a balanced analysis. Ideally, the approach requires a fairly high number of detailed case studies, and should differentiate between different sectors, such as external economic relations, diplomatic relations, and military affairs. One also could require an assessment of the impact on various international events and developments. But even a complete guideline would not allow me to address the issue I want to raise. This chapter's focus is on the sources from which observers draw to support their conclusions about international successes and failures. In particular, it strikes me that the criteria used to distinguish success from failure rarely have been considered or presented in explicit terms. On the following pages, instead of creating my own yardstick or analysing yardsticks developed by others, I want to inquire into the nature of the yardsticks themselves. I begin by asking: from where should our standard of measurement come? Basically, three sources seem available: 1) from the actors involved in the political process; 2) from outside observers; and finally, 3) from some sort of combination of the two. After discussing the three options, I demonstrate how we can gain insight about standards of success by employing an inside/outside distinction, that is, by considering how the EPC/CFSP functions inside and outside the EU. Next, I argue that comparison is a powerful measurement standard and offer two types of comparisons: one informed by a time perspective, and one including non-EU international actors. In the subsequent section, I change from a deconstructive to a constructive approach, i.e. I present six suggestions for studying the success, failure, and progress of the EU's performance in world politics.[2] Thus, I do not point out problems without suggesting possible solutions.

WHO SHOULD PROVIDE STANDARDS OF MEASUREMENT?

In my view, any EU observer should contemplate whether success criteria can and should be externally defined. In other words, should analysts knit together various objective standards? Or should we use standards that policy makers find relevant and appropriate for the analysis of *their* political aims and achievements, *their* successes and failures? Or should we use a mixture of both? I would argue that CFSP analysts on the whole have been too inclined to use self-made standards. Their standards have been predominantly implicit, that is, they have not presented in explicit terms the pros and cons of their analytical frameworks. I do not suggest that from now on we should depend solely on standards defined by the actors involved – if the Council of Foreign Ministers decides that a certain policy has been a great success, obviously, analysts should be free to disagree. Why, then, do I argue that we have been too inclined to use objective standards? Simply because, in Kratochwil and Ruggie's convincing words,

> there exists no Archimedean point from which regimes can be viewed as they 'truly' are. In the final analysis, the 'reality' of regimes resides in the principled and shared understandings of desirable and acceptable forms of behaviour among the relevant actors. Adaptations to new and unforeseen developments, attenuating circumstances, the rationales and justifications for deviations that are proffered, as well as the responsiveness to such reasoning on the part of other states, all are critical in assessing the efficacy of regimes.[3]

Though Kratochwil and Ruggie write about international regimes, their observation clearly applies to our analysis of the European Union's performance in world politics.

Drawing from intersubjective 'principled and shared understandings' has very important consequences both for research design and research findings. For example, if the aim of the EPC during the 1970s was simply for the actors involved to get to know each other and create 'procedure as substitute for policy'[4] then we can celebrate the success of EPC's first decade. But, the outsider analyst taking the rhetoric at face value or dreaming about a European superpower would necessarily be deeply disappointed and would conclude from the empirical findings that the EPC was, on the whole, a failure. There are similar examples in the 1980s and 1990s: if the purpose of declaratory diplomacy during the 1980s was to give Europe's citizens some 'comfort' in believing that European governments were doing something about the problem of superpower tension,[5] then the policy was not at all a failure. At least to some degree, Europe's public was reassured and 'felt' better. Yet, if the purpose of declaratory diplomacy was to influence world politics, 'to give Western Europe a greater say in international politics';[6] or to have an impact on developments in the Middle East, South Africa, or other hot spots, then the success was limited, at best.

Similarly, it is interesting to note how differently the EU's institutions have assessed the work of the CFSP, in preparation for the IGC 1996-1997. It is noteworthy that the Council of Minister's evaluation of the CFSP is not at all that negative.[7] True, it acknowledges that not everything worked as well as the Council had hoped and that there have been 'shortcomings'. Yet, the Council contends that certain unfortunate developments are due to the irresponsible behaviour of the European Parliament, which has tried to conquer some turf in the EU's inter-institutional power game. By contrast, the European Commission's report is highly critical of the current functioning of the CFSP. European Commissioner, Hans van den Broek, claims that the CFSP experience has been, quite simply, a big disappointment.[8] A similar analysis was presented in an *International Herald Tribune* article[9] with the telling title: 'Much Distress in Europe Over Talk, Talk, Talk'. I wonder whether the article described the state of CFSP affairs at the time, or was a carefully designed, informal contribution to the IGC process (if things are as described in the article, institutional reform is an imperative if CFSP is to survive).

One common method of measuring the EU's successes and failures is to use the EU's declared aims and objectives as a point of departure.[10] It is often used in public policy analysis, especially when dealing with implementation. In connection with the CFSP, however, there are a number of problems with using the method. First, Title V in the Treaty on the European Union lists the five principal objectives of the CFSP:
- safeguarding the common values, fundamental interests and independence of the Union;
- strengthening its security;
- preserving peace and strengthening international security;
- promoting international cooperation;
- developing and consolidating democracy and the rule of law, and respect for human rights and fundamental freedoms.

It would be fairly difficult to attempt to measure whether or not these objectives have been met, and it could easily become a meaningless exercise.

Second, even when the EU states, clearly and explicitly, its objectives serious problems may still arise when attempting to evaluate its success. The EU's policy of applying economic sanctions on ex-Yugoslavia is an illustrative example. When they were introduced in the autumn of 1991, economic sanctions were used as a coercive instrument to get Serbia to sign a peace agreement. Presumably, since Serbia did not sign, coercive diplomacy failed. However, the function of the sanctions was later changed from a coercive measure to playing a punitive function, and also represented EC solidarity. In other words, the policy became an end in itself rather than a means to a particular goal. As time passed, the sanctions became more difficult to lift because they constituted a sensitive part of EU policy making; they were used as placebo politics by EU politicians who opposed military intervention. This example illustrates how clearly stated policy objectives can change though the policy's name and substance remain the same. Was the EU's use of sanctions in ex-Yugoslavia, then, a success or a failure? The answer is easy – the question is wrong.[11]

Third, there are examples where policy outcomes perfectly match previously stated objectives, but where the full achievement of objectives constitutes a policy disaster. Unintended consequences and changed circumstances can be mentioned as possible explanations for policy disasters. The deployment of NATO mid-range missiles in the early 1980s can serve as an example. Deployment was put on the agenda in 1977 as an optional solution to Europe's lack of confidence in the American nuclear security guarantee. At that time, superpower relations were in a détente mode. But, when the missiles were deployed in the early 1980s, superpower relations had changed into an unstable tension mode. Missile deployment obviously added to this tension, in part because the rationale for deployment had been changed: it seemed to be a response to the deployment of Soviet SS20 missiles. In the late 1980s, however, when a mid-range missile disarmament agreement was signed by NATO and the Soviet Union, the SS20 rationale disappeared and the policy reintroduced the transatlantic nuclear linkage problem. Thus, the policy did not solve problems – it created them. In other words, despite full implementation we got a policy failure.

In sum, I have serious doubts about the conventional, one dimensional analytical procedure. My argument is not that it is always impossible and futile to judge the EU by its own declared and explicit objectives. I hope to point out only that it is not always a straightforward task.

SUCCESS ON THE INSIDE AND THE OUTSIDE

A well-known method of evaluating EU performance is to list examples of non-compliance with its policies, the incongruity of the EU's words and deeds, its lack of influence in world politics, and its tradition of inaction.[12] Of course, the predictable conclusion of such studies is that EU failures are emphasised more than its successes. The point I want to raise is not whether this method is fair or unfair, but rather to point out that inevitably we measure outcomes against imagined and qualitatively 'better' outcomes. Take the tradition of EU 'inaction'. In this context, Weiler and Wessels have argued interestingly that Europe's long-lasting vice of inaction can also be seen as a virtue. They emphasise the obstructive function of the EPC and argue that as a result, Europe has avoided getting itself dragged into all sorts of trouble: 'Europe has managed – through its procrastination, mixed responses, apparent confusion and ambiguous outputs of EPC – to sail through a host of international crises in the last two decades with no significant damage done to her chief economic and trade interests nor to her stability and security interests'.[13] Although a full-blooded functionalist would appreciate the functionalist perspective embedded in this view, it raises our awareness of the different possible objectives of the EPC/CFSP. In other words, if Europe aims to conduct its foreign policy in this ungraceful, muddling-through style, is there any reason to expect the straightforward, 'vulgar' policy style of a super-power?

Many observers seem to take for granted that the EPC/CFSP exists solely to meet external challenges. Yet, when we move our attention from the 'outside' to the 'inside' effects of EPC/CFSP, we see that there are legitimate reasons to doubt that assumption. Keukeleire[14] argues that the domestic function of European integration was and is to preserve peace and stability in Western Europe. Following this line of reasoning we can conclude that, while the CFSP may be less successful in solving problems outside the EU, it has been very successful as a shock-absorbing mechanism

– protecting outside conflicts from causing problems internally. Thus, if CFSP policies and procedures were designed with this function in mind, it is quite irrelevant when an observer, applying various objective standards of measurement to the external effects of CFSP, declares it a 'failure'.

Two other versions of EU 'inside' stories belong to the field of European public administration. The first version concerns the survival and adaptation of national foreign ministries. Most diplomats probably deplore the fact that foreign ministries are largely ignored in studies of EU foreign policy. When reading the exceptions to this rule, we learn that the establishment of the EPC was based in part on the idea that national foreign ministries would lose their pre-eminent role in national foreign policy-making if they were not 'Europeanised'.[15] Evidence confirms that most foreign ministries in EU member states have retained a 'coordinating' role in the process of national preference formation, i.e. 'Europeanisation' seems to have been successful: the foreign ministries have been able to fend off other ministries' attempts to conquer their turf. It is also noteworthy that foreign ministries have not been scaled down in terms of personnel or budgets. An in-depth study of foreign ministry adaptation reveals the degree to which ministries – to paraphrase di Lampedusa – have changed everything in order to keep everything as it is.[16] It is also worth considering Moravcsik's argument that European integration strengthens the executive branches of the state.[17] A similar argument has been made concerning the control of foreign policy-making, and currently it is accepted widely that national parliaments have lost ground to the executive, including, of course, its administrative level. Again, had strengthening the executive branch of each member state been among EU objectives, there would be reason to celebrate its great success.

Finally, another problem arises when we follow the reasoning – so common in recent literature – that international institutions serve, at least partly, a scapegoat function. The theory goes that institutions exist to take the blame for failures, while politicians from member states exist to be credited with policy successes. For example, the European Commission could do a good job, successfully promote a genuine common foreign policy, and be more active than expected, but regardless of its success, the Council of Ministers or national capitals, could choose not to see it as a success when it suits their interests to do so. It is time to put on the brakes. What can an analyst do in this paradoxical situation when the apparent success becomes a failure in 'reality'?

How Success is Influenced by Time Perspectives

Teleology in Practice. The observer's image of a desirable conclusion to European integration can have a significant impact on definitions of EU success. In other words, strategic vision can have a powerful impact on analysis. The 'United States of Europe'-minded observer is therefore bound to view the EPC/CFSP as a failure because it is not a genuine foreign policy and a genuine foreign ministry has not been established. This is a perfect example of today's CFSP being judged by its imagined performance in the future: if institutional dynamics do not point in the direction of a particular end point of European integration, the observer can only conclude, with affliction and frustration, that so far success has been absent. Sometimes, the telos-informed analysis is backed by an apocalyptic vision of the future, if the EU does not adopt their proposed policy prescriptions.[18] All in all, it is a very powerful diagnostic package.

Escape from the Past. Some observers are in their analysis strongly influenced by certain images of Europe's negative past. This is one of the real classic schools of thought.[19] Similar thinking most likely prompts Keukeleire to state that, 'The European integration process can be considered as one of the most successful conflict management operations in 20th century European history'.[20] When the Secretary-General of the Western European Union, José Cutileiro, argues that the organisation serves as a guardian against the revival of an ugly past, he provides a similar example. In theoretical terms, the argument equals what Mearsheimer criticises as 'the promise of institutionalism',[21] that is, the idea that European institutions mitigate potential conflicts among European states and help them redefine their identities and interests. The problem with the institutional success argument is that it is extremely difficult first to isolate different explanatory factors and then rank their explanatory power. Thus, has the EU single-handedly succeeded in mitigating conflicts between EU member states? Or was it NATO? Could it have been the balance of power – as the crudest version of realism would have it? Or did the existence of 'peace-loving' democracies in Western Europe – as some Kantians would argue – lead to 50 years of peace in Western Europe? Basically, we do not know. It is very difficult to obtain conclusive answers and, by extension, to credit specific institutions for the long peace.

Those Were the Days. Brian Breedham[22] raises the question, 'where has Europe's power gone?' But why does he ask this question? Well for starters, he notes that Europe did not have much to say at the so-called Europe-Asia Summit in February 1996. Secondly, he asserts that 'Europe of 1996 stumbles around the world in a daze', it did not intervene in the rows between Greece and Turkey, it 'missed the main point' of the disaster in the former Yugoslavia; and he reports that to 'a visitor coming to Europe from Washington or Tokyo, the foreign policy horizon of most European politicians remains astonishingly narrow'. Explanations for this state of affairs are offered too. One reason is that 'It takes a long time for a wounded continent to recover from a century like this', another is that Europe has no common will to 'drive the machinery', because a common will requires that Europeans 'see the world in roughly the same way'. In my view, Breedham's analysis contains an interesting diagnosis and includes powerful explanatory factors. In fact, it is more strategically framed than many of the other studies on the topic. Yet, it remains curious to me that Europe's present external relations are compared with its glorious past, when Europe was the undisputed centre of the world – 'Britannia rules the wave' and all that. In other words, should we expect failure upon failure until that glorious past is eventually re-established? If so, it's going to be a long, long, frustrating wait. Furthermore, what would a success story look like: would internal disagreements completely disappear? Would member states never 'go it alone', become non-compliant, or stick to their own idiosyncratic world views?[23] Would the European Union intervene in every crisis around the world? Would the Western European Union send the marines? Should good old *Clemenceau*, the French aircraft carrier, plough the waters of the South China Sea?

The Worst is yet to Come. Many analysts seem to have a positive attitude towards the EPC/CFSP. But while some project high aspirations for their object of study, other analysts are informed by what they regard as a very negative Utopia. Though Johan Galtung did not write specifically about the CFSP, he can, nonetheless, serve as a representative for this analytical tendency. In *The European Community: A Superpower in the Making*, he argues that the EC is destined to become a superpower, which is about the worst thing Galtung can imagine.[24] Because Galtung's analysis of the present is highly consistent with his nightmarish visions of the future, it is hardly surprising that Galtung offers a very negative assessment of the EC's role.[25] The EU is *a priori* stigmatised by this event and no matter what the EU did or did not do it was bound to be perceived negatively. Galtung shares his views with a considerable part of the Nordic peace research community.

Cassandra's Problem. In Greek mythology, Cassandra, the daughter of Priam and Hecuba, manages to manoeuvre herself into a situation where she possesses the power of prophecy. But her prophecies were never believed. The CFSP community is full of Cassandras. Along these lines, I would like to add that the image of a bleak future opposes to the *Worse is yet to Come* option. In other words, the problem is not that the EU is a new international actor, it is the lack of EU responsiveness. Analysts of the Cassandra breed see the problems of the future, problems that require CFSP action in the present. A plan of action unfortunately remains absent, which prompts analysts to conclude that the CFSP is a fatal failure. But, as a Danish poet reminds us, the pleasure of being proven right in a pessimistic forecast is short and bitter.[26] In the political sphere, Cassandra-like analysis was common in the late 1980s, when Jacques Delors kept insisting that 'History doesn't wait, we have to act.' Similarly, very soon we can expect that the 'demands' of the 21st century will enter into various CFSP studies – in fact, the first has already appeared.[27] Jacques Delors's approach is also interesting for its blending of concepts of past and future. Not only did he act like a technocratic Cassandra, but he also entered into discussions about neo-medievalism with historians like Jacques le Goff, that is, neo-medievalism as a diagnosis of the near future.

How is the Contemporary World? We need not limit our attention to the influence of various imagined futures and pasts. Similarly, the present is a time frame with its own powerful ways of influencing our analysis. According to Duchêne's classical prescriptive analysis, the EC *is* and *ought* to continue to be a 'civilian power'.[28] Any attempt to merge civilian and military dimensions in the process of European integration must therefore be seen by Duchêne, not as a success, but as something to be avoided. Hedley Bull basically agrees with Duchêne that Europe is 'civilian' yet disagrees with the prescriptive conclusion.[29] Bull regards Duchêne's concept of 'civilian power' to be a contradiction in terms, and proposes that the EC should develop its military power. If the EC does not, he asserts, it will never become a successful international actor.

A different version is provided by conjunctural analysis. A perfect example emerged around the time of the fall of the Berlin Wall. The New World Order *in statu nascendi* was supposed widely to be an ideal context for an international actor like the

EC, if not because 'power' was expected to disappear altogether, then because military power was expected to be outmoded and replaced by economic-political power. Yet, instead of an ideal foreign policy environment for the EU, an expectation capability gap emerged,[30] and frustration and pessimism became a widespread outlook, fuelling the well-known European optimism-pessimism cycle.

Dynamic conceptions present a different perspective from which we can measure success. The following concepts all connote change and progress: *plateau*, *saut qualitatif* and *acquis politique*. Regelsberger introduced the concept 'plateau' in order to argue that the EPC and CFSP have become more ambitious over time.[31] Similarly, Schoutheete argues that it was the limited ambition of the EPC's founders to define a 'common denominator' between the fairly diverse sets of national foreign policy traditions and that the EPC became 'the expression of the common denominator'.[32] Later on, higher ambitions were introduced and EPC reached a higher plateau. Thus, when we allow dynamic processes to enter our framework for analysis it becomes clear that what constitutes success at T1 easily can become a failure at T2. Goodwin adds further complexity to our measurement when he writes in the following succinctly framed terms, 'However, a good deal of this [EPC] activity [until 1977] has been procedural in nature rather than substantive and at times such modest progress as has been achieved has been extolled beyond its due if only to conceal the lack of progress on the internal side'.[33] Following, if not actually founding, a conventional analytical fashion, he notes the procedural character of early EPC, yet he also notes that limited EPC progress has been exploited to cover even more limited progress in communautarian affairs. What is certain is that it becomes extremely difficult to distinguish success from failure.

Comparisons with Other Actors

For Better or For Worse. Comparison with other actors is sometimes assumed to be an appropriate method for gaining insights about success and failure. But who are the relevant actors to include in our analysis? What is comparable? Some consider the US to be the obvious 'other'. One example is Birch and Scott who analyse European defence integration. Thus, when reading Birch and Scott, we learn, among other things, that Europe's 'most serious weakness, however, stems from a lack of fleet carriers' and that 'Europe's need for a satisfactory airlift wing is acute, as combined national capabilities are not impressive'.[34] That may be true, but what defence missions require a carrier fleet? What causes the 'acute need' for an airlift wing? What is 'satisfactory' and 'impressive'? What imagined conflict theatres demand a significantly strengthened European airlift wing? Why does it make sense to compare Europe to the US, given that the US armed forces in a global context is a 1st division one-of-a-kind force, some 20-30 years ahead of any armed force in the global 2nd division. In other words, Birch and Scott's analysis may be very precise in its identification of problems in contemporary European defence policy, but some of the failures seem only to exist because the US is used as the standard for comparison.

However, not only the US is used for comparison. Note the fashion in which Commissioner van den Broek slips, *en passant*, comparisons in time and between actors into his analysis,

> Either the Union will be enlarged as a genuinely integrated structure, bound by common interests, based on unity, while respecting the diversity of the Member States, and speaking with one voice in world affairs; or a wider Union will become a kind of Congress of Europe, with little internal coherence and, consequently, little external clout; a largely intergovernmental organisation, slow at taking decisions, fragmented in its policies, and unable to compete on an equal basis with the USA, Japan and the world's other major powers.[35]

Other analysts compare the actions of the European Union to those of individual member states. For example, Ludlow argues that in its policy on Yugoslavia, the European Community was 'condemned to succeed by one basic fact, which is that the member states have long reached the limits of their power in circumstances such as the Yugoslav crisis – they may scream at their Community but if they did not do it through that instrument they will not do it through any other'.[36] In this context, the point is not so much whether Ludlow's argument is valid or not, but that he makes his argument by way of comparison.[37]

A somewhat different comparison is made by a diplomat, quoted by Tonra: 'what's more important for a (minor) state; to move the policy of The Twelve, with their enormous economic and political weight two or three inches, or to run ahead a mile with little or no real impact?'[38] In this example, criteria for success depend on whether policies are designed with the actual impact on external environments in mind, or designed for the well-being of policy-makers and their domestic audiences. If success equals influence, there can be no doubt about the answer. Yet if the prime aim of policy is to celebrate one's 'self', then it probably feels wonderful to be a mile ahead.

Comparisons between the European Union and member states can also be presented in different ways and lead to different conclusions. The excessive expectations that the European Union would be the significant new international actor is an obvious point of departure. These were really 'puzzling' expectations given that the two former imperial European states, France and the UK, have been declining for years, and that Germany only acquired full sovereignty in the early 1990s, and that a well-informed observer writes about 'declining immobilismo' in Italian foreign policy[39] and another about the tradition of *isolationism* in Spanish foreign policy,[40] and that minor states are usually just that in international affairs. Given all these factors, how can anyone expect that the fore-mentioned actors could be able to provide the impetus for a qualitative leap into great-power status on the international scene?

Should the EU be Compared with International Organisations? If we take a look at the EU's own position on this issue, it is noteworthy that there has been a certain pronounced reluctance to enter into comparisons with other international organisations. The reason seems to be that such an endeavour runs counter to the claim that the EU is a *unique, sui generis* institution. A clear conception of *exceptionalism* is at play here.[41] In connection with this view, it is sometimes claimed that the EU experience has been so successful in Europe that it can function as a role model and be exported to other regions needing integration, democracy, and progress.

When the EU actually does engage in comparing itself to other international organisations, it tends foremost to see different categories of institutions. The EU seems to regard most international institutions as arenas for EU action. This is, in essence, an elevated model of the familiar concept of member state-EU relations. In a sense, the metaphor 'concentric circles' expresses the relationship between the EU *actor* and the international organisation *arenas*. The actor-arena relationship applies in the UN (minus the Security Council) and the OSCE, in which the EU, as often as possible, presents itself as a unitary actor. For various reasons it is more tricky for the EU to do so in NATO. The then-Assistant Secretary of State, Richard Holbrooke, provides one reason: 'an inescapable but little realised fact: the United States has become a European power in a sense that goes beyond traditional assertions of America's 'commitment' to Europe. In the 21st century, Europe will still need the active American involvement that has been a necessary component of the continental balance for half a century'.[42] The prime multilateral framework for this American 'presence' has been, and continues to be, NATO. How it works in practice has been summarised concisely by Michael Brenner.[43]

In some cases, other international organisations are seen as being inferior to the EU, as something the EU must resist being degenerated into. For example, EFTA has been regarded as a mere 'free trade area' and, as noted above, Hans van den Broek warns against the EU becoming 'a kind of Congress of Europe'. Conceptions of success and failure are here, for once, spelled out in clear language. Current debates on flexibility vs. coherence precisely determine the Union's identity between member states and international organisations.

From Deconstruction to Construction

Some may think that this chapter so far has a more deconstructive than encyclopaedic nature. My aim has been to deconstruct a few key terms that are widely used in studies of European Union performance in world politics. I hope to have demonstrated that the use of these terms tends to obscure things more than necessary. So, is my argument that everything is relative? In a sense, yes, but I hasten to add that one should remember the difference between *is* and *ought*. The rationale of the chapter has been to demonstrate just how casually and implicitly these key terms are used. In that sense, everything *is* relative, and the chapter can be seen as a plea to change this current state of affairs.

Hence, to paraphrase Lenin: What ought to be done? I limit myself to six suggestions. First, in order to present the actually existing relativism in CFSP research, I have been forced to point out the existence of 'multiple realities'. I know that this term makes some scholars allergic to, paradoxically, relativism, Cartesian anxiety, and related evils.[44] Nonetheless, I think we can change this into our advantage. Hence, I contend that a first step to get a better understanding of the European Union's performance in world politics is to acknowledge the existence of multiple realities. And actually, it is a less radical, and indeed a more common sense idea than many science-minded scholars are ready to accept. Note, for instance, how Christopher Tugendhat describes his experience as an EC Commissioner:

> To attempt a description of the European Community is rather like trying to explain a psychic experience. It exists on so many different planes: the one on which it presents itself; the way in which politicians try to mould it; the actual; and the potential. The overlap between them is often small, and the first two vie with each other in unreality.[45]

As the quotation demonstrates, a practitioner like Tugendhat does not reject the idea of multiple realities, so why should scholars? Furthermore, it may comfort some that the idea of multiple realities has strong philosophical and sociological underpinnings.[46] I cannot possibly outline all the lines of argument which can be deduced from such a constructivist stance. Yet, in the previous section, I have demonstrated the existence of multiple realities within the sphere of European foreign affairs. It seems plausible to me that a link between these observations and the general idea can be constructed by some of Searle's theoretical constructs: theory of speech acts, of intentionality, and of rule governed behaviour. However, that is for another occasion and for others to demonstrate.

My second suggestion logically follows the first. Having accepted the idea of multiple realities, the next step will be to identify the most prominent realities in the sphere of European foreign affairs. Imagine a spectrum of conceptions ranging from 'flat denial of EU performance' over denigration of the EU's international 'actorness' to the euphoric enthusiasm displayed from 1989 to 1990; expect differences between conceptions held in national capitals, European institutions, and external actors who either recognise or do not recognise the EU as an international actor; and note the advantage of applying a dynamic perspective on these matters (i.e. dynamic as the opposite of static). A second line of inquiry begins with the question: Where do social realities reside if not in collective ideas? Hence, we should trace and identify the mentalities of decision makers, and the relationship between current collective ideas and trends in European foreign policy.[47]

Third, from the vantage point we have reached now, we should proceed to discuss predictable contradictions between different conceptions of what constitute reasonable criteria for success within each social reality. It is hardly surprising that the Council of Ministers, the European Commission, and the European Parliament have different ideas about what foreign policy successes and failures are, how they come into being, and how failure can be turned into success. Equally unsurprising are the differences between member states of different sizes and status. Note the tension between the following two quotations. A senior diplomat from a minor member state reflects on CFSP habits: 'Even a rather stupid German minister will be listened to because he speaks for Germany'.[48] And a newspaper quotes a senior European diplomat: 'When a little country is speaking, you can see the faces of Kinkel and de Charette saying, 'Why do I have to listen to this guy?' They think it is a waste of time.[49]

Fourth, it would be a pity if the many meanings of success led to the abandonment of the concept. This step would repeat previous mistakes of abandoning essentially contested concepts from the language of scientific inquiry.[50] Yet, if we are not going to abandon these terms, then what? We must continue to analyse successes and failures, but avoid implicit assumptions about criteria for success, abstain from one dimensional analysis, and approach the subject matter from different perspectives.

Fifth, to some degree I think that different conceptions of success and failure reflect the fact that we are dealing with a moving target. In order to create insightful understandings of our subject, it seems advantageous to me to leave the general statements, the *grosso modo* perspectives, and the paintbrush descriptions of success and failure behind us. If for no other reason, we should do this because the outcomes of this type of analysis often say more about the observer than about the object of research.

Sixth, instead of *grosso modo* perspectives, we should consider how to construct an issue and time differentiated framework for analysis, and then conduct in-depth systematic cross-issue, cross-temporal comparative analysis. To give an example, it seems fair to assume more successes in the realm of international political economy than in international military crisis management.[51] Holland has previously made a plea for comparative analysis, yet his plea has sadly gone largely unnoticed.[52] Finally, it is worth noting Tugendhat's observation that 'It is when it [EPC/CFSP] is out of the limelight and involved in a continuos negotiation of the sort that enables diplomats and ministers to follow a consistent line of policy and build on what has gone before that the system of Political Co-operation works best.'[53] By concluding that the EU's joint action on the Non-Proliferation Treaty was 'an outstanding success', Müller and van Dassen's findings support Tugendhat's hypothesis.[54]

Obviously, this list of suggestions is in no sense comprehensive. My aim is merely to present a few platforms and guidelines for future research on the European Union's performance in world politics.

CONCLUSION: SUCCESS IS (MAYBE) NOT WHAT IT USED TO BE

The European Union's performance in world politics is likely to provoke continued and increased attention among observers. It probably reflects the fact that the Union plays an ever-increasing role in international affairs. To be sure, residual traditions in foreign policy-making can be found, but do they really matter? When the British Royal Yacht, *Britannia*, sailed out of Hong Kong harbour on 1 July 1997, it was to escort the last British Governor out of the country. Afterwards the royal yacht was decommissioned and not replaced: an exit of one of the prime symbols of the British Empire. In general, national foreign policies tend to fade away from our horizon. A quick browse through major book catalogues reveals that it has indeed been a while since a major work on a European national foreign policy has emerged.

Accordingly, we have to accept the 'messy' state of European foreign affairs in which we find an erosion of the domestic-foreign policy divide and where the boundary of the European Union remains blurred. Indeed, there was no political rationale to codify the protection of the Union's external borders and its territorial integrity in the Amsterdam Treaty. The foreign policies of member states and of the European Union are still in the process of being thoroughly reconsidered after the end of the Cold War. This messy state-of-affairs ought to be acknowledged when successes and failures in international politics are analysed.

If I have been fully successful in my endeavour, your notion of success will by now be different than hitherto. Yet, even if I have only managed to create a few cracks in the citadel of one dimensional analysis, or certain doubts about self-confident announcements of success and failure, I will consider the writing of the chapter a worthwhile activity. Equally so if my suggestions for a research agenda can serve as a source of inspiration for future studies.

NOTES

* I would like to thank Ulla Holm and Jan Zielonka for valuable comments on a previous draft of the article. The usual disclaimer applies.

[1] Cf. Ludlow, et al., 1995; Progress Report, 1995.

[2] By a 'deconstructive' approach I mean merely 'questioning' implicit assumptions, 'breaking down' things taken for granted, and 'undermining' structures of meaning presented in numerous studies of the CFSP. Readers should not expect applications of, say Derridaian deconstructive theory.

[3] Kratochwil, Friedrich and John G. Ruggie, 'International Organisation: A state of the art on an art of the State,' *International Organisation* 40: 753-776 (1986).

[4] Wallace, William and David Allen, 'Political Cooperation: Procedure as Substitute for Policy,' in *Policy-Making in the European Community*, eds. Helen Wallace et al. (Chichester: John Wiley and Sons, 1977).

[5] Guéhenno, Jean-Marie, 'Sicherheit und Verteidigung in Europa,' *Dokumente*, 48:2: 121-127 (1991).

[6] Scheel, Walter, 'Preface,' in *European Political Cooperation in the 1980s. A Common Foreign Policy for Europe?* ed. Alfred Pijpers et al. (Dordrecht: Martinus Nijhoff, 1988).

[7] Council of Ministers, Report on the Functioning of the Treaty on European Union, May 1995.

[8] Report on the Operation of the Treaty on European Union, European Commission, 10th May 1995. Hans van den Broek has presented his views on several occasions, see for instance, 'Why Europe Needs a Common Foreign and Security Policy', *European Foreign Affairs Review*, 1(1): 1-5; 'The Common Foreign and Security Policy in the Context of the 1996 Intergovernmental Conference', speech at the Royal Institute of International Affairs, Brussels, 4 July 1995; Further contributions from the Commission include Dr. Günther Burghardt, The Potential and Limits of CFSP – Implementing Maastricht, *CFSP Forum* 3/94; see also the expert report, *European foreign, security and defence policy: towards stronger external action by the European Union*, AVT95/BZ 40141, 30 March 1995.

[9] *International Herald Tribune* (30 April, 1997).

[10] I am grateful to Peter Viggo Jakobsen and Karen Elizabeth Smith for proposals to include reflections on the method.

[11] See my analysis of successes and failures in the EU's policy on ex-Yugoslavia, 'The European Union as an Actor in World Politics: the Case of Yugoslavia', *Quaderni Forum* 4 (1996).

[12] Inaction has many faces: 'As Martin Wight reminded us, respect for multilateralism is always in danger of becoming an excuse for doing nothing' (quoted in Inis L. Claude, 1993: 225). Does inaction at European Union level merely mirror inaction at the level of member states?, and does the European institution function as a shield, designed to fend off criticism of inaction?

[13] Weiler, Joseph and Wolfgang Wessels, 'EPC and the challenge of theory', in *European Political Cooperation in the 1980s. A Common Foreign Policy for Europe?* ed. Alfred Pijpers et al. (Dordrecht: Martinus Nijhoff, 1988): 252.

[14] Keukeleire, Stephan, 'The European Community and Crisis Management', in *The Art of Conflict Prevention*, eds. W. Bauwens and Luc Reychler (London: Brassey's, 1994).

[15] Hill, Christopher, ed., *National Foreign Policies and European Political Cooperation* (London: George Allen & Unwin, 1983).

[16] Further in Hocking, Brian and David Spence, eds., *EU Member State Foreign Ministries: Change and Adaptation* (Forthcoming).

[17] Moravcsik, Andrew, 'Why the European Community Strengthens the State: Domestic Politics and International Cooperation', paper presented at the Conference of Europeanists, Chicago (April 1994).

[18] Weiler, Joseph and Wolfgang Wessels, 'EPC and the challenge of theory,' in *European Political Cooperation in the 1980s. A Common Foreign Policy for Europe?* ed. Alfred Pijpers et al. (Dordrecht: Martinus Nijhoff, 1988): 241-242.

[19] Duroselle, Jean-Baptiste, *Fra fortid i splittelse til fremtid i fællesskab* (København: Lademann, 1990). The title chosen for the Danish edition of Duroselle's book is more telling than its British counterpart (in translation: *Europe: from a Past in Conflict to a Future in Community*).

[20] Keukeleire, Stephan, 'The European Community and Crisis Management,' in *The Art of Conflict Prevention*, eds. W. Bauwens and Luc Reychler (London: Brassey's, 1994): 137.

[21] Mearsheimer, John, 'The False Promise of Institutionalism', *International Security*, 19:3: 5-49 (1995).

[22] Breedham, Brian, 'Where has Europe's power gone', *The Globe and Mail* (9 March, 1996).

[23] This point concerns the relationship between principles and pragmatism, or law and politics. A lot of CFSP analysts are strong defenders of principles and legal rules. If only the CFSP were to become governed by *communautarian* rules, success after success in international performance would be secured. Healthy antidotes of pragmatism in the analysis of foreign affairs have been presented by John G. Ruggie (1991) and Inis L. Claude (1993).

[24] Galtung, Johan, *The European Community: A Superpower in the Making* (London: Allen and Unwin, 1973).

[25] Galtung, Johan, 'Reflection on Peace Prospects for Yugoslavia', in *Yugoslavia, War*, eds. Tonci Kuzmanic and Arno Truger (Schlaining and Ljubliana: Austrian Study Centre for Peace and Conflict Resolution/Peace Institute, 1992). However, when compared with the image of a potent superpower, the analysis of the present CFSP could, in principle, also result in a conclusion like this: The CFSP is not, after all, too bad, yet. But it could, easily, because of the European *mystique*, turn into something really bad, pretty soon.

[26] Henrik Nordbrandt, 'Istanbul under mine vinger', *Morgenavisen Jyllands-Posten*, 22 April 1997.

[27] European Security, *European Security Policy Towards 2000: ways and means to establish credibility, First Report*, 19 December, Brussels: European Commission (1994).

[28] Duchêne, Francois, 'Europe's role in world peace', in *Europe Tomorrow*. ed. Richard Mayne (London: Fontana, 1972).

[29] Bull, Hedley, 'Civilian Power Europe: A Contradiction in Terms', *Journal of Common Market Studies*, 21:1-2: 149-164 (1982).

[30] Hill, Christopher, 'The Capability-Expectations Gap, or Conceptualizing Europe's International Role,' *Journal of Common Market Studies* 31:3: 305-328 (1993).

[31] Regelsberger, Elfriede, 'EPC in the 1980s: Reaching another Plateau?,' in *European Political Cooperation in the 1980s*, eds. Alfred Pijpers et al. (Dordrecht: Martinus Nijhoff, 1988).

[32] Schoutheete de Tervarent, Philippe, 'Political Cooperation and National Foreign Policies', *European Affairs* 4: 62-67 (1987).

[33] Goodwin, Geoffrey, 'The external relations of the European Community – shadow and substance,' *British Journal of International Studies* 3: 39 (1977).

[34] Birch, Timothy J. and John H. Scott, 'European Defense Integration: National Interests, National Sensitivities,' in *The State of the European Community: The Maastricht Debates and Beyond*, eds. Alan W. Cafruny and Glenda G. Rosenthal, (Boulder: Lynne Rienner, 1993): 273-274.

[35] Broek, Hans van den, 'Why Europe Needs a Common Foreign and Security Policy', *European Foreign Affairs Review* 1:1: 2 (1996).

[36] Gow, James and James D.D. Smith, *Peace-making, Peace-keeping: European Security and the Yugoslav Wars* (London: Brassey's, 1992): note 95.

[37] In other contexts, I would take issue with Ludlow's analysis. It seems to me that Europe's response to the Yugoslav imbroglio demonstrated that EU member states could act individually or in smaller groupings than the EU. These potentials should not conceal, however, that states acted through the EU longer than would typically be expected.

[38] Tonra, Ben, 'The Impact of Political Cooperation', in *Reflective Approaches to European Governance*, ed. Knud Erik Jørgensen (London: Macmillan, 1997): 197.

[39] LaPalombara, L., 'Italian Foreign Policy – Declining Immobility,' *Relazioni Internazionali* (September 1989): 95-105.

[40] Ortéga, Andrés, 'Spain in the Post-Cold War World', in *Democratic Spain: reshaping external relations in a changing world*, eds. Richard Gillespie, Fernando Rodrigo and Jonathan Story (London: Routledge, 1994).

[41] Most major global power centres probably have tendencies to claim that they are exceptional. Such claims are somewhat paradoxically mixed with reasoning in universal terms. On the other hand, it is not uncommon to meet the following line of reasoning. 'It is because of our exceptionality that we are obliged to reason in universal terms'. I am grateful to Ulla Holm who made me aware of this point.

[42] Holbrooke, Richard, 'America, a European Power', *Foreign Affairs* (March/April 1995).

[43] Brenner, Michael, Multilateralism and European Security, *Survival* 35:2:138-155 (1992).

[44] Bernstein, Richard J., *Beyond Objectivism and Relativism: science, hermeneutics, and praxis* (Oxford and New York: Basil Blackwell, 1983).

[45] Tugendhat, Christopher, *Making Sense of Europe* (London: Penguin Books, 1987): 15.

[46] Searle, John R., *The Construction of Social Reality* (New York: The Free Press, 1995). See also Schütz, Alfred, *Collected Papers Vol. 1: The Problem of Social Reality*, ed. Maurice Natanson (The Hague: Martinus Nijhoff, 1967).

[47] 'Mentalities' refer to individual, shared and collective ideas. It is somewhat paradoxical that a fairly old book like Federico Chabod's, *Italian Foreign Policy: The Statecraft of the Founders*, can serve as inspiration.

[48] Tonra, Ben, 'The Impact of Political Cooperation', in *Reflective Approaches to European Governance*, ed. Knud Erik Jørgensen (London: Macmillan, 1997): 196.

[49] *International Herald Tribune* (30 April 1997).

[50] On the term 'essentially contested concepts', see Connonly, 1983: 9-44; on criticism of the term 'balance of power', see James E. Dougherty and Robert L. Pfalzgraff, 1971: 30-36.

[51] Jørgensen, Knud Erik, ed. *European Approaches to Crisis Management* (The Hague, London, and Boston: Kluwer Law International, 1997).

[52] Holland, Martin, *The Future of European Cooperation* (London: Macmillan, 1991).

[53] Tugendhat, Christopher, *Making Sense of Europe* (London: Penguin Books, 1987): 65.

[54] Müller, Harald and Lars von Dassen, 'From Cacophony to Joint Action: Successes and Shortcomings of European Nuclear Nonproliferation Policy', paper presented at the Second Pan-European Conference in International Relations, Paris (13-15 September 1995).

CHAPTER VII

Defining the European Security Policy

Guido Lenzi

These are again times when events tend to unfold faster than the human ability to foresee and steer them. Attempts at fitting them into pre-existing structures may prove elusive and even lead to unexpected drawbacks. Over 50 years ago, Gramsci lamented that the old order had faded while the new one was not yet recognisable. In his Zurich speech of 1946, Churchill called for 'recreating the European fabric.' He was followed, in 1950, by Robert Schuman who, setting the course for European integration, declared that 'world peace cannot be ensured without creative initiatives.' Today, we are once again 'at the creation,' as Dean Acheson then put it, with extensive new challenges and opportunities confronting Europe, from within and outside its borders, in political and economic terms.

EUROPE'S SECURITY: FROM DETERRENCE TO COOPERATION

The wide-open fields of globalisation and of network society compete with the assertion of micro-identities in a cause and effect relationship. This apparently contradictory mixture of transnational impositions and self-defence reflexes, branded as 'glocalism,' has already produced a mutation of the international system – an evolution of the species catalysed by economic diasporas criss-crossing national boundaries at will.[1] 'Global economy, local mayhem' was a title of *The Economist*, though 'the world economy may be on the brink of its first synchronised growth since the first world war.' From its Olympus, the Davos Economic Forum agreed. And Karl Lamers, writing from Bonn to a French sceptic,[2] argued that 'polity must be oriented with respect to ... the diktat of supranational reality, namely of global competition; this reality offers no alternative.' The European Monetary Union, when it finally happens, will consecrate the supremacy of economics over politics, and constitute the ultimate vindication of Monnet's vision. Common Foreign and Security Policy cannot lag behind any longer.

Security matters are not immune to this groundswell. These structural changes involve a broader concept of stability and security, and imply a renovated military posture that addresses crisis prevention and management rather than actual warfighting. Brushing aside the clear-cut equations of bi-polarism, too many variables are at play today, which defy the ability of individual states to control them, assuming that they are actually prepared to do so. Unpredictability and instability emerge as the reverse side of the liberalisation and democratisation coin. Any confusion that exists is not about general concepts, but has more to do with the present unwillingness of European states to undertake international commitments after years of being comfortably tucked beneath the strategic cover of the US. Apparently, no danger (not even Yugoslavia falling bloodily apart!) is perceived as sufficiently imminent to persuade states to do something decisively, either individually or through the available international mechanisms. The fact is that a process of domestic adjustment is under way in every European country, to the East as much as to the West of the former continental divide, which is not conducive to international security endeavours beyond the most elementary call of duty. Humanitarian intervention is the most that Europeans have so far been able to accept, in so-called 'non Art.5' (the former 'out of area') contingencies, leaving the Americans in charge of any peace-enforcement mission. Residual respect for the principle of territorial integrity, combined with a reluctance to get in harm's way, may account for this. The result is that any attempt at a re-appropriation of specific European security responsibilities will be postponed until the tangle has become so intricate as to defy any effective intervention. The establishment of a European security policy therefore requires a vision and determination of the kind that was in the end lacking in 1954, when the European Defence Community failed the scrutiny of the French National Assembly. The situation may be much more favourable today than it was then, precisely because all states, big and small, are either unable or unwilling to go it alone in the international security field. The Madrid and Amsterdam summits have provided important indications to that effect, with the convergence of the reform processes undertaken by both NATO and the EU, and WEU positioning itself consequently at their intersection.

In the meantime, however, many national sensitivities, antagonistic trouble-spots, and national stiffnesses have re-emerged from under the Cold War glacier, increasing the potential of possible crises. As Yugoslavia amply demonstrated, addressing them early rather than waiting to contain their consequences, in a proactive, rather than reactive, political posture is not only a commonsensical response but also a way of overcoming the reluctance of states to intervene militarily in conflict management abroad. For the purposes of developing a wider concept of security, full-fledged military means have been made available for non-military policing tasks. These developments have blurred many distinctions, complicated the calculations of political analysts, and confounded the electorate. Simplistic traditional solutions are thrown at radically new situations, while any innovative and voluntaristic approach of the kind expressed in Maastricht remains buried under the rubble of the Soviet empire. What is more, for the first time decision-makers are confronted with the need to involve the public fully in an extensive debate about national security interests and the most appropriate means of protecting them. While territorial defence is a self-evident constitutional duty, the projection of forces abroad for international solidarity or the promotion of a yet ill-defined international order are not, and therefore arguments to support such measures must be presented convincingly to the electorate. In order to forestall a 'democratic deficit' in matters of security and defence, a new impetus has been given to multilateral formulas which has produced a renaissance of the universalist concept of a concert of nations, in its constant tug-of-war with the realist balance-of-power kind of approach.

The Wilsonian dream of a new international order, re-enacted at the San Francisco Conference, is therefore surfacing again. And yet, given the diffuse system of multiple polarities and moving targets, the UN cannot be saddled with the utopia of world government. Multilateral contexts must not substitute for national responsibilities or be scapegoats for nations' failures. They should constitute instead a tool that Europe has a vital interest in using to avoid sinking again into a free-for-all and collective irrelevance. This time, Europe itself is at stake. Its Common Foreign and Security Policy ambitions may have been set too high at Maastricht: integration may remain elusive in defence and security matters where state prerogatives are still paramount. But European nations are aware that the challenges before them cannot be dealt with single handedly, and that they cannot continue to sublet their own security to the United States. The parameters of a European security strategy and the organisations to implement it already exist. But they must be rearranged, keeping in mind that no all-purpose solution can be devised, whilst a sense of direction must indicate that the European Community of nations is determined and able to use them, instead of giving in to isolationist or unilateralist tendencies. This adjustment has been termed 'the road back to Carolingia' (or is it simply to the Congress of Vienna?), involving at the same time a deepening of the common resolve and a widening of its solidarity. The two processes have different motivations, but their convergence must eventually lead to a recognisable common institutional framework.

In the meantime, in spite of the many invocations, no world leader is available and no all-purpose core group or other pre-established *directoire* is likely to emerge.[3] With no barbarians at the door, these can hardly be heroic times; at best, explorers could venture out to the uncharted territories that ancient maps used to indicate with the inscription 'hic sunt leones' (here dwell lions). The adjustments that are called for, in fact, do not always imply complex institutional engineering. It is managers, rather than architects, that are needed to ensure that the behaviours of states converge. Institutional interlinkages ought to encourage the sharing of responsibilities rather than impose structural hierarchies. Improved world governance needs the contribution of Europe as a distinct international actor. Western Europe, apart from its NATO connection, already exerts a stabilising gravitational and catalytic effect, to the extent that a demand for Europe exists in the new democracies and in the world at large. Things are already happening which politicians are hesitant to recognise and label accordingly. An impression of improvisation is thus spreading, with the recurring disputes between proponents of positive law and common law pragmatists, who shield from each other the commonalities of their purpose.[4] No wonder the demand for Europe has been shifted to the back-burner by applicants who now only queue for NATO, as if it were the cure for all ills. Instead, all European governments are increasingly aware that in security matters they will often have to fend for themselves. Even the recognised lone surviving superpower is reluctant and ineffective, although still able to wield its influence globally, aware as it is that the new multilateral conditions reduce its ability to shape events. Even nuclear deterrence is affected by this alteration in the international fabric.

Managers in Demand, Architects in Abundance

No grand design is available for the world, and therefore for Europe, to deal with the transition from the Cold War situation of 'no war, no peace' to a scenario where both war and peace can coexist. Things just happen, out of benign neglect at best. An enlarged security concept has thus emerged, where military and non-military factors interplay, and threats become multifaceted and uncontrollable by using traditional means. No strategic thermostat is applicable. Confronted as we are with such ambiguous challenges, cooperative security has become a matter of participation in a preventive mode, with differentiated interventions tackling separately the various potential crisis factors, a matter of empowerment rather than of imposition. New modalities of cooperation are being devised that overcome the traditional concepts of national sovereignty, and improve interaction where gaps appear in institutional arrangements and intergovernmental agreements. Political mentalities must evolve from the automatisms of traditional security structures that can no longer provide for every conceivable contingency, to a more voluntaristic approach that brings together only the willing and able. Hard cores, and variable speeds and geometries are already at play, regardless of institutional arrangements. They must now be more coherently interconnected. In Europe, the issues of enlargement and institutional reform have so far monopolised attention, as if they could in themselves absorb the variety of conditions, perceptions, and aspirations liberated by the disintegration of the bipolar system. Nowadays, different postures characterise even the full members of Western European institutions. That does not prevent the quite distinct approaches and perspectives of Germany, Sweden, Norway, Estonia, and Poland from cooperating effectively in the Baltic Sea area. Elsewhere, subregional cooperative possibilities have not been fully explored, subordinated as they are to the gold rush towards NATO or EU. Institutional solutions may buttress the eventual achievements within an overall structural coherence, but they cannot in themselves substitute for the *ad hoc* coalition building that today's situation calls for.

Collective defence cannot extend to every possible scenario. Nor can any alliance possibly establish automatic solidarities with respect to ill-defined scenarios.[5] In non Art. 5 cooperative security contingencies, regardless of whether they take place in NATO or EU/WEU, decisions will be taken pragmatically, spurred on by events as they unfold and under the leadership of the most resolute and operationally involved.[6] The broader continental scenario has been repeatedly laid out: in the 1975 Helsinki Final Act and all of its offspring, including the Charter of Paris and the Pact on Stability in Europe; in the New Strategic Concept and the Enlargement Study that NATO produced respectively in 1991 and 1995; in the Common Concept of WEU, in 1995; in the Euro-Mediterranean Partnership of Barcelona, also produced in 1995; all of which, the forthcoming EU Common Foreign and Security Policy will now somehow formally absorb as the political capital of The Fifteen. Compared to other geostrategic regions, Europe is overendowed with political declarations and institutions – a whole spaghetti-junction of them. They must not be rebuilt so much as allowed to interact more accurately, with their respective comparative advantages made more complementary and not exclusive, in a more coherent framework. Consultative and decision-making mechanisms must be readied, apart from any pre-established commitment to crisis management and contingency planning. A shift is occurring, among Europeans and between transatlantic allies, from strategic uniformity to tactical role-sharing, not only in terms of command and control, and logistical adjustments, but also, most importantly, within a broader consultative process extended to global issues, ranging from trade to terrorism. A mixture of multilateral, bilateral, and variable geometry relationships will result, as situations may suggest, tailoring responses to actual needs.

A SPAGHETTI JUNCTION OF INSTITUTIONS

In order to sustain each and all of these relationships, along with the necessary consensus, legitimacy, credibility, and effectiveness, their functional interlinkage must be improved, steering clear from a strict hierarchical subordination that would diminish the needed flexibility of responses. For the countries already members of European organisations, for those who aspire to membership, for those that will make it soon, and those that will not, a common security denominator will be provided by the interconnection of the existing organisations. The United Nations Charter establishes the legitimising chain, in a devolution of responsibilities, that include Art.51, which spells out the right of individual and collective self defence, and Chapter VIII, concerning regional cooperation. The Security Council remains the supreme authority in matters concerning the use of force, which can, and increasingly does, approve 'enabling resolutions,' conferring mandates to other organisations or associations of states better suited to addressing specific crises as they arise. In Europe, the following functional chain could ideally apply, which would lead to the re-empowering of Europe on the world scene: the OSCE would generate the necessary overall political consensus, in its capacity as the regional security organisation recognised by the UN Charter; NATO would provide the politico-military transatlantic link that constitutes the essential European common denominator; the Council of Europe would ensure the spreading out and observance of civil rights; the EU would provide the money, together with the coherence and sense of purpose of an increasingly integrated community, supplemented by a Common Foreign and Security Policy and pillar III's legal and law enforcement provisions; the WEU, finally, would act as the instrument for specifically Western European political-military consultations, planning and eventual operations, involving other countries as needed.

And yet, today the OSCE's overarching context is discarded as ineffective, the EU is confined to a purely economic role, and the WEU is diminished as a needless duplication of NATO. NATO's June 1996 Berlin communique singles out WEU 29 times (and the Madrid Declaration 20 times), but mentions the EU only once in passing, thus confirming Washington's reluctance to utter the two acronyms in the same breath. At a moment when coalition building and variable leadership are needed, NATO enlargement is perceived as the sole institutional remedy for political and operational requirements alike. In present strategic conditions and with dwindling budgets sacrificed to illusory peace dividends, no national Parliament would object to the US preserving and expanding its predominance in European security matters. Why try something new, if a clear-cut distinction can be drawn between the military and economic aspects of Europe, with NATO continuing to take care of the first and the EU addressing the second? Besides, the countries of Central Europe make NATO protection the priority – it is the simple way out compared with the intricate conditionalities of economic integration. But will the new generation of US Congressmen accept these implications? Or should Europe start to organise itself at the lower reaches of the security spectrum, concerning prevention, while keeping in store the decisive transatlantic strategic connection for times of real need? Besides, the two processes of EU and NATO reform are not linear: they must sustain and complement each other, as the new democracies proceed toward a consolidation involving domestic institution building as much as external protection and overall deterrence.

Broad, preventive security does not allow pre-established scenarios and indiscriminate commitments. The pragmatic proactiveness and 'ad-hocery' that circumstances suggest would call instead for diversified responses, tailored to changing needs, and therefore promoting a 'differentiated integration' framework,[7] within which an undiminished, rather than abstractly undivided, European security could be nurtured. This 'separable, but not separate' concept has already been enshrined in NATO doctrine. In the CFSP provisions, too, this distinction should be allowed: applicant countries could be accepted gradually into the intergovernmental second and third pillar common positions and joint actions, without waiting for the completion of their much stricter structural and economic integration into the first pillar.[8] This approach would eventually lead to a looser relationship between Art.5 of NATO and WEU,[9] without detracting from their inherent political and strategic interconnection. It would also ease the development of their respective links with other institutions and towards the prospective applicants for membership.

Without detracting from the specific role that other European organisations would be best suited to perform, the EU is particularly well suited for the 'enlarged security' tasks, not only in its present mostly civilian configuration, but also in its more extensive Maastricht ambitions. The European institutions must however all improve their networking and proactive relationship, to borrow formulas that are applicable to other managerial endeavours. No institutional obsession should be allowed to set in since, as Monnet used to say, 'we are uniting people, not forming coalitions.' Besides, NATO, the EU, WEU, and the OSCE, alongside the UN or the Council of Europe, are all presently acting for what are mainly political purposes, promoting consensus and convergence, national and international compatibilities and interlinkages, an incremental process that must not be allowed to turn into competing cooptations, but lead instead to aggregations and task-sharing.[10] There is life outside and between institutions which can and must disaggregate in order to cope with the variable challenges of European reintegration.

An important development in this direction already occurred in 1991 when, with the 'new strategic concept' approved at its Rome summit, NATO indicated that it was ready to consider responsibilities beyond territorial defence, thus overriding Art.5 implicit geographic constraint, that the US itself had originally established in order to circumscribe its military involvement in Europe. Washington's present reluctance to issue a blank cheque for European security responsibilities in former 'out-of-area' contingencies is therefore conceivably motivated by the conviction that European initiatives not sustained by a credible common political underpinning may erode the credibility of (and Congressional support for) the transatlantic commitment, equated so far primarily with the US contribution. Instead of seeking American concessions as a matter of principle, the Europeans should first establish the political decision-making procedures and operational mechanisms appropriate for their own 'separable, but not separate' security purposes. Only then will they be able to go and get from NATO the necessary supplementary assets, provided of course that NATO does not decide to deal with the issue itself. The two processes do not need to be interconnected from above, with all the relevant requests and concessions, devolutions of authority and institutional subordinations: they can proceed in parallel and in full view of each other, especially since (as is often overlooked in the heat of the debate) each of the ten full members of WEU is also a member of EU and NATO, which should in itself preclude any disconnection between the three organisations.

The 'combined joint task forces' (CJTF) concept approved at the Berlin Council in June 1996 constitutes a demonstration that NATO itself intends to diversify and choose between different formulas best designed to address hybrid situations. Indeed, not every security contingency ought to be dealt with by the full might of NATO, which may often be excessive, overshoot its target, or prove counterproductive.[11] More credible forms of specifically European responses should therefore be prepared. The Berlin Ministerial has singled out the WEU to be entrusted with 'the political control and strategic direction' of any distinct European action that may need the support of the Alliance. Maastricht, with its Art. J 4, had established the basic terms of reference for a European CFSP. The two must now meet.[12] With the implementation of the CJTF provisions, either NATO or European multilateral *ad hoc* task-forces are an alternative to full-fledged NATO intervention. Their 'double-hatting' would be for unforeseeable contingencies, as would any EU/WEU general defence staff or other command arrangement.[13] WEU would then have the means to assess the feasibility of a European-led military operation, determine whether it should be conducted under WEU leadership or under the leadership of a nation or nations, and advise and coordinate accordingly. Such a supplementary capability cannot be misconstrued as a challenge to transatlantic solidarity.

The fact that five EU Member States are not full members of WEU (former 'neutrals,' non-NATO members, or the special Danish case) should not in itself constitute a stumbling block, since the types of military tasks presently being considered by the Europeans are in the lower spectrum of security contingencies, which do not involve the full multilateral capability that only NATO can for the moment provide. The revised EU treaty approved at the Amsterdam Ministerial incorporates the 'Petersberg' cooperative security tasks.[14] This happened too late for the EU-WEU relationship to be tested in Albania, but new opportunities will no doubt soon come up. A joint endeavour has been undertaken when WEU contributed to the organisation of the EU administrative mission in Mostar, with specific policing tasks, the result of which cannot be considered conclusive. The implementation of the Dayton civilian annexes, alongside the SFOR follow-up mission in Bosnia should provide ample opportunities to enhance EU/WEU operational visibility in the field. Clearer multilateral decision-making procedures linking EU and WEU in foreign policy and security matters are, however, indispensable in supplementing, with the appropriate political credibility, the economic gravitational force of the EU as well as of the individual European governments.

If WEU is already fully equipped and legitimised to take upon itself a range of military tasks,[15] its political credibility and, consequently, its operational efficiency still depends on the interlinkage EU and NATO. It is in fact at the intersection of the respective reform curves that WEU will eventually position itself. The deepening and enlargement processes of the two organisations are therefore the necessary preconditions for WEU to derive either a new lease on life or to be grafted in the other institutional structures. So far it has had to stand still in practical terms, but WEU has however prepared generic plans for future contingencies. A WEU paper on 'criteria and modalities for the effective use of CJTF' was produced in June 1994 for NATO to consider; and six 'WEU illustrative missions' (on conflict prevention including monitoring, protection of humanitarian corridors, enforcement of sanctions and embargoes, containment, and interposition missions) were forwarded to NATO in 1996, as well as a more detailed document on 'practical arrangements for evacuation operations.' So far, WEU has been preparing particularly for the monitoring of sanctions, for the assistance in peacekeeping in Africa,[16] and for de-mining operations.

Short of institutional integration with the EU, which the Maastricht process preserves as a possibility, and assuming that an operational requirement is presented to it (by the EU or NATO, but also by the UN or the OSCE), WEU has declared its readiness and willingness to proceed. Its ability to deal with the incremental possibilities of the Petersberg spectrum would of course need to be gradually tested, for purposes of operational effectiveness as well as political credibility. The decision making would occur in the Council, which has appropriately included, since 1984, both Foreign and Defence Ministers. The Planning Cell, Situation Centre and Intelligence Unit, supported by the Satellite Centre, would provide the necessary feasibility assessments and possible force-packaging, drawing on the forces put at their disposal (FAWEUs, including the Eurocorps, Eurofor, Euromarfor and other joint contingents pre-organised by some, not all, members) or on the CJTF provisions of NATO.

With respect to the interrelationship between EU and WEU, short of a full merger, two intermediate options were presented in 1995 by a WEU Reflection Group to the IGC: either a reinforced partnership preserving the autonomy of each, or a gradual convergence implying political or legal subordination of WEU to EU. Article J4.1 of the 1991 Treaty on European Union established that the CFSP 'shall include all questions related to the common security of the union, including the eventual framing of a common defence policy, which might in turn lead to a common defence.' The new Treaty modified that phrase to read 'including the *progressive* framing of a common defence policy... which might lead to a common defence, *should the European Council so decide*' (emphasis added). This represents a hesitant step back, relying on a Darwinian evolution of the second pillar which diminishes the significance of the EU-WEU interlinkage: the Amsterdam Council replaced the terms 'requests the WEU' with 'will avail itself of the WEU' (to elaborate and implement decisions and actions of the Union). Events will, however, press ahead upsetting the ideal Maastricht flow-chart, as the three phases may develop separately and in parallel: common security actions could be undertaken before a common defence policy, let alone a comprehensive CFSP, have been worked out fully.[17] No abstract conclusion can be drawn until sufficient experience and evidence has been built up to sustain the practicability of a more decisive WEU course of action. Pragmatism and feasibility will show some of the possible substance of things to come, but the final purpose, the *acquis* and the common commitment must be progressively reinforced, lest the external credibility of the whole process be greatly undermined, as well as that of the individual nations partaking in it.[18]

COPING WITH AN ENLARGED SECURITY SPACE

Deepening aspects are important, but widening aspects are even more crucial. As for the enlargement process, it must be underlined that, while common defence remains necessary for the prospective newcomers and belongs in the realm of NATO and WEU deepening commitments, it is cooperative security that is the most immediate issue of enlargement, in territorial and functional terms. Cooperative security relies on ad hoc, precisely tailored participation. In effect, it can be argued that applicants seek the enlargement of existing institutions more for reasons of political solidarity than for military interoperability. It is widely accepted that forward deployment of NATO will not be necessary, as much as the establishment of interoperability and rapid reinforcement capabilities. By the same token, EU enlargement is expected to provide political reassurance and practical cooperation in the second (CFSP) and third (law and order) pillars, before the more demanding first pillar conditionalities are met. The expansion of EU will therefore be much more gradual and intricate than NATO's, but it will have far wider socio-economic implications. WEU has in the meantime surged forward, developing a comprehensive and multilateral process of conceptual exchanges, political consultation and some operational cooperation between the more than 30 countries of Europe and the Mediterranean, a process that has somewhat blunted the military alliance implications of the Brussels Treaty.[19] The issue of a 'European security space' must now be addressed by NATO, EU, and WEU in complementary fashion, responding to events as they actually unfold and not in mechanical, separate, and self-contained ways which could result in developments steering clear of real events. The result should not lead to abstract uniformity but rather to the diversification of tasks, the asymmetry of responsibilities and the flexibility of actual commitments that circumstances may demand. Common principles are more than ever indispensable; they admit however differentiated undertakings.

The review process of the TEU has not produced a straightforward insertion of national security policies into the second pillar, which most of the unpredictable international circumstances (apart from the sovereign prerogatives of states) would not warrant. Amsterdam, however, called for a more coherent political expression of common interests and priorities, structural linkages, and a clearer political solidarity.

The EU Council had been entrusted with defining principles and general guidelines, as well as with deciding on common strategies (setting out objectives, duration, and means), which would lead – as required – to common positions (defining approach) and joint actions (addressing specific situations where operational action is deemed to be required). Against this backdrop, common operational decisions may be taken pragmatically, possibly involving only some of the member countries and even non members, on an *ad hoc* basis. EU will propose and stimulate; WEU will prepare and coordinate; governments and events will decide the course of action. In non-Art.5 contingencies, where flexibility and multi-bilateral approaches are called for, no pre-established commitments can apply. Nor have institutionalised *directoires* or even permanent 'contact groups' proven possible.[20] Furthermore, no institutional primacy can assert itself (with the sole exception of the UN Security Council), nor can formal delegations of authority be sought or attributed as a precondition for action.[21] The basic principle that would apply is the opting-in of the willing, instead of the opting-out of the unwilling: it is in this sense that the concept of 'constructive abstention' should be formed, together with the political solidarity clause that will result from it, implicitly or explicitly. The decision-making mechanism would thus remain intergovernmental, and individual national sovereignties would be safeguarded. The 'enhanced cooperations' repeatedly invoked by Bonn and Paris[22] would reconcile the deepening and enlarging processes. They would provide the flexibility clause necessary to circumvent unanimities hardly practicable in security issues that cannot be subjected to supranational enforcement. It is worth mentioning that such an escape clause from institutional uniformity is allowed by Art. J 7.4.[23] Its inclusion in Treaty provisions would provide a broader political solidarity underpinning any practicable variable geometry. Inside the European project cooperative security is not simply a matter of belonging, but of participating in the work in progress, or sometimes stepping aside from projects that do not require the compulsory participation of all and cannot allow obstruction from Member States whenever they have no vital interests at stake in the issue at hand.

An essential element of any European security framework must of course be the involvement of Russia as an active participant in the common endeavour, with no privileged status, no veto power or *droit de regard,* and therefore no re-establishment of the bipolar tutorship on European matters, which circumstances no longer warrant. Moscow insists that any form of NATO 'expansion' must be 'militarily neutral,' and not involve any forward deployment of nuclear or other significant military hardware. Only Washington could nudge the Kremlin forward towards a more proactive relationship with its other European partners. But, after years of superpower pre-eminence, the United States seems equally unwilling to stoop to conquer, as it could if it would engage in deeper consultations with the Europeans, either in NATO or in OSCE.[24] While retaining its function of independent common denominator of any European equation, Washington could play the more open role of a facilitator and coalition builder, and thus make the difference in any decision-making forum. If the NATO and EU reform processes do not proceed in full view of each other, they may result in a pile-up of disparate initiatives instead of initiating the intended cross-breeding effects. In the meantime, WEU remains on hold: if all goes well, it would naturally find its place as the interface – maybe the intermediary peg – between NATO and the EU, and not the third party interfering with both, which many observers implicitly accuse it of being.

Capping it all, of course, the overriding requirement remains that of maintaining the indispensable linkage with public opinion through parliamentary process. Democratic involvement is particularly necessary in matters of cooperative security, where the prerogatives of the executive must be constantly sustained by a well-informed and involved public that must be properly fed with persuasive information, especially since the resulting solutions will be subjected to ratification processes and referendums.

THE NEW SECURITY AGENDA FOR THE UNION

The 'new security agenda' is basically about stability and predictability in the transitional and evolutionary process affecting every nation, irrespective of whether or not it is a full member of security institutions. Common defence automaticities have been overtaken by flexible cooperative security arrangements, which take into consideration a much broader concept than simply territorial defence. The clear-cut Cold War strategic environment with which NATO was designed to cope, implied homogeneity of military postures and nuclear deterrence. The response to the heterogeneous – and at times ambiguous – new challenges is now more about participation, diversification, and persuasion.

The 'demand for Europe' is two-fold: it is about reintegration after years of forced partition; it is also about participation into a brave new world. The issue lies between the terms of reference that former President Giscard d'Estaing called 'Europe espace' and 'Europe puissance.' When power is sought, the knee-jerk reaction is towards the United States and NATO, the admission to which is the obvious quick-fix solution. Accession to the EU has far broader socio-economic consequences, the pinch of which is felt even by those who already belong to it. And yet, a European security and defence policy within the CFSP has become an ever-increasing requirement, especially after the 'first wave' of NATO enlargement. By developing a political visibility and a preventive security capability, the EU will also stimulate a participatory multilateralism, involving common interests more than common values, operating in and around existing security institutions and blurring the difference between the ins and the outs, thereby integrating a stabilisation process far more complex than military options could ever afford. The issue of whether WEU will eventually integrate the EU and become its security arm should not stall its function as a complementary instrument for the most appropriate downsizing and destructuring of either NATO or EU, in the many, not always foreseeable, circumstances that will be assessed on their own case-by-case merits.

The issue of security, stability, and crisis prevention on a continental European scale cannot only be a matter of belonging or not to the existing organisations. It should instead pursue the convergence, compatibility, and complementarity of different national contributions. Institutions ought to provide a legitimising and organising factor, underpinning what has been achieved and providing it with greater coherence and political visibility, not project abstract solidarities or replace national responsibilities. An incremental process can accommodate diversity and respect specificities, while promoting the common wealth of behavioural principles established in the OSCE. It is pragmatism and flexibility rather than institutional uniformity that will be needed. In an international situation where challenges and risks are diverse and multifaceted, security reassurances can be provided by interrelating the existing institutions, so that even the nations that lag behind in the process of reform can implicitly benefit from it. A European security space already exists that blurs the difference between the institutional haves and have-nots.[25] Pan-European security cannot be bestowed or imposed from above: it must be built from the bottom up by interlinkage and interaction of organisations and national efforts. Core countries and variable geometries, opt-in formulas and *ad hoc* multinational forces composed of the willing and able, whether or not they are members of existing institutions, will best contribute to the overriding requirement of an undiminished security on the continental scale. Producing their CFSP for the benefit of the whole continent should be the special concern of West Europeans.

NOTES

[1] François Sauzay (European Press Officer of the Trilateral Commission), *Anti-Prince* (Rome 1996).

[2] 'Non Monsieur Seguin, il n'y a pas d'autre politique,' *Le Monde* (12 October 1996).

[3] Pierre Lellouche in 'Légitime défense,' Paris 1995, calls for the establishment of a European Security Council within the OSCE, which Russia however has not as forcefully promoted as it was expected to do in the organisation's last ministerial meeting, in November 1996 in Lisbon.

[4] In spite of their declared different attitudes to greater European integration, France and Britain came together in the Rapid Reaction force in Bosnia, after UNPROFOR, that made IFOR possible.

[5] Nicole Gnesotto, 'Lessons of Yugoslavia', *Chaillot Paper* 14 (Paris: Institute for Security Studies of WEU, March 1994).

[6] Robert S. Chase, Emily B. Will and Paul Kennedy invoke 'Pivotal States,' *Foreign Affairs* (1996/1); Joseph Nye, in his *Bound to Lead: the Changing Nature of American Power* (New York: Basic Books, 1990) spoke of a co-opting power.

[7] Joseph Janning and Werner Weidenfeld, *Politique Etrangère* 3 (1996).

[8] An Italo-British proposal along these lines was presented in1994.

[9] Institutionally, the connection is established by art. IV of the modified Brussels Treaty which states that the two organisations shall 'cooperate closely,' in order to 'avoid any duplication'; subsequent political interpretations have imposed a stricter relationship.

[10] The German Foreign Minister Kinkel in *International Herald Tribune* (24-25 December 1996) called for 'a coherent division of labour,' among 'radically reformed multilateral organisations.'

[11] Alyson Bailes, 'Europe Defence Challenge,' *Foreign Affairs* 1 (1997) Europeans 'also want to be free to take their own risks with smaller or more offbeat missions that are uncongenial for the US or perhaps too delicate for the heavy hand of NATO.'

[12] The French Foreign Minister put it in the following terms to the members of the WEU Assembly on 3 December 1996: 'WEU is a hinge between the Alliance and the Union: from the former it must extract its full operational dimension; from the latter, its political legitimacy.'

[13] Some operational NATO/WEU task-sharing has already been tried with the 'Sharp Guard' mission for the enforcement of UN sanctions against Serbia in the Adriatic, a marine environment which lends itself

best to multilateral security cooperation (with the exception of AFSOUTH, which has very special politico-military connotations).

[14] Adopted at the June 1992 WEU ministerial, they include humanitarian and rescue tasks, peace-keeping tasks, and crisis management, including peace-making, tasks.

[15] Even before the Yugoslav crisis, in 1988, during the Iraq-Iran war, WEU had undertaken a de-mining operation of the Persian Gulf sea-lanes, that went largely unnoticed, for want of appropriate political solidarity; then, on the Danube, WEU cooperated with the riparian countries, for the implementation of the embargo on Serbia.

[16] In conjunction with the Organisation for African Unity or in support of the UN, as was attempted in the Great Lakes crisis. See Winrich Kühne et al., 'WEU's role in crisis management and conflict resolution in sub-Saharan Africa', *Chaillot Paper* 22 (Paris: Institute for Security Studies of WEU, December 1995).

[17] See also Laurence martin and John Roper (eds.), 'Towards a Common Defence Policy', a study by the European Strategy Group and the Institute for Security Studies of Western European Union (Paris: Institute for Security Studies of WEU, 1995).

[18] The former French Prime Minister Juppé put it in the following terms: 'Let's have the courage to say it, the Union of tomorrow will no doubt be constituted by two different levels: a Union of common law, comprising the fifteen present members as well as those that have a vocation to adhere to it; at the heart of this Union, of this first circle, a second circle, narrower but modular, composed of a smaller number of States around France and Germany, nations at the same time willing and able to go further or faster than the others on issues such as money or defence' (Translated from *Le Monde* [14 March 1996]). And the 'strategic concept' agreed by France and Germany on 9 Dec. 1996 has also been set 'at the centre of a solidarity framework.'

[19] Christopher Hill of the London School of Economics draws the distinction between 'action organisations' and 'framework organisations,' and raises the possibility that NATO itself may change to the point where it performs both functions separately (the concept was expressed in part during his intervention at the WEU Institute annual seminar for policy planners on 23 January 1997).

[20] As the separate Franco-German and Franco-British initiatives in security matters have so far demonstrated.

[21] In the CJTF concept, WEU would ask for assets, not necessarily for authorisation; but the problem of a possible 'mission creep' would subsist.

[22] The de Chârette-Kinkel letter of 17 October 1996 spells out the concept, specifying that they should develop 'within the single constitutional context of the Union.' Such a differentiated integration should not jeopardise common policies or marginalise any country. An Italian draft proposal presented on 20 January 1997 along the same lines is intended to stress that the reinforcement of the security of the Union and its member States should be implemented 'at different levels of intensity.' The Franco-German bi-lateral strategic concept of December 1996 spells it out in terms that are far more innovative for Bonn than for Paris.

[23] 'The provisions of this article shall not prevent the development of closer cooperation between two or more member states on a bilateral level, in the framework of the WEU and the Atlantic Alliance, provided such cooperation does run counter to, or impede that provided for in this Title.'

[24] Ronald Asmus and Stephen Larrabee, 'NATO and the Have-Nots,' *Foreign Affairs* (November/December 1996).

[25] The 'European Security Space' working papers by the European Strategy Group and the WEU Institute, 1996. See also Karl W. Deutsch, et al., *Political Community and the North Atlantic Area* (Princeton: Princeton University Press, 1957).

CHAPTER VIII

Balancing Europe's Eastern and Southern Dimensions

Esther Barbé

After the fall of the Berlin wall, Vaclav Havel was rumoured to have said that European history had 'started walking again.' In a sense, the disappearance of the most important border in Europe,[1] separating the OECD countries from those of the Warsaw Pact, meant that once again both sides could independently pursue their goals. Since that moment a kind of *Drang nach Osten* has filtered the process of European construction. The 'return to Europe' of the Warsaw Pact countries became one of Europe's most important aims. Even before Maastricht, European foreign policy concentrated on Central and Eastern Europe, most notably through projects like the PHARE Plan in 1989, EBRD in 1990, and EU Association Agreements with the Visegrad countries in 1991. Other new institutional arrangements between Eastern and Western Europe include the Stability Pact (1994), the statute of WEU Associated Partnership, NATO Partnership for Peace, and the strategy for EU enlargement approved by the European Council in Essen (December 1994). Clearly, Europe has begun the process of integrating these countries in terms of political institutions and security concerns.[2]

But, while the EU presumably has been concentrating its efforts on Central and Eastern European Countries, it has also dedicated more attention than ever before to non-EU Mediterranean Countries. The November 1995 Euro-Mediterranean Conference, organised under the leadership of the Spanish EU presidency and held in Barcelona, is the best example of the EU's paradoxical strategy.[3] Much like Central and Eastern Europe, the Mediterranean countries have established political dialogues with the EU (Barcelona process), WEU, and NATO. How can the EU's dual affection be explained? This chapter examines the EU's paradoxical strategy and its links to the national policies of the Southern and Northern EU Member States. The explanation offered in this chapter may also help to answer one of the main questions raised in this book: are the EU's policy objectives different from its Member States?

GEOGRAPHY RISES AGAIN

Experience shows that among the many ways in which countries cooperate with each other, foreign policy coordination has always been the most difficult to achieve. Regelsberger and Wessels point out that the difficulty is due to the 'DDS (discreet, discretionary, sovereignty) syndrome;' that is, that coordination of foreign policy and security raises immediately, and most visibly, the issue of national sovereignty.[4] According to Regelsberger and Wessels, the success of foreign policy coordination depends on bilateral efforts to accommodate differences in historical traditions, and an awareness of public prejudices in each country.

The divergent traditions and conflicting interests in the foreign policy of the European Political Cooperation (EPC) countries were obvious, but for two decades, this policy coordination mechanism functioned quite well. Since the end of the Cold War, however, cooperation has been shaky. The interests among EU countries have diverged in this period due to the so-called *forces profondes*.[5] Elements of national power[6] and traditional factors,[7] such as geographical location, historical experience, and cultural links to non-EU countries, have also become stronger during this period. Examples of paradoxical behaviour abound: the negotiations on the transformation from EPC to Common Foreign and Security Policy (CFSP), were held while Member States were simultaneously renationalising their security policies due to the 'open space' atmosphere. Such discrepancies show that the disappearance of the Iron Curtain has produced not only centripetal forces, deepening the European construction process, but also centrifugal forces that have driven the process of sub-regionalisation and created 'spheres of influence' among EU Member States. Southern European countries (Spain, France, Italy), motivated by the fear of a destabilised Arab world, have created a Mediterranean *spécificité*. In the North, Germany and the Nordic countries hope to recreate the Hanseatic world, now made possible by the disappearance of the Soviet Union. 'Mental maps,' based on geography, history, and culture, have emerged in the European collective consciousness: 'Mittleuropa,' or the Baltic sea as a 'mythical source of identity'[8] may now propel the foreign and security policy of certain Member States.

Geography-based division of labour poses a clear danger to coordinated security. A Bertelsmann Foundation report warns that while

> there may be some scope for the idea of some form of 'military division of labour' between WEU member states on functional lines...this should not be extended to a geographical division of labour, since, by appearing to endorse the idea of national 'spheres of influence,' it would tend to undermine rather than strengthen a common European approach. Some countries may have more military resources available for particular areas by virtue of geography -for example Sweden in the Baltic or Italy in the Mediterranean. But a primary purpose of a common defence policy is to ensure that members can rely on other members for support, wherever that support is needed ... The organisation of ad hoc 'coalitions of the willing' in response to particular crises is unlikely to contribute to the strengthening of CFSP. Rather, there is a danger that such coalitions will be regarded as a reflection of the CFSP's weakness, illustrating the very real risk that, with the Soviet threat gone, European defence will become increasingly 'renationalised'[9]

Evidence exists that the renationalisation process (converting European policy into policing each country's sphere of influence) has already begun. Two cases demonstrate this shift: the German policy, favouring the diplomatic recognition of Slovenia and Croatia in 1991, and the post-Cold War Spanish policy of linking European construction to Mediterranean stability. In both cases, the national strategies pursued by individual countries were converted into EU policies. In the first case, Germany's unilateral move to grant the rapid recognition of the two former Yugoslav republics, was a complete departure from all the collective policy commitments it had made, but nevertheless forced other European countries to follow its lead. Different theories have been offered to explain Germany's behaviour. Traditional power-politics explanations (based on Germany's geo-economic and geopolitical sphere of influence) have clashed with institutionalist approaches. The latter is best described by Bulmer and Paterson who argue that 'Germany's unilateralism was the product not only of domestic pressure for recognition [of Slovenia and Croatia] but also of dissatisfaction with the faltering nature of EPC decision making on Yugoslavia ... German power will become more evident where European institutions prove to be weak.'[10] (1996:17).

Spain could not act unilaterally as Germany had in pursuing its policies in the Mediterranean due to the high financial costs associated with stabilising the region. Instead, Spain undertook a traditional lobbying approach and was able to convince European organisations to commit to Spanish objectives. By May 1989, Spain, along with other EU-Mediterranean countries, were defined as EU 'mentors' for the Maghreb countries in the final resolution approved by the second Forum on the Western Mediterranean Countries.[11]

SHIFTING AND BALANCING

Even before the fall of the Berlin wall, the relations between the EC and certain East-bloc countries had changed dramatically. Domestic changes in Poland and Hungary combined with Germany's assertiveness in the EC brought about a pledge for a privileged relationship between the EC and Central and Eastern European countries. During the Paris Arch Summit held in July 1989, the EC was assigned the task of coordinating the PHARE Plan. This move also meant that the Community was assuming comprehensive responsibilities in Central European countries, beyond simply economic assistance[12]

From that moment, lobbyists for the Mediterranean policy feared that the EC's attention and resources would be completely shifted to the Central and Eastern European countries and away from the Mediterranean countries. To pre-empt this shift, Abel Matutes (the Spanish EC Commissioner in charge of Mediterranean policy, relations with Latin America and Asia, and North-South relations) suggested that the Community establish a 'parallel program' for Eastern Europe and the Mediterranean region.[13] Matutes's opinion was in complete agreement with the official Spanish position, which has been a driving force behind EU Mediterranean policy.[14] After Matutes's term expired in 1992, his portfolio was given to another Spaniard, Manuel Marín. The Spanish policy has always been clear: Felipe González has repeatedly emphasised the dangers related to shifting the focus away from the Mediterranean countries. One clear example was his visit to Morocco in December 1995, where

120 *Barbé*

González advised the Moroccan prime minister to put pressure on Brussels to maintain its Mediterranean focus.[15]

In other words, the Arab and the ACP countries' status as the EC's geopolitical and geo-economic 'most favoured region' ended in 1989.[16] In the early 1990s, the ratio of EC aid to the Central and Eastern European Countries in comparison with that of the Mediterranean Countries was 2.5 to 1. When population differences are added, that ratio translates into one ECU of EC economic assistance for each Mediterranean citizen to five ECU for every East European citizen. This difference is greater still when taking into consideration other quantitative items, like bilateral economic assistance and private investment.

The paradox of this uneven ratio becomes evident when you consider Europe's energy dependence on the Arab countries or Euro-Mediterranean trade figures,[17] which alone could have justified a privileged relationship with the EC. The seemingly paradoxical behaviour of granting more aid to Eastern Europe is based on feelings of European 'solidarity' and historical responsibility for the region,[18] while EC's interest in the Mediterranean countries is solely based on security. Referring to the beginning of the post-Cold War era, Dinan points out that 'the Community's preoccupation with Eastern Europe almost blinded Brussels to developments in the South, where economics and political instability threaten the Community's security.'[19] Southern EU members lobbying for Mediterranean countries began emphasising the security concerns in the region in an effort to compete with the excitement of EU's Eastern expansion. As a result Matutes's suggestion for a parallel policy for both Eastern Europe and the Mediterranean region evolved conceptually into a balancing strategy, based on the so-called solidarity vs security approach.

Balancing is a familiar concept in European construction. In fact, the life of the EU has been a history of balancing small and large countries, rich and poor countries, supranationalism and intergovernmentalism, and European aims and national priorities. Therefore, balancing Eastern and Mediterranean policies is a progressive step in the process of the European construction-and it is an important one.

MEDITERRANEAN STABILITY MEANS EUROPEAN CONSTRUCTION

Many believe that the EU's relationship with the Mediterranean countries will influence European construction. At the height of the Persian Gulf Crisis Felipe González said: 'I think, like François Mitterrand, that the construction of Europe cannot be attained without first trying to resolve the explosive problems that are building up in North Africa with respect to demography, development, religion and the standard of living.'[20] The belief in Euro-Mediterranean interdependence has made the region a diplomatic priority for Spain, France, and Italy. These countries and the Commission have promoted diplomatic initiatives in the Mediterranean region, based on the global security approach,[21] as well as a multidimentional agenda involving environmental, socio-economic and cultural issues. One such initiative was the Spanish-Italian proposal of convening a Conference on Security and Cooperation in the Mediterranean (CSCM). This initiative was presented by the flamboyant Italian foreign minister, Gianni de Michelis in September 1990. The CSCM proposal was based on a comprehensive approach to Mediterranean stability; tackling economic, social, political, and military dimensions of security. It adopted the CSCE's methodology of dividing the areas of cooperation into three 'baskets': political and security, economic, humanitarian and cultural.[22] The Gulf War prevented any meeting from taking place, but it did not invalidate the economic, social and cultural need for European involvement in the region. On the contrary, anti-Western demonstrations in some North African countries were a warning sign of the social and economic unrest existing in those societies. But Italian interest in Euro-Mediterranean relations faded once de Michelis resigned,[23] and domestic instability became a priority in Italy.

The Euro-Mediterranean relationship emphasised the traditional civil power policy,[24] based on economic, social, and cultural relations, whereas the Gulf War prompted certain EU member countries to promote the creation of a European military structure to face post-Cold War threats. During the Maastricht Treaty negotiations, these demands clashed with countries in favour of NATO. Article J.4 of the EU Treaty is the cautious result of that clash.

Mediterranean security risks have grown since the end of the Gulf War. Civil war in Algeria, Libyan support of terrorism, and the slowness of the Middle East peace process have compelled South European countries to strengthen their pro-Mediterranean lobbying policy in the EC. At the same time, the desirable incorporation of Central and East European countries into European organisations has led to the creation of a new set of institutions like WEU associate partnership (1992), NATO partnership for peace, and, at the European Council of Essen in 1994, EU structured dialogues.

The EU-Mediterranean lobby have supported that similar institutions be set up for the Mediterranean countries, although without the implication that these countries will eventually be included in the EU. This 'parallel program' is illustrated by many examples: the 1990 Italian proposal to create a Mediterranean Bank similar to EBRD; the Spanish and French proposal of creating a PHARE Plan for the Mediterranean;[25] Spain's proposal to organise a Mediterranean Partnership for Peace during a September 1994 NATO meeting in Seville;[26] France's proposal for a Stability Pact for the Mediterranean during the Euro-Mediterranean Conference in Barcelona (November 1995) which Malta has also supported;[27] and the 1996 Italian plan to create a structured dialogue on the issues of security and diplomacy with the Mediterranean region.[28]

Manuel Marín (the Spanish Commissioner in charge of the EU's relations with non-member Mediterranean countries) was committed to adapting the partnership instruments, created for Central and Eastern Europe, to the Mediterranean area. In March 1995, Marín published an article in *Le Figaro* entitled 'La Méditerranée: une priorité au même titre que l'Europe ex-communiste.' The Commission's policy eventually adopted Marin's approach and he was personally supported by president Delors. According to Gillespie, Marín has been a central figure in the development of EU-Mediterranean policy since its former emphasis on cooperation to its current stress of partnership.[29] (1996:210).

EURO-MEDITERRANEAN PARTNERSHIP VS EASTERN ENLARGEMENT

Marks[30] points out that 'the Southern Mediterranean, along with the former Soviet Union is considered by Europe to be one of the two main strategic regions bordering a progressively enlarging EU.' The fact is, that both the emergence of the Mediterranean as a strategic region and the preparations for the Eastward enlargement of the EU are occurring simultaneously. This parallel course has been forcing the EU to link the two distinct projects and even make trade-offs between the two goals, in its attempt to balance the interests of the Eastern and Southern dimensions of Europe.

The balancing strategy initiated by the EU-Mediterranean lobby began to show results by mid-1994. In June 1994, the European Council of Corfu elaborated a new strategy towards both Eastern Europe and the Mediterranean. The Council agreed that enlargement negotiations with East European countries should start after the 1996 Intergovernmental Conference. Reciprocal concessions were made to the Euro-Mediterranean lobby. The Corfu summit decided to create a zone of cooperation in the Mediterranean and agreed that enlargement negotiations with Cyprus and Malta would start six months after the Intergovernmental Conference. It is worth noting that the Greek president fought very hard to get Cyprus included in the next stage of enlargement.

Committed to developing a partnership between the EU and the Mediterranean region, the EC established a new policy which departed greatly from its former policy emphasising cooperation. The document proposing the Euro-Mediterranean Partnership included the creation of a free-trade area, offered a substantial financial aid package, and designed a zone of cooperation leading towards a close association between the two regions.[31] This Partnership emphasises two goals: in the short term it will expand the trade bloc surrounding the EU, and in the long term, it will create a real Euro-Mediterranean network, cooperating in the sectors of energy, environment, terrorism control, culture, and tourism.

In December 1996, the European Council of Essen endorsed the partnership idea proposed by the Commission, with the Mediterranean region constituting 'a priority zone of strategic importance for the European Union.'[32] The Council accepted Spain's offer to organise a Euro-Mediterranean Conference in the second half of 1995. This decision is considered to be another reciprocal concession, given that the Essen summit simultaneously adopted a strategy of structured dialogue with Central and Eastern European countries on EU enlargement.

The Euro-Mediterranean Partnership project was presented by EC President Jacques Delors as an effort to mitigate the cleavage between the Mediterranean lobby, led by Spain and France, and the eastern lobby, led by Germany. Delors underlined that the French and Spanish presidencies will be able to make an 'ambitious' policy for the region, once the northern countries, particularly Germany, understand that it is necessary to send a *message fort* to the South.[33] Delors's statement seems to have foreshadowed the events of the European Council of Cannes in June 1995. During that summit, the ambitious Mediterranean policy of France and Spain clashed with German-led Northern interests when it came to the allocation of resources to the project.

Before the Cannes summit, the Commission had produced a document concerning the Union's relations with the Mediterranean countries. The communiqué proposed offering the Mediterranean program 5.5 billion ECU in an effort. According to Marin, this amount was hoped to re-establish the credibility of the EU's relationship with the Mediterranean countries, which had been neglected due to EU interests in the Central and Eastern European countries.[34] The idea of putting the Mediterranean and Eastern European regions on equal footing was insisted upon as the only way that the balancing philosophy could be fully implemented by the Commission. The East-South balance was also apparent in the first report adopted by the Council (on April 10, 1995), in preparation for the Euro-Mediterranean Conference. In fact, the report emphasised the EU's hope of creating complementary policies for both the East and the South in the interest of geopolitical coherence.[35]

Despite these preceding agreements, the balancing philosophy was put to the test during the Cannes summit. For the first time, the objectives of the Mediterranean lobby openly clashed with EU Eastern enlargement policy. France and Spain hoped to grant 5.5 billion ECU to the Mediterranean and 7 billion ECU. for Eastern Europe between 1995 and 1999. But the Northern countries (Germany, United Kingdom, Netherlands, and Denmark) favoured maintaining the policy in force from 1992 to 1996 and proposed grants be given to the two regions in a 5 to 1 ratio favouring Eastern European countries. The clash between Kohl and González finally resulted in increasing grants to the Mediterranean countries (4.685 billion ECU) by 22 percent while grants to Central and Eastern Europe were increased by 8 per cent.[36]

The outcome of the Cannes summit suggests two conclusions: first, that Spain was successful in playing a leading role in the Mediterranean lobby, and second, that trade-offs were inevitable given the dual aims of Eastern enlargement and creating a Euro-Mediterranean Partnership. According to Gillespie,

> Spanish lobbying to strengthen the Mediterranean policy has been linked at important junctures to other issues on which Madrid's support has been sought by Germany and other Northern member states, particularly in relation to EU policy towards Central-Eastern Europe. Spain has never opposed the European Union's eastward expansion, from which there will be costs and dangers for economies including Spain's, but González's last two governments were very careful about how Spain would give its consent, ensuring first that contrapartidas (reciprocal concessions), such as German acquiescence in the mid-1990s increase in the EU spending on the Mediterranean, were secured in return.[37]

CFSP AGENDA: MEDITERRANEAN PLUS CENTRAL AND EASTERN EUROPE

The June 1992 European Council of Lisbon adopted a report on the possible evolution of the CFSP. That report enumerated some factors that must be taken into consideration when defining the issues and areas of future cooperation, and included geographic proximity of regions, political and economic stability, and the existence of security threats.[38] The report indicated several geographic areas in which the EU must be engaged: Central and Eastern Europe, the Balkans, and the Mediterranean-particularly the Maghreb and the Middle East.

One can only wonder if CFSP has also adopted a balancing strategy in developing its joint actions. I argue that, apart from the Maghreb policy, the CFSP agenda focuses on the same geographic areas that were traditionally on the EPC agenda. Central and Eastern Europe, as members of CSCE, as well as the Middle East conflict were some of the first issues addressed by the EPC in the early 1970s. CFSP has not changed the scope of its agenda-which was always been determined by geography – but only the direction of their policies as a consequence of the new international order (the end of the Cold War and the peace process in the Middle East). For my purposes, the only CFSP-Central and Eastern European joint action deserving of attention is the Stability Pact, a kind of confidence and security-building mechanism mentioned in the Barcelona Declaration of 1995. As a result of the follow-up meetings after the Barcelona Conference, the European Council of Dublin (December 1996) proposed drafting a 'Charter for Peace and Stability in the Euro-Mediterranean Region,' with an aim to build security in the region through political dialogue, arms control, and Rule-of-Law mechanisms.

The Council has adopted two joint actions in support of the Middle East peace process. The first, adopted by the Council in April 1994, focuses on the organisation and observation of the Palestinian elections. The second policy, adopted in November 1996, appointed a European envoy to witness the peace process. These actions deserve two comments. First of all, it is necessary to emphasise the low profile role played by the Union in regard to the political dimension of the peace process. The above-mentioned joint actions left the crux of the negotiations in the hands of the United States. Even in its low-profile role, the Union has been much more engaged in Central and Eastern Europe, for example in its coordination of the PHARE Plan. As a matter of fact, the global coordination of international aid for the Middle East was entrusted to an ad hoc Liaison Committee and not directly to the Union which was the first donor to the area.[39]

Second, it is necessary to emphasise Spain's high-profile position in EU policy making. For instance, Madrid was the venue for the October 1991 Middle East Peace Conference, and in November 1996, the Council appointed a Spanish diplomat, Miguel Angel Moratinos, as the European envoy following the Peace Process. The high-profile role of Spain in the Middle East and as lobbyist for the Euro-Mediterranean Partnership, leads one to wonder if the EU-Mediterranean lobby has a leader, playing a similar role to that of Germany in its support of Central and Eastern Europe.

Also, the Lisbon report brought a new priority to the European foreign policy agenda-the Maghreb. The report asserted that the stability of this region is of 'great common interest for the Union. Demographic growth, the repeated social crises, large scale emigration and the increase of fundamentalism and religious *intégrisme* are problems that endanger this stability.'[40] On the basis of these dangers, the Lisbon Summit endorsed the idea of a Euro-Maghreb partnership in free trade, political dialogue, and economic, technical, cultural, and financial cooperation.

Since 1992, however, the problems for the Euro-Maghreb option have become obvious. The civil war in Algeria, the placement of economic sanctions on Libya by the CFSP (a common position adopted in November 1993), and the failure of the Arab-Maghreb Union have undermined the spirit of the Euro-Maghreb partnership. It became evident that the Maghreb is not a region in the process of economic integration, given its scarce horizontal exchanges. Nor is it an area of political *entente*. As a result, the Euro-Maghreb initiative was eventually turned into the Euro-Mediterranean Partnership.

The failure of the Maghreb option was a shock to the French leaders of EU-Mediterranean policy. France had always supported cooperation initiatives between Europe and the Western Mediterranean (for example, Mitterrand's proposal of convening a Western Mediterranean Conference in 1983 and the Western Mediterranean Group initiated in 1990). The Spanish-Italian proposal of convening a CSCM encompassing all of the Mediterranean countries was a challenge to the traditional French division between French-dominated Maghreb and Middle East. The French policy of *chasse gardée* in the Maghreb has muted in the 1990s in favour of Spain's pro-Mediterranean lobby.[41] According to Gillespie, 'by successfully competing for the European Commission portfolios relating to the Mediterranean, and making the Mediterranean a priority area for the diplomatic service, Spain in the first half of the 1990s was able to play a leading role in shaping this aspect of EU policy.'[42] In short, it is impossible to talk of a cohesive Mediterranean block within the EU because of the French-Spanish competition for the leadership role in the region.

Nevertheless, neither France nor Spain have been interested on bringing attention to the Maghreb area following the CFSP scheme (common positions, joint actions, declarations). For instance, neither the Algerian civil war nor the Western Sahara conflict have received special attention in the CFSP agenda. Far from being a major issue, the Algerian civil war rendered only three declarations from the CFSP out of the 300 adopted between the entry into force of the Treaty and the second semester of 1996. It is a paradox that the European Union, commencing an ambitious Euro-Mediterranean policy, has ignored, in diplomatic terms, the conflicts in Northern Africa. Could it be the result of differences between the Union's policy and some of its members' interests? Could it be the result of applying instruments created for the Central and Eastern Europe to the Mediterranean region?

CONCLUSIONS: PRIORITY AND MISTRUST

It is obvious that the Mediterranean members of the Union are directly affected by the developments on the Sea's Southern shore. This claim is supported by the fact that millions of Maghrebians live in France, that Spain is dependant on Algeria and Libya for gas, that Spain holds territories in North Africa, that drug traffic runs across the Strait of Gibraltar, and that there are territorial disputes in the Aegean Sea. In addition to these material concerns Europe and the Mediterranean countries share common experiences, and even 'past trauma,'[43] where colonialism left an important mark. The French-Algerian relationship is much more than a foreign affairs issue, but is a domestically sensitive issue. Moreover, Spain fought its last international war in the 1920s against Moroccan troops.

In other words, the relationship with some or all of the Mediterranean countries is a priority for the Southern European members of the Union, at both the low politics level (fishing, investment, trade, environment) and the high politics level (conflict mediation, migration, terrorism, weapons proliferation). Are national interests therefore clashing with the Union's policy objectives? If this is the case, can the Union meet the national expectations of its Member States?

This chapter argues that the East-South dilemma is an EU priority. Although the Southern members essentially support EU Eastern enlargement, these countries, especially Spain, have tried to make the Mediterranean policy an even bigger priority for the Union agenda and have tried to retain more resources and commitment to the Mediterranean region. In fact, creating a strong Euro-Mediterranean network was the main objective of the Barcelona Conference. The notion of interdependence, as the basis for increasing security in the region, is the main driving force of the Euro-Mediterranean partnership.

Northern EU Member States, feeling only indirectly affected by Mediterranean security issues, seem reluctant to accept some of the policies put forth by the Southern Member States, particularly when principles or financial resources are involved. But has the Union the means to meet the objectives of its Southern members? With regard to principles, the pragmatic policies adopted by Spain or France in the field of human rights in the Maghreb countries have already clashed with some European Parliament decisions.[44] Concerning resources, the Cannes summit is the best example that the Southern EU member-states were forced to temper their high expectations.

In any case, the Northern EU Member States have converging interests with their Southern partners on Mediterranean matters where trade and investment are concerned. In this sense, Marks points out that 'the creation of a free-trade zone encompassing both flanks of the Mediterranean – and linked in to an area stretching North to the Arctic circle and East to the confines of the former Soviet Union-fits into the 1990s dynamic of building large transnational trading and investment blocs.'[45] (1996:2). Inevitably, in terms of common foreign and security policy, sensitive issues for some members, like the Algerian civil war for France, will prevent a unanimous position on the matter. Apparently, the idea of a Euro-Mediterranean Partnership, resembling the Europe Agreements based on free trade, economic cooperation, and political dialogue, is too ambitious for the time being.

The EU-Central and Eastern Europe relationship is substantially different from the Euro-Mediterranean relationship. In terms of security, one can clearly see the difference. On the one hand, the relationship between the Union and Central and Eastern European countries is based on mutual confidence. In other words, these countries have psychologically agreed to be part of a pluralistic community of security formed by the Fifteen and, as far as they are concerned, these countries share an 'EU identity.' In Deutsch's words, the countries forming a community of security eliminate the use of force among them.[46] That is to say, they constitute a 'zone of peace.' The Franco-German reconciliation in the framework of the Union is the best example of this peace-making mechanism. Democratic regimes and the acceptance of the European integration principles constitute a basis for the community. On the other hand, the EU-Mediterranean relationship is more complex. In a sense, it is 'a group of states whose primary security concerns link together sufficiently closely that the national securities cannot realistically be considered apart from one another.[47] The existence of such a complex of security has been cited by Southern EU members as proof for the need to develop a partnership between both shores based the instruments used in the EU, WEU and NATO for Central and Eastern Europe.

The basic problem of that Partnership in matters of politics and security is the negative perception of the so-called complex of security. In other words, the mistrust between both shores. The Arab world has criticised the Euro-Mediterranean operation, arguing that the Europeans have turned Mediterranean economic and social problems into their own security problems. The mistrust stems as much from the traditional dimensions of security (military dimension) as from economic and societal dimensions, especially from factors relating to identity. A case in point is the interpretation of human rights between Europe and the Mediterranean region. Another point of contention is the reluctance of the Maghreb countries to accept NATO's new role in the Mediterranean. The Maghreb countries repeatedly have accused the Mediterranean lobby (France, Spain and Italy) of creating troops and units (Eurofor and Euromarfor) to interfere in South Mediterranean affairs.[48] At the same time, European countries have compelled Mediterranean countries to participate in political dialogues in an effort to build confidence, beginning with the Barcelona follow-up process and later with NATO and WEU.[49] These developments resemble more closely the defense-detente philosophy of the East-West period than the present relationship between the Union and Eastern Europe.

In short, EU's policy of balancing its Eastern and Southern concerns has been more a pragmatic measure than a long-standing planned policy. For the time being, the international priorities of the individual states have been reconciled with common security concerns, without endangering the Union's policy objectives.

NOTES

[1] R. Davy, 'The Central European dimension,' in *The Dynamics of European Integration*, ed. W. Wallace (London: Pinter, 1990): 141.

[2] The present chapter deals with the group of ten Central and Eastern European countries that are closer to Western Europe in terms of current institutional arrangements and future enlargement: Bulgaria, Czech Republic, Estonia, Hungary, Latvia, Lithuania, Poland, Romania, Slovakia and Slovenia. They are members of the Council of Europe, and prior to accession they have signed Europe Agreements with the EC, they have the statute of WEU Associated Partnership, they participate in a privileged way in the NATO structures for Eastern Europe (NACC and Partnership for Peace), and some of them even have forces in Bosnia (IFOR, SFOR).

[3] This chapter deals with the group of Mediterranean non-Union countries that have signed any kind of agreement with the EC. It's a group of eleven countries -Algeria, Cyprus, Egypt, Israel, Jordan, Lebanon, Malta, Morocco, Syria, Tunisia, Turkey- and the Palestinian Authority. Libya is the outstanding exception.

[4] E. Regelsberger and W. Wessels, 'The CFSP Institutions and Procedures: A Third Way for the Second Pillar,' *European Foreign Affairs Review* 1 (1996): 31.

[5] P. Renouvin, *Histoire des Relations Internationales* (Paris: Hachette, 1953).

[6] H.J. Morgenthau, *Politics among Nations. The struggle for power and peace* (New York: Alfred A. Knopff, 1948).

[7] M. Merle, *Sociologie des Relations Internationales* (Paris: Dalloz, 1976) and R. Aron, *Paix et guerre entre les nations* (Paris: Calman-Levy, 1962).

[8] J. Oberg, *Nordic Security in the 1990s. Options in the changing Europe* (London: Pinter, 1992): 161.

[9] Bertelsmann Wissenschaftsstiftung, *CFSP and the Future of the European Union*, Interim Report of a Working Group prepared in collaboration with the Research Group on European Affairs (University of Munich) and the Planning Staff of the European Commission (DG1A), (1995): 4.

[10] S. Bulmer and W.E. Paterson, 'Germany in the European Union: gentle giant or emergent leader?,' *International Affairs* 72:1.

[11] R. Aliboni, 'The Mediterranean Dimension' in *The Dynamics of European Integration* ed. W. Wallace (London: Pinter, 1990): 157.

[12] E. Barbé and R. Grasa, *La Comunitat Europea i la Nova Europa*, (Barcelona: Fundació Bofill, 1992): 101.

[13] Comisión de las Comunidades Europeas, *Hacia una política mediterránea renovada*, SEC (89) 1961 (23 November 1989).

[14] R. Gillespie, 'Spain and the Mediterranean: Southern Sensitivity, European Aspirations,' *Mediterranean Politics* 1:2 (1996): 210.

[15] 'González insta a Marruecos a presionar a la CE para que no olvide el Magreb,' *El País* (14 December 1995).

[16] B. Khader, *Europa y el Gran Magreb* (Barcelona: Fundación Paulino Torras Domènech, 1992): 177.

[17] In 1993, the trade between the EC and the Mediterranean countries implied 78.8 ECU billions meanwhile the EC-Central and Eastern European Countries implied 46.4 ECU billions. In the Mediterranean case the balance of trade was much more positive for the EC (12.4 ECU billions) than in the Eastern case (5.8 ECU billions). See B. Khader *Le partenariat euro-méditerranéen* (Louvain: CERMAC, 1995):19.

[18] D. Moïsi. and J. Rupnik, *Le nouveau continent. Plaidoyer pour une Europe renaissante* (Paris: Calman-Levy, 1991).

[19] D. Dinan, *Ever closer Union? An Introduction to the European Community* (London: Macmillan, 1994): 459.

[20] 'Un entretien avec M. Felipe González,' *Le Monde* (20 November 1990).

[21] B. Buzan, *People, States and Fear: An Agenda for International Security Studies in the Post-Cold War Era* (New York: Harvester-Wheatsheaf, 1991).

[22] E. Barbé, 'Espagne: une redécouverte de la Méditerranée,' *Confluences. Méditerranée* 2 (1992): 72.

[23] D. Dinan, *Ever closer Union? An Introduction to the European Community* (London: Macmillan, 1994): 459.

[24] F. Duchêne, 'Europe's Role in World Peace,' in *Europe Tomorrow: Sixteen Europeans Look Ahead* ed. R. Mayne (London: Fontana, 1972).

[25] *Europe* 6326 (30 September 1994a): 10.

[26] E. Barbé, 'Reinventar el Mare Nostrum: el Mediterráneo como espacio de cooperación y seguridad,' *Papers* 46 (1995): 20.

[27] *Europe* 2821 (31 May 1996): 4.

[28] *Europe* 2805 (3 April 1996): 4.

[29] R. Gillespie, 'Spain and the Mediterranean: Southern Sensitivity, European Aspirations,' *Mediterranean Politics* 1:2 (1996).

[30] J. Marks, 'High Hopes and Low Motives: The New Euro-Mediterranean Partnership Initiative,' *Mediterranean Politics* 1:1 (1996): 2.

[31] European Commission, *Strengthening the Mediterranean Policy of the European Union: Establishing a Euro-Mediterranean Partnership* (Communication from the Commission to the Council and the European Parliament), Brussels, Com (94) 427 final (19 October 1994)): 2-3.

[32] *Europe* 6376 (11 December 1994): 1.

[33] *ibid.*

[34] *Europe* 6436 (9 March 1995): 6.

[35] EU Council *Conférence Euro-Méditerranéenne de Barcelone. Rapport de Synthèse*, 6532/95 (10 April 1995): 2.

[36] E. Barbé, 'The Barcelona Conference: Launching Pad of a Process,' *Mediterranean Politics* 1:1 (1996): 32.

[37] R. Gillespie, 'Spain and the Mediterranean: Southern Sensitivity, European Aspirations,' *Mediterranean Politics* 1:2 (1996): 206.

[38] 'Informe al Consejo Europeo de Lisboa sobre el posible desarrollo de la Política Exterior y de Seguridad Común (PESC) con vistas a determinar los ámbitos en que pueden desarrollarse acciones comunes con respecto a países o grupos de países particulares' (Anexo I), *Boletín de las Comunidades Europeas* 6 (1992): 20.

[39] E. Barbé and F. Izquierdo, 'Present and Future of the Joint Actions for the Mediterranean Region,' in *Common Foreign and Security Policy: The record and reform*, ed. M. Holland (London: Pinter, 1997).

[40] 'Informe al Consejo Europeo de Lisboa sobre el posible desarrollo de la Política Exterior y de Seguridad Común (PESC) con vistas a determinar los ámbitos en que pueden desarrollarse acciones comunes con respecto a países o grupos de países particulares' (Anexo I), *Boletín de las Comunidades Europeas* 6 (1992): 21.

[41] B. Khader ed., *L'Europe et la Méditerranée* (Paris: L'Harmattan 1994).

[42] R. Gillespie, 'Spain and the Mediterranean: Southern Sensitivity, European Aspirations,' *Mediterranean Politics* 1:2 (1996): 207.

[43] C. Hill, 'The Capability-Expectations Gap, or Conceptualizing Europe's International Role,' *Journal of Common Market Studies* 31:3 (September 1993): 308.

[44] L. Feliu, 'La apropiación de la temática de los derechos humanos por los regímenes marroquí y tunecino: retórica y realidad,' *Papers* 46 (1995): 92.

[45] J. Marks, 'High Hopes and Low Motives: The New Euro-Mediterranean Partnership Initiative,' *Mediterranean Politics* 1:1 (1996).

[46] K. Deutsch et al., *Political Community and the North Atlantic Area* (Princeton: Princeton University Press, 1957): 6.

[47] B. Buzan, *People, States and Fear: An Agenda for International Security Studies in the Post-Cold War Era* (New York: Harvester-Wheatsheaf, 2nd. ed., 1991): 190.

[48] F. Faria and A. Vasconcelos, *Security in Northern Africa: Ambiguity and Reality* (Paris: Institute for Security Studies [*Chaillot Papers* 25] 1996): 11.

[49] NATO has started dialogues with Egypt, Morocco, Tunisia, Israel, Mauritania and Jordan. WEU has dialogues with Morocco, Tunisia, Algeria, Mauritania, Egypt and Israel.

CHAPTER IX

Policies without Strategy: the EU's Record in Eastern Europe[*]

Jan Zielonka

Eastern Europe is now the European Union's major preoccupation – if not obsession.[1] No other region demands from the Union more diplomatic skills, financial sacrifice, and political involvement. During the Cold-War period, the European Community could easily ignore geography, culture, and history: relations between the EC and the Eastern part of the continent were practically non-existent.[2] But since the demise of the communist system, disintegration of the Soviet empire, and demolition of the Berlin Wall, the European Union can no longer dismiss Eastern Europe or hide behind America's back when dealing with its Eastern neighbours. In particular, the Union can no longer confine the integration project to the Western core of the continent.

Since the late 1980s the Union embraced this challenge by gradually developing active policies vis à vis all the corners of the postcommunist region, from the Baltic states to the Balkan states, from Poland to Ukraine, Belarus, and Russia. Yet the Union's ten-year hyperactivity in the region has proved controversial. Some experts praise the Union for a bold, wise, and flexible strategy that brings peace, democracy, and prosperity to the region. As Karen Smith forcefully argued: 'With respect to Eastern Europe since the late 1980s, the Community/Union has formulated and implemented an active, consistent, common policy ... The evolution of the policy is remarkable in and of itself; the speed with which it occurred even more so.'[3]

However, such a generous evaluation of the Union's foreign policy record is not shared by the majority of experts. They accuse the Union of lacking any strategic vision and doing too little too late in various parts of postcommunist Europe. As Wolfgang Wessels put it: 'The EU showed a lack of will and capacity in presenting any serious offers which would be of real use to the Eastern and Central European countries ... The EU has not proven itself to be the purposeful, coherent and successful actor which would be capable of making "widening" its new historical vocation to be tackled with energy and confidence.'[4]

Critics argue that the Union's lack of an identifiable strategy has irritated, demotivated, and confused its Eastern European neighbours. It also has weakened the Union's influence in Eastern Europe, especially in comparison with the influence displayed by the United States. Did not the US succeed in the Balkans where the Union had failed? Was it not the US rather than the Union that orchestrated the series of historic disarmament deals with the Kremlin that led to the withdrawal of the Red

Army from several Eastern European states? Was it not the US that 'pushed' for speedy NATO enlargement into Eastern Europe, while the EU enlargement project remains uncertain for nearly a decade? One can dislike the style and contents of US policies, but it seems increasingly evident, critics argue, that although Western policies in Eastern Europe are largely financed by the Union, they are usually designed by the US.[5]

This chapter will examine the EU's Eastern European record and will try to establish whether the Union's policies represent a well-conceived strategy or a chaotic response to external pressures.[6] Does the Union know what its aims in Eastern Europe really are and by what means it should achieve them? Is the Union helping the postcommunist region or is it merely helping itself? How can we be sure that the Union's policy towards Eastern Europe is not just an expensive, inconsistent, and largely purposeless exercise?

Although examples presented in this chapter show the EU's policies to be generous, timely, and comprehensive, I will argue that most of these policies emerged by default rather than by design. The Union has invested enormous financial and political capital in Eastern Europe, but this investment has lacked a clearly-defined strategic purpose. This is due to three major deficiencies in the Union's policy towards the region. First, the Union has never articulated the vision of Europe for which it is striving. Second, policies towards Eastern Europe have been dominated by the Union's internal agenda rather than broader strategic considerations. Third, the Union has failed to reform its own institutional structure – a necessary step if the EU hopes to implement any strategy.

In conclusion I will admit that a well designed and executed strategy is difficult in the complex postmodern and post-Soviet environment of contemporary Europe. However, strategic deficit is one of the inherent features of the Union as an international actor. The Union has a long tradition of defining the aims and means of its policy in a highly ambiguous manner which prevents it from designing and executing any sound strategy. The Union's policies towards Eastern Europe illustrate this point very well.

A POSITIVE HISTORICAL RECORD

The EU's record in Eastern Europe for the last ten years should not be underestimated. First of all, the EU's response to developments in the region was remarkably speedy. As early as July 1989, the Union (or more precisely the Community, as it was still called then) assumed the task of coordinating all G24 aid to Poland and Hungary.[7] That year the Union also rewarded the reforms undertaken by Mikhail Gorbachev by offering Moscow MFN treatment for tariffs and duties, and political dialogue through a Joint Committee (the Trade and Cooperation Agreement). The Union was also first in trying to manage the ensuing armed conflict in the Balkans following the declarations of independence by Slovenia and Croatia on 25 June 1991.[8] When instability in Moscow heightened the threat to the Baltics during the

August 1991 coup, the Union responded quickly by recognising the three Baltic States' independence and offering them its technical aid program.

Of course, speedy involvement does not necessarily imply 'correct' or 'sufficient' involvement. Nor does it suggest that the Union is quick in responding to emergencies – when decisions are needed virtually overnight. That said, it is unfair to accuse the Union of being slow in responding to some broader historic developments in Eastern Europe, especially in comparison with other actors.

Moreover, as events in Eastern Europe evolved, the Union has been progressively upgrading its involvement. And thus the initial aid program for Hungary and Poland gradually has been extended to other countries in the region and organised in two separate regimes; PHARE and TACIS (the latter for the New Independent States including, among others, Ukraine, Belarus, and Russia). The substance of the EU's Eastern European involvement also has been upgraded regularly. In 1992, the Community moved beyond the technical aid PHARE program and began to conclude the so-called Association Agreements, which progressively reduced trade barriers with no less than ten postcommunist countries. In 1993 the Copenhagen Council officially envisaged the prospect of eastward enlargement and specified the main criteria for possible accession to the Union. Soon afterward the so-called 'structured dialogue' enhanced political contacts between the EU and associated countries, and the Commission published the White Paper, which provided associated countries with a guideline for moving towards the EU's single market. All this was proudly labelled a 'pre-accession strategy.' In July 1997, the Commission published an enormous document entitled 'Agenda 2000: For a Stronger and Wider Union,' which suggests a detailed blueprint for future EU enlargement.

Relations with Moscow also have been upgraded by signing the Partnership and Cooperation Agreement in June 1994, in which the Union committed itself to supporting Russian accession to GATT and WTO, removed most quotas on Russian exports, and promised to consider creating a free-trade zone in1998. Later, Partnership and Cooperation Agreements also were signed with Ukraine, Belarus, Kyrgyzstan, Kazakstan, Azerbaijan, Armenia, Georgia, and Moldova.

The Union's involvement in the former Yugoslavia has been more complex. The EU decided to withdraw its monitoring mission from Bosnia in May 1992 and later, following the fiasco of the London Conference, it has somewhat down-played its political involvement in the Balkan conflict. However, the Union up-graded its financial involvement in the region following the Dayton Peace Accord: nearly half of $1.8 billion pledged for supporting Bosnia's reconstruction comes from European states, as opposed to the mere 15 per cent promised by the US.

This leads us to another feature of the EU's policy in the region, namely its financial generosity. The lion's share of money that the G24 countries have committed to Central and Eastern Europe during the crucial period of 1989-1991 came from the EC: 72 per cent of all grants (ECU 4.1 billion), and half of all loans and credits (ECU 7.0 billion). In comparison, at that time the US had allocated only ECU 763 million for grants and ECU 179 million for loans.[9] The 1997 'Agenda 2000' program envisages an 'enlargement package' of no less then ECU 75 billion: 'a veritable Marshall

Plan for the countries of Central and Eastern Europe,' as President Jacques Santer described it.[10]

True, not all EU money has been wisely invested, and some of it actually went right back into 'EU pockets.' For instance, the European Investment Bank and OECD estimate that 75 per cent of PHARE money was channelled via Western consultants operating in Central and Eastern Europe. It is also true that the EU is more generous to its current members from Southern Europe than to its future members from Central and Eastern Europe: for the next five years the EU intends to spend no less than ECU 178 billion for the so-called structural funds supporting poorer EU members.[11] It is also true that the amount of money allocated to Russia and other NIS states is relatively lower than for the PHARE states: the current TACIS package amounts to ECU 2.2 million for the period of 1996-1999.[12] That said, one can nevertheless conclude that the Union's financial contribution to Eastern Europe is significant, by most standards. It is difficult to expect any international organisation to be more generous to outsiders than to its own members. Likewise, it is only natural that the countries just outside EU borders are the major beneficiaries of the EU aid.

The Union has not limited its role in Eastern Europe to crediting and accounting, but has been active in many different fields; from politics and security to environmental protection and culture. Granted, the Union was at its best when applying civilian rather than military means. For instance, the Union successfully engineered the Stability Pact aimed at preventing ethnic and border disputes between Central and Eastern European states, but was unable to agree on the application of military force (via WEU), either in the former Yugoslavia or later in Albania. There is little doubt, however, that the EU's involvement in Eastern Europe has been multi-dimentional and fairly comprehensive.

In addition, the EU's involvement has been largely institutional. Its policy was neither about secret pacts nor about grandiose public declarations. Instead its policy was about negotiating and signing a very complex set of legal and institutional arrangements, such as the Europe Agreements and the Partnership and Cooperation Agreements.

Finally, the Union's involvement in Eastern Europe has been conditional: the promise of EU membership and various forms of assistance have been linked to democratic and market reforms and to conflict-prevention measures. For instance, the 1993 European Council in Copenhagen decided that Eastern European applicants must meet three basic criteria for the EU membership: 1/stable institutions guaranteeing democracy, the rule of law, human rights and the protection of minorities; 2/the existence of a functional market economy as well as the capacity to cope with the competitive pressures and market forces within the Union, and 3/the ability to take on the obligations of membership including adherence to the aims of political, economic, and monetary union. Four years later, the Commission reviewed applicants' progress in meeting these criteria and concluded that only five of the ten applicant countries have made sufficient progress to be invited to begin admission negotiations with the EU.[13]

The principle of conditionality has also been applied towards Russia and the Balkan countries – albeit with less success. For instance, in 1995 the EU temporarily suspended completion of an interim trade accord with Russia because of the atrocities committed by the Russian army in Chechnya. But as Karen Smith points out in her chapter, the EU soon decided to reverse its policy and proceed with the trade agreement even though fighting in Chechnya was still raging.[14]

In conclusion, the EU's record from the last ten years shows not only grandiose words, but many deeds that follow a plausible logic: the more Eastern Europe resembles the 'civilised' West, the more is offered by the Union. EU policies in the region were relatively speedy, progressively up-graded, financially generous, and multi-dimentional. Why then is the Union under fire from critics? Why do critics claim that the Union lacks a sound strategy?

AN AMBIGUOUS VISION OF EUROPE

The major problem with the EU's policies is that they do not fit into any concrete design for Europe. The Union obviously supports democracy, prosperity, and peace throughout the continent. But here clarity ends and ambiguity begins. For nearly a decade since the fall of the Berlin Wall, the Union has failed to produce answers to some basic strategic questions such as: Which countries are going to join the Union, why, and when? What is the basic aim of enlargement? What kind of relationship does the Union want to develop with countries that are unlikely to become EU members? By not answering these questions the Union's policy in Eastern Europe becomes accidental, inconsistent, and shaped by short-term parochial interests. By not answering these questions, the Union is unable to design and execute any sound strategy.

Let us start with the confusion concerning EU's aims, especially in the context of the forthcoming eastward enlargement. Is the aim of enlargement economic: creating a vast free-trade area? Is it political: preventing instability just across EU borders? Or maybe the aim is cultural: bringing under one roof all 'truly' European countries?

Of course, various economic, political, and cultural aims may well be in harmony. For instance, liberals always argue that the best way to achieve peace and democracy is via free trade. However, on a lower level of abstraction various aims are often in conflict, presenting politicians with difficult choices. For instance, economic aims yield basically policies of financial profit, while political aims yield policies of financial sacrifice. Economic aims argue for embracing stable and prosperous countries, while political aims argue for embracing weak and unstable ones. Countries with strong European credentials in terms of culture are not always the most attractive economic targets. Nor can one guarantee that the list of most culturally 'European' EU candidates will overlap with the list of countries deserving EU's political embrace.

Different aims behind enlargement also call for different institutional solutions. For instance, if security in Central Europe is the greatest Western concern, then membership in NATO and WEU seem to be most crucial, and one can wait with the eastward enlargement of the EU which, after all, is basically about economics.

Because the aims of enlargement remain vague, the admission criteria are subject to voluntaristic if not conflicting interpretations. Consider, for instance, the economic criteria for admission spelled out by the Copenhagen European Council: applicant countries must have a functioning market economy as well as the capacity to cope with competitive pressures and market forces within the Union. Is there a way to interpret these criteria in any 'objective' manner? Should the level of growth be decisive or the size of the economic market? Should one watch inflation and the budget deficit or the progress of privatisation? The Agenda 2000 found all the abovementioned economic factors equally important and spelled out their meaning in detail. No weighting of individual criteria was attempted however, and no system of judging the importance of each of the criteria was suggested. As a consequence, the picture became extremely complex and probably even more confusing. The road to EU membership for individual applicant countries is now rife with economic hurdles, but with neither signposts indicating the required direction nor instructions indicating which hurdles to jump over first.

In a more specific fashion, it has also been pointed out that the macroeconomic criteria of the Maastricht treaty indicated in the Agenda 2000 are convergence criteria rather than accession criteria per se, even though new members need to adjust to the new rules guiding the EMU project. In fact, macroeconomic criteria set up in Maastricht are as yet not being met by all current EU Member States. Moreover, macroeconomic criteria ignore such crucial issues for the postcommunist economies in transition as growth and employment. Meeting macroeconomic criteria in a particular moment does not guarantee that the economies of applicant countries will continue to grow sufficiently fast to catch up with the economies of the current EU Member States.[15] The European Council's Copenhagen decisions and the Commission's Agenda 2000 are also silent about the interplay between economic and political factors, and there is no mention of cultural factors.[16]

Cultural criteria should not be dismissed, however, because without cultural cohesion the whole concept of a distinct European identity will be built on sand. In fact, EU officials explicitly use cultural criteria in deterring the EU aspirations of Turkey and the countries of the Maghreb. But if cultural criteria are important can one prevent Russia from entering the Union at some point?

Many other important questions concerning the exact route to membership are still open to debate and conflict. For instance, the Agenda 2000 rules out the partial adoption of the *acquis communautaire* by applicant countries. This is neither realistic nor fair. The history of previous enlargements shows a degree of flexibility in the time schedule of the adoption of the *acquis*. Even the 'old' Member States had been granted many derogations, for example in the field of environmental regulations, while the United Kingdom had been allowed to opt out of the Social Charter. Why should Eastern European applicants be treated differently? Moreover, the *acquis* itself has expanded considerably since previous enlargements, regarding such crucial issues as the Single Market, CFSP, EMU, and justice and home affairs. Is it realistic to expect that Eastern European applicants will quickly adopt such a broad, multidimentional, and comprehensive *acquis*?

Thus, in reality we are faced with two largely incompatible options. One is to schedule a long pre-accession period, allowing the applicant countries to adopt the ever-growing *acquis*. The other is to allow partial or gradual adoption of the *acquis*.

These considerations highlight a major point: we do not really know the time frame for enlargement. Will enlargement proceed in stages, and how many stages are envisaged? And what exactly is offered to countries initially or definitively left out of EU borders?[17]

Ambiguity and confusion concerns not only the Union's geographic reach, but also its basic mode of involvement. One of the problems with the Union's involvement in the former Yugoslavia was that the Union created the impression that it is prepared to use military means if economic and diplomatic means fail. This proved to be a costly bluff, and it took much precious time before other actors felt compelled to replace the EU as the leading external actor in the Balkans.

The Union's non-committal, ambiguous, and vague policy is defended on practical grounds: is it not better for the Union to keep all options open? For instance, keeping the prospect of enlargement open provides the Union with an effective international leverage. Many countries in Eastern Europe are willing to modify their behaviour in line with the EU's wishes in the hope of obtaining EU membership. Fixing EU borders would deprive the Union of part of its appeal and would demotivate if not frustrate countries that are left out. However, the opposite might in fact be true: granting EU membership to democratic and economic champions in the region is the best motivation for laggards to improve their records. In other words ambiguity is demotivating rather than motivating. That said, the most salient explanation for the existing ambiguity is found elsewhere. The ambiguity of the enlargement project and other policies towards Eastern Europe emerges, first of all, from the inherent ambiguity of the European Union's integration project itself. After all, one can hardly identify the aims and criteria of enlargement without first determining the aims of the European Union itself. Is the Union primarily about economics or politics or culture? The problem is that the Union's basic purpose and profile are still being debated, re-articulated, and re-adjusted. The Union's basic aims and functions are purposefully being kept ambiguous in order to prevent an excessive clash of interests among and within its 15 diverse members. And if the Union's integration process is conducted in disguise, little wonder that the enlargement project – or any other foreign policy project – is also ambiguous and enigmatic.[18]

And thus the Union's ambiguity in foreign policy results from the Union's ambiguity about its own identity. The Union can hardly be more specific about its policy towards Eastern Europe without defining first its own profile.

ASSERTION OF DOMESTIC INTERESTS

Another problem is that the Union's Eastern European policy has become a hostage of the Union's own parochial agenda. In other words, the Union's internal, selfish interests dominate broader strategic considerations. Sometimes the Union's policy towards Eastern Europe has been undermined by the EU's own power ambitions, however misguided. For instance, there are good reasons to believe that the Union's initial involvement in the Balkan conflict was more about the EU's ambition to become a full-fledged international actor than about addressing the war situation on the ground. Moreover, policies towards Eastern Europe have been overshadowed by the Union's ambition to introduce a single currency: the Euro. In the last few years, EU leaders invested most of their time and political capital in the Euro project, clearly at the expense of other important projects such as eastward enlargement. Until now, the Union has not managed to explain how introduction of the Euro is likely to reshape its relations with the eastern part of the continent.

At other times, Ostpolitik has been the victim of squabbling between individual EU members. As Esther Barbé mentions in another chapter of this book, the Union's policy of financial aid to Eastern Europe has been subject to internal squabbles between northern (led by Germany) and southern (led by Spain and France) EU Member States. Clearly this has more to do with the internal balance of power within the Union than about the needs of Eastern Europe and Maghreb.[19] Selection of new EU members from Eastern Europe is currently subject to a similar type of internal squabble. Some candidates, such as Estonia, are backed by Scandinavian EU members, Slovenia's membership is advocated by Italy and Austria, while France is the champion of Romania's cause. Despite the end of the Cold War, geopolitics seems again to be in vogue in national capitals, which has damaging implications for the Union's collective interests and little regard for developments in Eastern Europe as such.

Divisions concerning the preferred model of European integration also hamper the Union's policies towards the East. Arguments continue between those who favour widening the Union by quickly including new members from Eastern Europe and those in favour of deepening the level of integration within the Union before admitting any new states. Moreover, those in favour of widening usually are more concerned with preventing deepening than with Eastern European issues. Likewise, those in favour of deepening are often prepared to sacrifice broader strategic considerations on the altar of the federalist project.[20]

EU policies in Eastern Europe were not only undermined by the selfish policies of individual Member States, but also by sectarian pressures by various interest groups within the Union. Time and again the Union has created the impression that its strategy in Eastern Europe is primarily about protecting the interests of EU bankers, farmers, steel workers, and trade unions.[21] Protectionism was the order of the day in EU policies towards Eastern Europe even though an open-door policy towards the region could hardly affect the EU as a whole. After all, EU economic relations with Eastern Europe are still of marginal overall significance. For instance, Central and Eastern European countries' share of total extra-EU trade is around 5 per cent. But time and again the Union has used its enormous political and economic leverage in Eastern Europe to enhance the interests of a relatively small group of EU producers. Broader strategic consideration obviously did not count when Member States objected to the Commission's extremely modest proposal of importing two extra lorry loads of Bulgarian strawberry jam or an extra 12 kilos of Slovak ham per Member State per day.[22] In those first crucial years of transition, Eastern Europeans were deprived of easy access to the EU market in all their leading sectors such as steel, textiles, and agriculture. Eastern European labour was also virtually prevented from entering the EU. Even the Association Agreements with their asymmetrical reductions in tariffs and quotas could not prevent the continuously increasing Eastern European trade deficit with the European Union.[23]

Of course, the Union is not the only international actor with a foreign policy agenda dominated by internal, parochial concerns. However, there are at least three crucial factors that make this problem greater for the Union than for 'traditional' international actors such nation states. One of them has already been mentioned: the Union prefers to maintain an ambiguous profile in terms of its basic purpose and interests. But in the absence of a clear hierarchy of collective interests, parochialism has a greater chance of asserting itself.

Moreover, the Union is a collection of still largely sovereign states with largely diverging agendas, and the Union's decision-making process is still largely based on intergovernmental bargaining. No wonder that parochialism has good chances to prevail over strategic arguments.

Finally, individual Member States usually opt for a fragmented institutional approach to European politics which, in the words of six academic experts from the Sussex European Institute, 'tends to feed positions which reflect particular interests into the European-level policy process.'[24] The experts offer the example of the German government which is, in principle, most receptive to Eastern European demands for market access and early membership in the EU. Nevertheless, during the negotiations on Association Agreements with Eastern European countries German representatives argued against greater market access, alongside protectionist Member States, in those sectors where German producers feared Eastern European competition, such as coal, agriculture, and steel. Broader considerations, such as enhancing economic opportunities, advancing industrial restructuring, or promoting geopolitical stability, seemed to be less relevant than the fear of increased unemployment in the above-mentioned sectors. And the experts argue that the existing policy process and structure of the Commission makes it difficult to counter sectoral pressures and shape EU policies along a broader strategic lines. This leads us to another crucial problem: the lack of institutional reform within the Union itself.

EU'S RELUCTANCE TO REFORM

The Union has always demanded institutional reform in Eastern Europe, but it has been doing little to reform itself. Both in Maastricht in 1992 and five years later in Amsterdam, the Union failed to reform its decision-making system, re-adjust its structural aid funding, or reformulate its common agricultural policy: all steps required by the prospect of eastward enlargement. Several weeks after concluding the Draft Treaty of Amsterdam, the Commission called for a new Intergovernmental Conference to meet as soon as possible after 2000 to prepare for enlargement with far-reaching institutional reforms. Similarly the Union was unable to improve the institutional set-up of its Common Foreign and Security Policy (CFSP) to allow it to cope with military or diplomatic crises in the postcommunist part of the continent. As the Commission's own report observed: 'The experience of the common foreign and security policy has been disappointing so far.'[25]

The message is loud and clear: had the Union designed a serious strategy towards Eastern Europe it would have re-adjusted its own institutions along the way in an effort to allow this strategy to work. It is difficult to imagine that the forthcoming eastward enlargement will be a success without serious institutional reforms within the Union. An enlarged EU cannot function at the minimum level without re-adjustment of the system of weighting votes within the Union, extension of the qualified majority voting, reduction of the number of Commissioners from each Member State, and introduction of some serious flexibility clauses in EU law. Moreover, to function effectively, an enlarged EU probably even needs to significantly extend the area in which majority voting applies, simplify the entire decision-making system, and drastically reform the existing competence division between the Commission and the Council. The existing institutional set-up was originally created for six Member States and it is already strikingly inefficient with the current 15 members. An addition of five or more new members will totally paralyse the Union and deprive it of any remaining legitimacy. This is why the 1996–97 Intergovernmental Conference was conceived and its participants were issued the task of reforming EU institutional system and preparing it for the eastward enlargement. But several months of deliberations produced extremely disappointing results in the form of a new Draft Treaty adopted in Amsterdam: the most crucial decisions (on the future size of the Commission and the re-weighting of the Council's voting arrangements) have been postponed until the first wave of enlargement. True, there was agreement that the large Member States will give up one of their Commissioners, but only if the weights of the votes in the Council are eventually re-adjusted. The qualified majority vote was also allowed in a few more areas and a group of EU states will now be able to move together without waiting for others, but again, only in some limited policy areas. In short, all these changes stopped short of meeting some basic requirements for the new wave of enlargement.

The Union is similarly reluctant to reform its budget as required by eastward enlargement. Enlargement will not be cheap, but extending the Union's current spending on the Common Agricultural Policy and regional aid to new Eastern European members would require an increase in the Union's budget that surely will be unacceptable to taxpayers. Estimates of additional annual expenditures for the Common Agricultural Policy range from ECU 12 billion for all ten applicant states to ECU 38 billion for only four Visegrad countries.[26] Application of the current EU rules concerning the structural funds to the four Visegrad candidates would increase spending to ECU 26 billion over a five-year period. If Bulgaria, Romania, and the three Baltic states are also included, the structural funds would need to rise by ECU 54 billion.

In the Agenda 2000 the Commission suggested far-reaching reforms of both the Common Agricultural Policy and the costly regional aid budget. But it faced immediate opposition from the powerful farm lobbies across the Union as well as from countries benefiting from structural aid, such as Greece, Spain, and Portugal.[27] Thus, the Union is faced with an insoluble dilemma: how will it maintain budget discipline, reassure beneficiaries of the current budgetary system, and admit new Eastern European members on equal terms?

A workable Common Foreign and Security Policy (CFSP) could help the Union design and implement policies in Eastern Europe. But again, no substantial institutional changes to the CFSP system were endorsed by the 1997 Summit in Amsterdam. As Reinhardt Rummel and Jörg Wiedemann point out in their chapter, the coherence of the system is still undermined by the pillar structure, separating trade and economics from foreign policy and preventing the link between policy ends and means. As a consequence, the CFSP has very few instruments at its disposal. These are either to be found in the first pillar of the Union or outside the Union structure, in the Western European Union, for instance.

The CFSP decision-making process is still largely based on the principle of unanimity and as such cannot avoid being slow, conflict-ridden, and subject to the lowest common denominator. The whole institutional arrangement lacks the clarity, hierarchy, and coherence which would allow the Union to act in an accountable and effective manner, especially when coping with Eastern European crises. The system produces inertia, indifference, and inconsistency. And there are plenty of examples indicating that the existing CFSP institutional system undermines the Union's Ostpolitik.

The reasons for institutional stagnation within the Union are very complex. Some would argue that the Union's built-in intergovernmentalism prevents any substantial self-reform. A single government unhappy with the prospect of institutional change can always use its veto power. Others argue that European citizens rather than European governments oppose further reforms of the Union because they fear further loss of democratic control over administration and politics. Whatever the explanation, one conclusion seems to be justified by the above analysis: EU institutions are badly suited to meet the challenge of designing and implementing EU strategy.

WHY DOES THE UNION NEED A STRATEGY?

International strategy was not a Cold War invention, but it is hard to deny that Cold War circumstances facilitated a strategic approach in foreign policy. During the Cold War, one could easily distinguish between friends and foes, US leadership was firm and indispensable, and generals knew how to respond when conflict arose. The collapse of the Soviet empire produced what the West had always wanted, but it also produced an entirely new Europe in which old diplomatic and security concepts look obsolete and new ones have yet to be created. Western Europe has lost its major enemy, but it also has lost the sextant by which its ship has been guided for the last five decades. Brave visions of a new pan-European security structure brought forth in the aftermath of the Cold War soon proved ill-conceived and hopelessly optimistic in their anticipated schedules and goals. Long-proclaimed principles and values were repeatedly compromised in day-to-day practice. The European Union itself has lost its vitality and sense of direction. Many European politicians now are turning inward, and the people of Europe seem increasingly confused and uninterested in any ambitious European project. How can any European strategy be conducted in an atmosphere of growing public cynicism, individualism, and disinterest? How can any strategy be conducted without a sense of direction? Contemporary Europe represents a very complex political, cultural, and economic environment that is hardly suited for crude political crafting. Although the Union is equipped with a unique leverage over Eastern Europe it no longer has the ideological compass that guided its policies throughout the Cold War.

Given the rapidly-changing circumstances of today, the multiplicity of diverse actors, and the on-going re-assertion of political values, there is no point in denying that designing and implementing any strategy presents a difficult challenge. However, this does not necessarily mean that the Union should abandon all strategic ambitions. First of all, strategy is about leadership; making difficult choices amidst conflicting evidence and multiple pressures. Without strategy EU policies will always be pushed around by chaotic sequences of events and sectarian pressures. Second, strategy is about efficiency, which means that policies are geared towards achieving only selected objectives and are equipped with adequate instruments. Third, in a democratic body politic, strategy is also about democratic accountability. The European electorate can hardly execute democratic control over EU bureaucrats and politicians if it does not really know what choices are being made by them in terms of policy aims, preferential or discriminatory treatment, and the scale of investment. Fourth, strategy is also about communication with other international actors. Friends and foes of the Union ought to be given clear signals about the Union's objectives. They should also be given good reasons to believe that the Union is able and determined to achieve those objectives.

Besides, the Union's problems with strategic deficit are not necessarily emerging from the post-Cold War confusion and complexity. They are largely products of the Union's tendency towards political and institutional ambiguity. Throughout its entire history the Union (or Community) never specified its basic purpose, functions, and geographic reach. As I pointed out in the introduction of this book, the ambiguity of the successive cooperative arrangements was basically rooted in the persistent differences between EU Member States concerning the very nature of integration (federalism vs. intergovernmentalism), the functional scope of integration (high politics vs. low politics), and competing national agendas (e.g., French and Spanish 'anti-Americanism' vs. British and Dutch 'pro-Americanism'). Ambiguity has helped achieve the necessary consensus across Member States, but it also has prevented the Union from acquiring a minimum degree of strategic purpose. The damaging implications of this fact are evident when we examine the European Ostpolitik. EU policies in Eastern Europe have been found to be prompt, generous, and comprehensive, but they are reactive rather than pro-active, vulnerable to accidental and parochial pressures, guided by short-term rather than long-term considerations, and lacking in sound institutional support.

NOTES

* I would like to thank Knud Erik Jøergensen, Adriaan van der Meer, and Karen Elizabeth Smith for their critical comments on early versions of this chapter, and to Nida Gelazis for her splendid editorial assistance.

[1] The following countries fall under the term Eastern Europe in this chapter: Albania, Belarus, Bulgaria, Bosnia-Herzegovina, the Czech Republic, Estonia, Hungary, Latvia, Lithuania, Macedonia, Moldova, Poland, Russia, Romania, Slovakia, Slovenia, Ukraine, and the Yugoslav Federation (Serbia and Montenegro).

[2] For a comprehensive analysis of the history of the EC involvement in Eastern Europe see: John Pinder, *The European Community and Eastern Europe* (London: Pinter Publishers, 1991), especially pp. 8-36. Also Peter van Ham, *The EC, Eastern Europe and European Unity. Discord, Collaboration and Integration Since 1947* (London and New York: Pinter Publishers, 1993), especially pp. 15-143. It is worth keeping in mind that the EC was not formally recognised by the USSR and COMECON. Moreover, one should distinguish between collective policies of EU Member States towards Eastern Europe and bilateral links between individual Eastern and Western European states. For instance, before 1989 the Federal Republic of Germany had much more developed relations with Eastern European countries then other EC Member States. Since 1989 bilateral cooperation programs between Western and Eastern European states represent a significant addition to the collective EU policies in the region.

[3] Karen Elizabeth Smith, *The Making of Foreign Policy in the European Community/Union: the Case of Eastern Europe, 1988-1995*, Ph.D. thesis defended at the London School of Economics and Political Science in 1996, pp. 352-353. (Soon to be published by Macmillan). As a matter of fact, Smith's argument relates only to the EU's policy towards six Eastern European states, and not towards the former Yugoslavia and the former Soviet Union.

[4] Wolfgang Wessels, 'Problems and Perspectives of the EU-Political and Institutional Options,' in *East-Central Europe and the EU: Problems of Integration*, Karl Kaiser and Martin Brüning, eds., (Bonn: Europea Union Verlag, 1996), p. 68.

[5] As David Allen put it: 'In the middle of 1997 a new European order still has to emerge and the central role of the European Union is under some question. Whilst it is still possible to contemplate an image of a future European order based upon an enlarged European Union linked in close cooperation with the non-Member States of the Mediterranean and the former Soviet Union, the immediate reality is of a Europe whose fundamental structures are being shaped and problems solved (albeit in the short term and probably for all the wrong reasons) by the resurgent power and influence of the United States. It was the Americans who recognised the imperatives of German unification (although the EC provided an essential framework), who assisted in the withdrawal of Russian forces from the Baltic States, who negotiated the agreements between Russia and all other former Soviet States that removed all nuclear weapons from their territory and control, who moved from a 'Russia First' policy to one that advocated NATO enlargement, who intervened militarily and politically to prevent the Bosnian war spreading to Kosovo or Macedonia, who finally intervened to broker and police a peace settlement in Bosnia, who resolved the latest outbreak of potentially lethal Greek-Turkish squabbling 'whilst European leaders slept' and who have apparently negotiated an acceptable deal between Russia and NATO that should allow NATO enlargement in the near future.' See David Allen, Reuniting Europe or Establishing New Divides?: The European Union, the States of Eastern and Central Europe and the States of the Former Soviet Union,' Paper presented at the 5th Biennial Conference of the European Community Studies Association, Seattle, WA, 29 May-1st June 1997, p. 2, (unpublished).

[6] This chapter tries to interpret the already existing and relatively well-known evidence. New historical data are coming out each year, however. For a good example of a major research project collecting many as yet unknown factual details see e.g., José Ignacio Torreblanca Payá, *The European Community and Central Eastern Europe (1989-1993): Foreign Policy and Decision-Making* (Madrid: Centro de Estudios Avanzados en Ciencias Sociales, 1997).

[7] In fact, the European Community was negotiating trade and cooperation agreements with individual Eastern European countries since 1988. As communist parties were still in power in the region, these negotiations have often been criticised, especially in the United States. See e.g., Heinrich Vogel, 'East-West Trade and Technology Transfer Reconsidered,' in: *After the Revolutions: East-West Trade and Technology*

Transfer in the 1990s, eds. Gary K. Bertsch, Heinrich Vogel and Jan Zielonka (Boulder: Westview Press, 1991): 171-185.

[8] Initially both the WEU and NATO took limited back-up roles and became more deeply involved only in the second half of 1992. The United States was also reluctant to get involved in the conflict. Ralph Johnson, a US State Department official responsible for European Affairs, stated in his address to the Senate Foreign Relations Committee that 'since Europe accounts for nearly 80 per cent of all Yugoslav trade...it is appropriate for the EC to take the lead.' See Reneo Lukic and Allen Lynch, *Europe from the Balkans to the Urals. The Disintegration of Yugoslavia and the Soviet Union* (Oxford: Oxford University Press, 1996): 261. Also James Gow, 'Nervous Bunnies: the International Community and the Yugoslav war of Dissolution, the Politics of Military Intervention in a Time of Change,' in *Military Intervention in European Conflicts*, Lawrence Freedman, ed. (Oxford: Blackwell Publishers, 1994): 14-33.

[9] Since the July 1989 decision to launch the PHARE program to aid Poland and Hungary, and after its extension to include Bulgaria, Czechoslovakia, Romania, and Yugoslavia, by January 1991, the G24 had allocated to PHARE ECU 5.7 billion in grants, as well as ECU 9.9 billion in loans and credits from governments and the Community, together with ECU 3.9 billion from the World Bank. The EC contribution mentioned came both from the EC institutions and from the EC Member States. See John Pinter, *The European Community and Eastern Europe*, op.cit...p.88.

[10] Intervention de M. Jacques Santer, Président de la Commission européenne devant le Parlement européen, Agenda 2000, Strasbourg, le 16 juillet 1997, internet source: http://europa.eu.int/comm/agenda2000/rapid/9716fr.htm.

[11] See *The Economist*, July 19, 1997. The amount indicated concerns the 1998-2002 budgetary years. It must be stressed that southern European states are not the only Member States benefiting from the Structural Funds. However, the preferential treatment of the current EU members is not likely to change after the first wave of eastward enlargement. According to the 'Agenda 2000,' spending on structural policies will remain pegged at the current limit of 0.46 per cent of GNP, providing ECU 275 billion for the entire period between 2000-2006. Of this ECU 210 billion would be for operations in the existing Member States, including ECU 20 billion for the Cohesion Fund. From accession, the new Member States would receive a total of ECU 38 billion.

[12] The PHARE budget for the same period is ECU 6.93 million. In all, PHARE will have delivered a total of ECU 11 billion in assistance to the applicant Central and Eastern European countries over the ten years from 1989 to 1999. See Günter Burghardt and Fraser Cameron, 'The Next Enlargement of the European Union,' *European Foreign Affairs Review* 1:2 (1997):18.

[13] The five countries praised by the Commission were Hungary, Poland, the Czech Republic, Estonia, and Slovenia.

[14] The EU was anxious not to isolate Russia and its President, Boris Yeltsin. Moreover, the EU was also afraid that its uncompromising position on the accord might increase Russia's opposition to the forthcoming enlargement of NATO and to NATO's bombing of Serbian positions in Bosnia. For a comprehensive analysis of relations between the EU and Russia see e.g., Andrei Zagorski, 'Russia and European Institutions,' in *Russia and Europe, The Emerging Security Agenda*, ed. Vladimir Baranovsky (Oxford: Oxford University Press, 1997): 519-540.

[15] See Horst Günter Krenzler, 'The EU and Central-East Europe: The Implications of Enlargement in Stages,' *The Robert Schuman Centre Policy Paper* (October, 1997): 8-9.

[16] The Agenda 2000 only states that 'the respect of the political conditions defined by the European Council in Copenhagen by an applicant country is a necessary, but not a sufficient, condition for opening accession negotiations' (p.49).

[17] The Agenda 2000 insists that the enlargement is 'an inclusive process embracing all of the applicant countries,' and the EU Commissioner Van den Broek argues that 'there are no "ins and outs" but rather "ins and pre-ins." Differentiation in no way implies discrimination.' So far however, no details have been given concerning the EU treatment of those countries that will not enter accession negotiations in the first round. The Agenda 2000 speaks vaguely about a 'framework which consists of the reinforcement of pre-accession strategy for these countries,' and about inviting them to a special 'European Conference.' The Commission also proposed to double 'pre-accession' assistance to the applicant countries, but this is still a matter of contention among the EU Member States. See Hans van den Broek, 'No new dividing lines,' *Financial Times* (September 22, 1997): 16.

[18] Elsewhere I have argued that ambiguity in the Union's basic aim and profile prevents it from acquiring the necessary democratic legitimacy and cultural identity, and is thus very damaging regardless of all arguments in favour of ambiguity that lies behind the neo-functionalist project of the integration by disguise. See Jan Zielonka, *Explaining Euro-paralysis* (London: Macmillan, forthcoming 1998).

[19] This is not to deny security concerns of EU Southern Member States related to recent developments in Algeria and other Maghreb countries. In the end, however, the Union tried little to address the hard core security agenda in the region. The Union focused on trade relations and humanitarian aid which might indirectly enhance security in Maghreb only in a very long term. See *Synergy at Work: Spain and Portugal in European Foreign Policy*, Franco Algieri and Elfriede Regelsberger, eds. (Bonn: Europa Union Verlag, 1996): 54-55.

[20] See e.g., an interview with the former EU Commissioner, Frans Andrissen in *de Volskrant* (March 16, 1996).

[21] This is not to argue that the EU should be a new 'altruist' type of international actor, but to point to the absence of an overall strategic assessment of various interests on the part of the EU. Nor is it to deny the damage caused to individual sectors such as steel, textiles, or agriculture by introducing a truly free trade with Eastern Europe. Such damage ought to be considered in a broader strategic context with various other relevant factors and each should be weighted in search of a proper balance.

[22] See Malcolm Rifkind, 'A Wider Europe: Britain's Vision,' Extracts from a speech by UK Foreign Secretary made in London on May 1, 1996, and published in: *European Document Series*, Institute of European Affairs, No. 14 (Summer 1996), pp. 58-59.

[23] As Czech Prime Minister Vaclav Klaus argued: 'We need to look beneath the surface at indicators such as the size of subsidies and various export promotion schemes and non-tariff barriers in the EU countries and we see that, in reality, asymmetry favours existing [EU] members.' Quoted in: Anthony Robinson and Robert Anderson, 'Czech premier attacks EU association agreements,' *Financial Times*, June 18, 1997. Of course, the EU's protectionism was not the only factor behind Eastern European trade deficit. Recession in Western Europe, the poor quality of Eastern European goods, lack of exporting experience, and other factors also should be mentioned.

[24] Alasdair Smith, Peter Holmes, Ulrich Sedelmeier, Edward Smith, Helen Wallace, and Alasdair Young, 'The European Union and Central and Eastern Europe: Pre-Accession Strategies,' *Sussex European Institute Working Paper*, No. 15 (1996), p.16.

[25] European Commission, *Report on the Operation of the Treaty on European Union*, SEC(95), Brussels, May 10th, 1995, p.5. See also Hans van den Broek, 'CFSP: The View of the European Commission,' in *The European Union's Common Foreign and Security Policy: The Challenges of the Future*, Spyros A. Papas and Sophie Vanhoonacker, eds. (Maastricht: European Institute of Public Administration, 1996), p.25.

[26] For a comprehensive overview of various estimates cited see: Heather Grabbe and Kirsty Hughes, *Eastward Enlargement of the European Union*, (London: The Royal Institute of International Affairs, 1997), especially pp. 38-46. Also Susan Senior Nello and Karen E Smith, 'The European Union and Central and Eastern Europe: The Implications of Enlargement in Stages,' *The Robert Schuman Centre's Working Papers*, (October, 1997).

[27] See Lionel Barber, 'EU alert over new members,' *Financial Times*, July 14, 1997.

CHAPTER X

From European Union to Atlantic Union

Charles A. Kupchan

Europe and the Atlantic community have arrived at a historic turning point.[1] With the wrenching ideological and geopolitical cleavages of the Cold War behind them, the Western democracies are seeking to consolidate their gains and extend peace, democracy, and free markets across Europe. To do so, the European Union is preparing for enlargement at the same time that it introduces a new level of supranationality through a single currency and a stronger defence identity. And NATO is embarking on its own plans for enlargement, getting ready to embrace in successive waves Europe's new democracies. At least on the surface, the West is triumphantly charting a course for the next century.

Beneath the surface, however, a profound disquiet accompanies on-going efforts to transform the institutions of the West. Preparation for monetary union is proceeding, but amidst widespread doubts about its economic desirability and political viability. NATO enlargement is on track, but also amidst deep reservations on both sides of the Atlantic about its purpose and consequences. Anxious self-doubt rather than triumphalism increasingly characterises debate about the future of the West.

This sense of unease is all too appropriate. Despite their good intentions, the leaders of the established democracies have embarked on a course that will lead to the demise of the West, not its renewal. At the core of the problem is that they are trying to broaden the community of peaceful, democratic nations even as they deepen it. But if enlargement is to be both politically feasible and strategically desirable, they must first loosen the West's structures.

Absent the Soviet threat, the vision of Europe embodied in the Maastricht Treaty is now but a legacy of a former era. Preparations for monetary union notwithstanding, efforts to move toward centralised governance of Europe and a common foreign and security policy are foundering as national states dig in and resist further attempts to whittle away their sovereignty. Worse still, the futile push toward federalism is absorbing the energy and resources that should be devoted to the EU's most important and urgent mission: its enlargement to the east.[2]

NATO, on the other hand, is addressing the task of enlargement with the urgency it deserves. But NATO has been misdirecting its energies into a heated debate over which Central European countries to admit and when to do so, failing to recognise that the problem is in the very nature of the alliance, not its membership. Formal military blocs and the rigor of territorial guarantees are no longer necessary or politically sustainable. Rather than asking 'who gets in when?' NATO should be asking 'what are they getting into?'

Unless the EU and NATO undertake fundamental reform, they risk coming apart just as they draw within reach of completing their historic mission to unite a peaceful and democratic Europe. The excessive ambition of current policies will overextend Western institutions, undermining the transatlantic community as Member States defect from unwanted commitments. Instead, Western leaders must scale back their vision and seek to strike a balance between institutions that demand too much and those that deliver too little. They must devise a framework that occupies a new and vital centre and that promises to match commitments and responsibilities to political realities.

The solution to the West's dilemmas is an Atlantic Union (AU) that would subsume the EU and NATO. The EU would abandon its federal aspirations and concentrate instead on the extension of its single market East to Central Europe and West to North America. NATO would become the defence arm of the AU, but its binding commitments to the collective defence of state borders would give way to more relaxed commitments to uphold collective security through peace enforcement, peacekeeping, and preventive diplomacy. The AU could then open its doors to the new democracies of Central Europe in a manner acceptable to both Russia and commitment-weary electorates in NATO countries. Once democracy takes root in Russia and other states of the former Soviet Union, the AU would include them in its security structures and single market. Institutions that promote civic engagement and legislative oversight at the transatlantic level should be created to undergird and legitimate an Atlantic Union of democratic states.

An AU would sacrifice depth for breadth. But a looser and more comprehensive transatlantic union would ensure that the bridge between North America and an enlarged Europe rests on solid economic and political trestles, not just on increasingly weak strategic ones. It would thus lock in, and eventually extend, perhaps the most profound transformation of our century: the creation of a community of democratic nation states among which war has become unthinkable. The Western democracies have built much more than an alliance of convenience among countries that are each out for individual gain. They enjoy unprecedented levels of trust and reciprocity and share a political order based on capitalist economies and liberal societies.[3] The consolidation and expansion of this democratic core holds the greatest promise for a stable peace in the Atlantic region and beyond, and it is a sensible and prudent starting point as the West casts about for a new grand strategy.

ASIA-FIRST VERSUS EUROPE-FIRST

Asia's economic ascendance and geopolitical instability have raised questions about the continuing relevance of a special Atlantic link. Just as Asia-firsters attacked America's Atlanticism during the early post-World War II years, they are now arguing that preserving the transatlantic community is not worth the effort.[4] Asia-firsters contend that Atlanticism has served its purpose and that the United States has far more pressing needs at home and in the Pacific. Now that threats to European peace are limited in geographic scope and severity, Europe no longer requires American attention and resources; Europeans can and should assume responsibility for their own security. Asia is far more deserving of the top spot in America's new geopolitics. It promises to emerge as the next century's engine of global economic growth.[5] The United States should be poised to tap into the region's new markets and capital flows. And unstable regional alignments, in combination with uncertainty about how China will cope with its new-found power, necessitate the deterrent and stabilising effect of a robust American military presence. With Asia's ascendance, the argument runs, must come the end of America's Euro-centrism and the beginning of a grand strategy anchored in the Pacific rather than the Atlantic.

The Pacific Basin's economic dynamism and political volatility notwithstanding, an Asia-first grand strategy is fundamentally flawed. Europe still matters for three potent reasons. First, despite the end of the Cold War, the US-European partnership continues to serve as the fulcrum for broader multilateral action in the international arena. A transatlantic coalition was behind all the central diplomatic initiatives of this decade – countering Iraqi aggression in the Persian Gulf, bringing to a successful conclusion the Uruguay Round of trade negotiations, paving the way for a lasting peace in the Middle East, helping to build democracy in the former Soviet bloc, and enforcing the Dayton Accord in Bosnia. In addition, the transatlantic partnership is at the heart of the institutional infrastructure that underpins ongoing efforts to liberalise the international trading system and prevent and stop conflict. To the extent that a set of norms and rules are gradually becoming embedded in the international system, the driving force emanates from the common values and efforts of the Western democracies. For the foreseeable future, no Asian power or coalition of powers will be able to fill the shoes of America's European allies in helping to construct an international order based on the principles of liberal multilateralism. The United States should by all means sustain a cooperative relationship with Japan and seek to channel China's coming economic and military might toward constructive ends. But a strong Atlantic coalition will enhance, not diminish, American leverage in East Asia.

Second, Europe itself would be deeply unsettled should the Atlantic connection wither and America disengage from the continent. Whether by design or default, NATO has greatly facilitated Europe's coming together by assuming responsibility for hard-core security issues, leaving the European Community (the EU's forebearer) free to pursue political and economic integration. As Europe's failure to act decisively and effectively in Bosnia made clear, the EU is not ready to take over the management of European security. Indeed, an American withdrawal would send shock waves across Europe, perhaps threatening even the Franco-German coupling by forcing Germany to reconsider its security needs. Should this unravelling of Europe come about, the bedrock of US foreign policy – a cohesive Western Europe at peace – would be shaken loose.

Third, to allow the transatlantic community to erode would be to miss an opportunity to lock in the zone of democratic peace that North America and Western Europe have succeeded in constructing. Countries within this zone have all but eliminated the security competition and jockeying for relative advantage that have characterised international politics for millennia. It may be that without a common threat, it will not be long before relations among the Western democracies again fall prey to traditional power balancing and the search for individual gain. But it is worth trying to do better and to make permanent the establishment of a grouping of nations among which war is no more.

THE FALLACY OF THE REST AGAINST THE WEST

The most effective and familiar means of ensuring the vitality of the West would be to find it a new enemy. A transcendent external threat would provide a new 'other' against which the Atlantic democracies could renew their common identity and sense of shared purpose. Whether motivated by concern about restoring the West's cohesion or by a sincere assessment that dire threats are looming on the horizon, the search for new fault lines is all the rage. Samuel Huntington, for example, sees other civilisations as the new enemy against which America and Europe should gird their loins.[6] Profound cultural differences, Huntington contends, will ultimately lead to a clash of incompatible civilisations. While Huntington sees the most serious threat to the West emanating from a Confucian-Islamic connection, others worry more about a coming divide between Western and Orthodox Christendom.

Robert Kaplan argues that the coming cleavage will fall along socio-economic rather than civilizational lines. Poverty, illness, and violence in underdeveloped regions promise only to worsen, threatening to engulf the industrialised West. In a variation on the same theme, Matthew Connelly and Paul Kennedy fear overpopulation and migration from the poorer south to the richer north. 'Demographic-technological fault lines,' they contend, 'will define the landscape of the twenty-first century.'[7] The wealthy West must now come together to combat poverty and overpopulation lest it be overrun by the world's poor.

These efforts to provide the West a new mission and *raison d'etre* are dead ends. Ideological and religious affinities do not translate into geopolitical alliance any more than ideological and religious differences necessarily trigger conflict.[8] The Confucian and Islamic worlds – let alone the two together – are hardly coherent political actors; both are riven by ethnic, religious, and national divides. And Orthodox Europe is not preparing to do battle with Western Christendom. Former Soviet republics are still in the midst of efforts to reclaim nationhood and rediscover their cultural distinctiveness. But Russia and its neighbours are, for the most part, looking westward with hope, not fear. A new east-west divide in Europe may ultimately take shape, but it should not do so because of a self-fulfilling prophecy set in motion by the West's own actions. The challenge for the West is to live comfortably alongside these other civilisations, not wilfully or by accident to orchestrate a collision with them.

Overpopulation and poverty are far more worrisome than trumped-up cultural clashes. The South's scarce resources will grow ever more strained as its population soars. Wealth inequalities between the North and South will widen. But the connection between social breakdown in, say, Africa and the well-being of the West is at best tenuous. As they have well demonstrated, the industrialised democracies are very good at tolerating and cordoning off suffering in far-away places. Efforts to instil public alarm by concocting visions of millions of diseased and dispossessed storming the beaches of New Jersey – or even the Cote d'Azure – are simply too far-fetched. The Western democracies should soberly assess how they might help avoid the humanitarian disaster looming in Africa, and get on with doing what they can. But a call to arms based on the imagery of 'the rest against the West' will neither help the rest nor galvanise the West.

TOO MUCH EUROPE

Decision makers on both sides of the Atlantic appear to recognise that the West must seek to hang together because of common values and purposes, not common fears. Increasing integration within Western Europe and the opening of the EU and NATO to the new democracies of Central Europe are supposed to invigorate the West while erasing, not recreating, geopolitical cleavages.

Because they have mapped out futures for the EU and NATO that are far too ambitious, however, the leaders of the West are in the process of bringing about the demise of these institutions, not their revitalisation. As they should, both bodies intend to take advantage of the historic opportunity to open their doors to Central Europe. But they have yet to loosen their internal structures, a necessary step if their plans for enlargement are to have the intended consequences.

The EU continues to move toward a federal Europe – monetary union and a common foreign and security policy are the next steps – even as it prepares to double its membership. But the ambitious vision laid out in the Maastricht Treaty no longer enjoys the popular support that it did five years ago, when the treaty passed national referenda by the narrowest of margins.[9] Indeed, the ongoing Intergovernmental Conference in Turin, Italy is primarily an exercise in damage control, masking the reality that nation states across Europe are reasserting their sovereignty, not giving it up.

Deepening European integration has lost not only its popular appeal, but also its strategic purpose. Enlargement is now the geopolitical necessity – and not just to the east. The EU's current plans for a Europe-only single market, even if it promotes the welfare of its Member States in the short run, will likely harm the global economy in the long run. Although the North American Free Trade Agreement (NAFTA) and the Asia-Pacific Economic Cooperation (APEC) Forum also aim to promote regional integration, they differ from the EU in one crucial respect: the United States links the two regions through its participation in NAFTA and membership in APEC. As trade within North America and Asia increases and becomes more liberal, so will trade between the two regions. In contrast, if the EU forges ahead on its own to build a single market, single currency, and central bank, Europe's integration into the global economy will be jeopardised. Enlargement to the east makes this drift all the more likely as the free flow of goods from Central Europe will threaten producers in Western Europe, generating new pressures for protection from non-EU imports. Because Europe's welfare state is more extensive and its corporate and financial structures less adaptive than their counterparts in North America and East Asia, lagging competitiveness will also create incentives for the EU to put up protective barriers.[10]

THE GEOPOLITICAL RISK OF EMU

A single currency is expected to help Europe climb out of its extended period of slow growth and become more competitive. And there is little doubt that the *Euro* will bring economic benefits. The economic gains a single currency is likely to produce, however, do not alone confirm the desirability of monetary union. Precisely because political objectives have been paramount in fuelling the push for a single currency, EMU must be evaluated in terms of its political as well as its economic merits. After all, elected leaders looking to endow Europe with a more pronounced supranational character, not corporate leaders looking to increase profits, have been monetary union's main sponsors.

Within Europe's dominant narrative, EMU is meant to fulfil two geopolitical objectives. First, it is intended to lock in the Franco-German coalition by transferring authority over monetary policy from the national to the supranational level and by abolishing one of the most powerful symbols of sovereignty – national currencies. Second, it is supposed to create an inner core of expanding, integrated economies that will act as a magnet, drawing the EU's smaller states toward the centre. A Europe of concentric circles should emerge, with successive enlargements of the inner core taking place as states not initially included in EMU meet the criteria and are prepared to keep pace with France, Germany, and those other EU Member States moving most rapidly along the path of deeper integration.

The appeal of this vision notwithstanding, it is by no means clear that a single currency will have these intended geopolitical effects. The integrity of the Franco-German coalition is, to be sure, essential to preserving an integrated, cohesive Europe. Indeed, the Paris-Bonn (soon to be Paris-Berlin) axis is the centrepiece of the European construction. It provides the EU an identifiable power centre and a hierarchical structure of governance extending outward from this centre. At the same time, the coalition also serves as an instrument that binds and moderates the influence of Europe's core. This dual function is what allows France and Germany to guide the EU without appearing to dominate it. Europe's smaller states are willing to enter the EU precisely because it provides reassurance that the continent's power centre will exercise its influence in a moderate and benign manner.[11]

The problem is that EMU may well strain, rather than strengthen, the Franco-German coalition. Less than 40 per cent of the German electorate favours currency union, largely because the deutsche mark remains a powerful symbol of national identity. Establishing a supranational monetary authority, by triggering a popular backlash against increasing integration, may well induce a reassertion of French and German sovereignty. So too might the economic austerity needed to meet the Maastricht criteria jeopardise the Franco-German relationship. Workers in France and Germany have resorted to strikes to protest the cutbacks in spending implemented by their governments. And the efforts of France's new Socialist government to renegotiate the terms of monetary union have already produced strains between Paris and Bonn. As austerity continues and squabbling intensifies over preparations for the single currency, the temptation will increase for French and German elites to blame each other for any setbacks. Monetary union, which is intended to lock in the Franco-German coalition, may have precisely the opposite effect.

Even if a common currency succeeds in locking in a prosperous and cohesive Franco-German core, the broader construction that results may well consist of concentric barriers rather than concentric circles. Monetary union will have the greatest payoffs among the advanced economies of northern Europe. Similar structures and levels of performance will maximise the benefits associated with larger economies of scale and lower transaction costs while minimising EMU's distorting effects on national labour markets. In the economies of southern Europe, however, EMU promises to cause considerable dislocation and substantial increases in unemployment because of its effect on wages.[12] EU members initially outside the inner core may therefore choose to remain where they are. Those that ultimately choose to join EMU may eventually wish they had not.

The symbolic politics of EMU will create its own barriers. In deciding to proceed with a single currency, the EU is entering a new phase of its evolution in which the *de jure* equality of its members will give way to their *de jure* differentiation. *De jure* differentiation, at least on deductive grounds, risks turning the centripetal force that has drawn Europe's periphery toward its centre into centrifugal force that will drive centre and periphery apart.

Exclusion from the inner core could raise concern about relative gains, concern that has thus far been sublimated by *de jure* equality. Even if the benefits of participation in the EU remain strong in absolute terms, new dividing lines might make peripheral states more sensitive to their position relative to the core.[13] EMU might also lead to relative losses in the periphery as the inner circle reaps the benefits of a single currency and leaves behind its less fortunate neighbours. Barriers could also result from the explicit relegation of some states to a second-class status, producing a sense of injury and rejection in affected states and an effort to distance themselves from the source of that injury. Finally, EMU could cause fragmentation in the construction of Europe by triggering competition among peripheral states to attain entry into the inner circle. Fearful of being left out of monetary union or other aspects of integration pursued by the core, neighbouring states may vie with each other to clear the hurdles for entry, triggering both old and new rivalries.[14] At a minimum, the EU needs to think through these issues before it goes ahead with a multi-speed construction, only to find that an inner circle, far from serving as the engine behind deeper integration, begins to delineate new fault lines across Europe.

Unlike in the past, Europe's wealthier states will no longer bear the cost of ensuring that the EU's poorer members stay on track. The EU has thus far been able to deepen and widen simultaneously in large part because less developed countries have been kept happy through side payments. The pie for aid is shrinking, however, even as claims on it promise to balloon. Germany, for one, is unlikely to continue covering almost one-third of the EU budget. The cost of integrating eastern Germany has been enormous. High wages are forcing major German firms to move production outside the country. And daunting demographic figures loom on the horizon. By 2020, there will be one German pensioner for every German worker.[15] Come the next century, Germany will not be expending resources to ensure that its neighbours join a European currency union. Despite all the talk of concentric circles and widening cores, monetary union between France and Germany may well leave much of Europe's poorer periphery just where it is.

CFSP ADRIFT

Political integration has lagged considerably behind progress on the economic front, ensuring that the Maastricht agenda will be more a mantra than a map. The EU has gone far in nurturing a European identity that sits comfortably alongside national identities. But Europeans are not, and may never be, ready to move from a fundamentally intergovernmental union to one that smacks of federalism. The hallmark of a federal system is the existence of a legitimate, representative arena of politics that operates above individual state units. The European Parliament, however, is still without real legislative authority and remains a forum for speech making, not decision making. The European Commission continues to churn out proposals for increased political integration, but most have to be approved at the national level. Even as borders become more porous, powerful cultural and linguistic dividing lines continue to fortify the national state. Opinion polls reveal that publics are at best ambivalent about further encroachments on national sovereignty, with support for a single currency hovering at about 50 per cent.[16]

The Maastricht Treaty envisioned a common foreign and security policy, but the outlook on this front is bleak as well. The Western European Union (WEU), the Europe-only defence organisation that has effectively lain dormant since its inception in 1948, is to develop the capability to operate independently of NATO and intends ultimately to extend collective defence guarantees to states that have recently joined the EU or intend to do so in the future. But if West European countries could not more fully integrate their foreign policies during the Cold War, why should they be able to do so now?

Absent a unifying Soviet threat, the security interests of individual states are drifting apart, not coming together. Germany is far more concerned about developments in Central Europe than is Spain, Portugal, or France, countries that at least for now are preoccupied with North Africa. The failure of the EU and NATO to take more effective and timely steps to stop the slaughter in Bosnia made clear that Europe's security is now divisible. Which EU members, for example, would today defend the Finnish border against a Russian attack, a task to which all should be committed in principle since Finland entered the EU in 1995?

The EU's notable lack of progress in forging a common foreign and defence policy stems from two main sources. First, the union continues to strive for a consensus among all its members, ensuring that it gravitates toward the lowest common denominator. Waiting for a union-wide foreign policy to emerge is a recipe for paralysis. Not until the EU is ready to act via ad hoc coalitions of the willing can it succeed in taking on more defence responsibilities. In practice, this approach means relying more heavily on the Franco-German coalition to orchestrate collective action, enlisting the participation of other EU members on a case-by-case basis.

Second, France and Germany share less common ground on defence matters than they do on matters of economic integration. Part of the problem is the weight of history and Germany's continuing reluctance to participate fully in multilateral military operations. But French and German leaders also hold incompatible conceptions of the ultimate objectives and character of the union. For Germany, Europe is a construct for binding, moderating, and managing power – in short, for ensuring that the continent never again falls prey to the destructive forces of national rivalry. This perspective is not just a reaction against World War II. It has deep roots in the Holy Roman Empire, which aimed to dampen ambition and diffuse power in Europe. For France, the EU is more about amassing and projecting power, aggregating the union's military and economic resources so that it can assert itself as a global actor. The EU is to do for Europe what the national state is no longer strong enough to do for France. This perspective too has deep historical roots that trace back to Napoleonic and Jacobin conceptions of France's destiny as a great power.

Melding these competing visions of Europe will be no easy task. Germans will need to become more comfortable with leading a Europe that is more engaged and active in global affairs. The French will need to adapt their conceptions of what constitutes a more assertive Europe, choosing to apply their efforts to facilitate Europe's equal participation in broad multilateral undertakings instead of pursuing an independent course under the illusion that doing so constitutes leadership. Unless they arrive at a common conception of the broad objectives of integration, Germany and France together will be unable to provide the guidance needed to forge a coherent European defence policy.

The Labour Party's recent victory in Britain raises the novel possibility that London might be able to help Paris and Bonn forge a compromise vision. Tony Blair shows signs of trying to push Britain toward much deeper engagement in the EU. The first trip of Blair's Foreign Minister, Robin Cook, was to Paris and Bonn, not Brussels or Washington. It is at least conceivable that Britain will not just cease being Europe's caboose, but that it will become one of the EU's engines. The British share Germany's perception of the EU as an instrument for binding and managing power, but also share France's appreciation of the importance of projecting influence beyond Europe. Britain could also help define a middle road between Germany's desire to sacrifice national sovereignty for a deeper union and France's Gaullist insistence on preserving a strong national state. It would indeed be a strange twist of fate should Britain become part of Europe's core and provide a vision of the EU that ultimately carries the day.

DEEPENING VS WIDENING

The EU's plans for simultaneous widening make these numerous obstacles to deepening only more formidable. Integrating the economies of the new democracies into the EU would bloat the organisation's budget and pit Central and Southern Europe against each other in a competition for regional development funds. Because of Central Europe's sizeable farming sector and the Common Agricultural Policy's price supports and export subsidies, the eastward enlargement would burden the EU with enormous outlays. Swelling the EU to twice its present membership would, by complicating decision making, put an end to Maastricht's already unrealistic political agenda. A common foreign and security policy that would reconcile the interests of some 30 states, for example, would be out of the question.

By overreaching, the EU opens itself up to two missteps of geopolitical consequence. First, in light of the trade-offs between deepening and widening, the EU's pursuit of a federal Europe comes at the expense of its eastward enlargement. The tighter the internal structures, the higher the hurdles for entry. The more energy and resources expended in deepening, the less left over for widening. Enlargement will require reform of the EU's cumbersome decision-making procedures, expensive agricultural subsidies, and regional development program. But to delay the inclusion of the new democracies into Europe's markets and councils while the EU pursues illusory aspirations of federalism is to miss a historic opportunity to widen the continent's zone of democracy and peace. Though less urgent, the westward enlargement of the single market to North America is equally important as a bulwark against Europe's drift from the global economy.

Second, the EU's excessive ambition could jeopardise the progress that Western Europe has already made in building an integrated union of democracies at peace. The vision only dreamed of by the original architects of European integration is now a reality. Trying to do more at this juncture risks overburdening institutions and triggering a backlash among nation states bristling at what electorates will view as unjustified and unwanted infringements on national sovereignty. If it continues to cling to a vision its Member States will summarily reject, the union will suffer irreparable damage. The EU should consolidate its achievements rather than gamble for more and risk Europe's undoing in the process.

Too Much NATO

Current plans for the enlargement of NATO are equally problematic. Despite the NATO-Russia Founding Act and the establishment of a consultative council open to Moscow, NATO is a traditional military alliance whose purpose is to concentrate power against an external threat; its enlargement will continue to alienate Russia. It will also leave in strategic limbo those states left between Russia and NATO's new eastern border. Expanding NATO in its current guise thus promises to resurrect, not eliminate, rivalry between Europe's east and west. Enlargement will also erode the alliance from within as current members balk at assuming new responsibilities. The days of expansive strategic interests are no longer; faced with shrinking threats, status quo powers are becoming less willing to take on defence commitments. As for ensuring American engagement in Europe, NATO enlargement promises to do just the opposite. If institutions evolve as planned, economic and security matters will still be addressed in separate bodies, leaving NATO as America's primary institutional link to Europe. But defence policy no longer enjoys a position of primacy among either electorates or their leaders, making NATO in virtually any form a weak foundation for bridging the Atlantic.

NATO must take the lead in consolidating a democratic peace in Central Europe and incorporating the region into a meaningful security structure. But these tasks need not and should not entail its eastward expansion as a Cold War military alliance. It is the formal extension of the mutual defence provisions of Article V of the 1949 North Atlantic Treaty that would irk Russia and relegate those Central European states not admitted to a grey zone of uncertainty. So too is it the formality and cost of treaty-based territorial guarantees that make NATO enlargement problematic from the perspective of America's domestic politics.

The risks of enlarging NATO as a traditional military alliance might be justified were a major external threat to Central European states to arise. But Russia is neither interested in nor capable of mounting such a threat. Moscow does not protest NATO's increasing engagement in Europe's east. Russia has joined the Partnership for Peace, watched passively as NATO troops conducted exercises with local forces in Poland and the Czech Republic, sent its own troops to the United States to train with US forces, and agreed in all but name to put under NATO command its soldiers enforcing the Dayton accord in Bosnia. What Russia objects to – justifiably – is the formal enlargement of a military bloc from which it would be excluded.

Similarly, electorates in NATO countries, if they care at all, are happy to see their militaries collaborate with former adversaries. But when successive waves of NATO enlargement require Senate approval, and the associated costs and responsibilities become apparent, the electorate will be neither apathetic nor acquiescent. Party discipline should ensure approval of the first wave of new entrants – Poland, Hungary, and the Czech Republic.[17] But it is hard to imagine that voters will continue to respond favourably as NATO embarks on second and third waves of expansion, asking electorates to extend iron-clad defence guarantees to a host of countries most could not locate on a map. Not just prospective entrants would suffer a setback were NATO legislatures to reject enlargement. If it stakes its future on moving east, only to have its plans shot down by the public, NATO would be dealt a crippling blow.

An Atlantic Union

America belongs in Europe, and Central Europe belongs in the West. But if Western leaders are to achieve these aims, they must scale back their aspirations and focus on consolidating what already exists – a peaceful, integrated community of democratic nation states. The challenge is to find a balance between an institutional structure that demands too much and falls prey to overextension and one that delivers too little and atrophies from irrelevance. In addition, strategic matters must no longer be divorced from economic considerations. National security concerns will not remain sufficiently salient to serve as the West's binding glue. The Western democracies ultimately will hang together only if their citizens sense that they occupy a unique political community and have vested interests in seeing that community preserved. Economic and political arguments will have to carry at least part of the weight once borne by strategic concerns.

An Atlantic Union that would incorporate the EU, WEU, and NATO fulfils these criteria.[18] The initial members of the AU would be the current members of these three organisations. The AU would then expand at a steady pace not just to Central Europe, but also to Russia and the other states of the former Soviet Union. The infrastructure of the EU and NATO would serve as a ready foundation for the new body. States joining the AU would take on three basic commitments: to introduce a single market, to uphold collective security, and to expand political engagement at the transnational level.

Calls for the negotiation of a free trade area encompassing North America and Western Europe have already surfaced on both sides of the Atlantic. Part of the impetus comes from economic prospects; the removal of today's barriers would, by 2000, increase transatlantic trade by at least 20 per cent.[19] The introduction of a single market would likely be accompanied by an investment protocol and more convergence on regulations and standards, increasing the flow of capital and prompting industrial restructuring in Europe and North America.[20] It would also help prevent both areas from drifting toward protectionism and emerging as regional trade blocs. Instead, the United States would serve as the pivot of an integrated global economy, connecting a transatlantic free trade zone with one encompassing the Pacific Rim.

The most potent appeal of the Atlantic Union's single market is, however, its political significance. The conclusion of the Uruguay Round of trade negotiations reduced trade barriers in most sectors to minimum levels. And the EU and the United States agreed at their summit in Madrid in 1995 to pursue a host of follow-up measures. The elimination of remaining impediments would threaten powerful sectors such as agriculture and textiles, and thus would call for heavy lifting. But just as the introduction of a single market in Europe made borders more porous, facilitated political integration, and promoted a sense of common identity, so would the creation of a single Atlantic market strengthen the underpinnings of the community of North American and European democracies. Winning congressional approval of a transatlantic free trade zone would not be easy, but a high-profile debate connecting America's prosperity with Europe's fate would drive home to Americans that they share a unique political space with Europeans.

Building an Atlantic community of strong national states that are closely integrated economically is a far more realistic enterprise than constructing a federal Europe that sublimates the nation state and that omits North America from its central project. Returning to some elements of the EU's current agenda for deepening may prove expedient down the road. A single Atlantic currency, for example, is not unimaginable. But first steps first. Deepening makes sense only when it will not come at the expense of the far more vital enterprise of consolidating and enlarging a stable, prosperous union of Atlantic democracies.

The Atlantic Union's commitments to collective security would be looser and less automatic than NATO's current commitments to collective defence, removing the key stumbling block to a broader Western security community.[21] The AU would replace

NATO's Article V guarantee and its emphasis on territorial defence with a focus on peacekeeping and peace enforcement; confronting external threats as well as those that might arise from within, it would coordinate multilateral operations across Europe. Members would affirm their intention to solve conflicts peacefully whenever possible and, when necessary, to use military force to defend against common threats. Case-by-case decision making and a broad mandate to preserve peace in the Atlantic area would be the organising principles of a new US-European security bargain and a revamped NATO. The elimination of NATO's Article V guarantee would weaken the alliance's deterrent power. But as long as Russia continues to pose no threat to Central or Western Europe, compromising deterrence and holding out to Russia and its immediate neighbours a realistic prospect of inclusion in the West makes good strategic sense.

Scaling back NATO's mission and relaxing the commitments its members are expected to uphold is both a logical necessity in the absence of an enemy and a manoeuvre that would circumvent many of the problems plaguing current plans for NATO's enlargement. Under the guise of the AU, a transformed NATO could soon open its doors to all the new democracies of Central Europe without appearing anti-Russian. Defence concerns would recede into the background; joining the AU would be joining a civic community, not a military alliance. Collective security commitments would provide the Central Europeans some, but not all, of the assurance they seek. American troops would stay in Europe. NATO's existing infrastructure would remain intact. Militaries in the new democracies would continue the planning and exercising already begun through the Partnership for Peace, furthering their integration into the Western security community and their ability to operate with the forces of current NATO members. But this steady integration would occur quietly, avoiding the fanfare and political histrionics that would make the admission of new members to today's NATO so problematic.

To be sure, these new arrangements would involve sleight of hand. Central Europe, via AU membership, would secure a place under the West's protective umbrella. But couching new commitments in a broader political context and making them more contingent on strategic circumstance and less formal would render Central Europe's early inclusion in the West far more palatable to Russia as well as to electorates in NATO countries. Central European states would get to join the club, even if that club proves to be less exclusive and selective than the new entrants would like.

Doing away with Article V commitments also permits a broader definition of Europe's boundaries. Because NATO is still a formal military alliance, only countries deemed of sufficient strategic value to warrant their defence will ultimately be eligible for membership. Some proponents of NATO expansion have already begun to argue that enlargement should go no further than Poland, Hungary and the Czech Republic, the countries that occupy the main corridor between Russia and Western Europe. But this plan leaves most of Central Europe out in the cold.

In contrast, states would join the AU as they demonstrate a commitment to democracy, markets, and international norms of behaviour, offering the prospect of inclusion to all of Central Europe as well as the former Soviet Union. A pan-European collective security system could become a reality, not just rhetoric to placate Russia as

Poland enters a NATO everyone knows will never go farther east. At the same time, should Russian democracy falter, the AU's military infrastructure could serve as the foundation for a new, enlarged anti-Russian alliance.

Finally, merging NATO with the EU and WEU avoids a looming crisis over the responsibilities of these institutions. The three already have incongruent memberships that will grow only more inconsistent should they independently pursue their respective plans for enlargement. If, as in the most likely scenario, the EU and the WEU incorporate ten or more Central European countries while NATO stops after accepting only three or four, the United States and its main European partners would no longer share parallel strategic commitments on the continent. The AU, on the other hand, would keep American and European commitments in step, preserving the sense of common purpose that undergirds the Atlantic community.

Regardless of how far east the AU ultimately reaches, its major powers should form a directorate to prevent the sequential entry of new members from making the body unwieldy. A small, flexible forum in which the major powers could forge a consensus, this directorate would guide the AU on both military and economic matters. The absence of a formal mechanism for great power leadership has prevented the Organisation for Security and Cooperation in Europe from fulfilling its potential. Moreover, an informal concert of major states already calls the shots on the continent. The Contact Group formed to seek a settlement in Bosnia consisted of the United States, Germany, France, Britain, and Russia. In practice, both NATO and the EU function through the fashioning of agreement among their leading members. A major power directorate at the core of the AU would only formalise present realities, while making possible effective decision making and timely collective action.

GALVANISING DOMESTIC POLITIES

The final pillar of an Atlantic Union is deepened civic engagement on the transnational level.[22] Civic society among nation states emerges from political participation and community association, just as it does within nation states. If the Atlantic community is to survive and prosper, its citizens must share a sense of belonging not only to their nation states, but also to a transnational political space that the Western democracies inhabit. The legitimacy that the institutions of the EU enjoy in its Member States, for instance, is not just a function of the services they provide. It is also a reflection of the degree to which Europe has come to compete with the nation state as a defining element of individual identity and allegiance.

The Cold War bequeathed to the West a rich network of public institutions and associations as well as private enterprises and groups that transcend national boundaries. Thickening this network so that it becomes the enduring social and political fabric of an Atlantic Union entails several tasks. The European Parliament should be enlarged into an Atlantic Parliament and charged with providing legislative oversight of the AU. National parliaments would retain the lion's share of legislative authority, but handing over a substantive portfolio of responsibilities to an Atlantic Parliament would nurture a Western political identity that complements national loyalties, thereby legitimating a transatlantic polity. The Atlantic Parliament's duties would include designing the AU's budget, aligning American and European social policies, and developing union-wide laws and regulations.

Public and private groups should ensure the flowering of the many forms of transatlantic association – business contacts, religious and cultural activities, social causes, and leisure activities. These associations will intensify citizens' engagement in and identification with a transatlantic polity. Educational and vocational exchanges and scientific and industrial collaboration should also be promoted. Finally, Western governments should launch ambitious education campaigns to inform their electorates of the importance of public engagement in preserving and widening the transatlantic community. The West is unravelling in part because it lacks the defining images and projects that galvanise domestic polities. Constructing an Atlantic Union of democracies will not call up the same sense of collective commitment and sacrifice as the struggle against communism. Yet it need not. Bold leadership in laying out a vision of a peaceful, prosperous union of Atlantic democracies and proceeding with the necessary institutional innovations will suffice to wean citizens away from domestic preoccupations and inspire them to construct a new West.

EUROPE, AMERICA, AND THE GLOBAL ORDER

Constructing an Atlantic Union is not just a prudent move aimed at making permanent the historic transformation of the Atlantic area from a zone of war into a zone of peace. It would also lay the groundwork for a more integrated and cooperative global order. To make the renovation of the West a top priority of US foreign policy is not to demote other regions or indicate that the Western democracies must prepare to do battle against them. On the contrary, locking in peaceful relations among the Atlantic democracies will free the Western powers to address challenges elsewhere. A strong Atlantic coalition will also increase the West's leverage in other regions. As they work to build an Atlantic Union, the United States and EU members should explicitly seek to augment cooperation with powers outside the Atlantic area and help promote stability in those areas. Although its results were less substantive than symbolic, the EU-Asia summit in Bangkok in 1996 was an important step in the right direction.

While strengthening its ties to other regions, the AU should also foster regional integration elsewhere. Linked by global trade and coordination among the great powers, regional unions along the AU model in Asia and Africa could eventually consolidate new zones of peace and provide the foundation for a more stable international order. The main reason for not inviting Japan, one of Asia's most democratic and prosperous nations, to join the AU is that a focus on the Atlantic community would distract Japan from facilitating further integration in its own neighbourhood. The AU is thus the first step toward the creation of a global concert of democratic great powers that would coordinate relations among and within regional organisations.

The AU would also serve as the driving force behind the liberalisation of global trade. Through successive accessions to NAFTA, a transatlantic free trade zone would gradually extend throughout Central and South America. Because the EU is already looking south as well as east, an Atlantic single market might eventually include the Middle East and North Africa. Fearful of being excluded from the AU's widening trade zone, other areas would face pressure to open their own markets in return for access. The geoeconomic move toward globalisation would balance the geopolitical move toward regionalisation.

Constructing an Atlantic Union is a conservative enterprise. Plans that call for further sacrifices and increased responsibilities, like monetary union and NATO expansion, have little public appeal in this era of waning internationalism. A more modest set of objectives is needed to fashion a new consensus. Rather than deepen institutions, the AU would merely extend their reach, reasonably asking electorates on both sides of the Atlantic to form a single market, uphold collective security, and send representatives to a common parliament. By solidifying a transatlantic community at peace, an Atlantic Union would do much more for the West and the rest of the world than monetary union among Germany, France, and Luxembourg or tank traps on the Poland-Belarus border. If the AU successfully consolidates democratic peace, what appears mundane today will, in the longer course of history, prove revolutionary.

NOTES

[1] This essay draws on analysis presented in two previous articles. See my 'Reviving the West,' *Foreign Affairs*, vol. 75, no. 3 (May/June 1996); and 'Reconstructing the West: The Case for an Atlantic Union,' in Charles Kupchan, ed., *Atlantic Security: Contending Visions* (New York: Council on Foreign Relations, 1998).

[2] EU officials argue that Europe's internal construction must be settled before it proceeds with taking in new members. See, for example, 'Reinforcing Political Union and Preparing for Enlargement,' *Official Commission Opinion* (February 28, 1996), prepared for the Intergovernmental Conference in Turin. I accept that some institutional change – in particular reform of voting rules and of agricultural and regional assistance policies – is needed to pave the way for enlargement. But, for reasons outlined below, I challenge the general proposition that deepening needs to precede or even accompany widening.

[3] See Daniel Deudney and G. John Ikenberry, 'The Logic of the West,' *World Policy Journal* (Winter 1993/94): 17-25.

[4] For discussion of this earlier debate between Asia-firsters and Europe-firsters, see Jack Snyder, *Myths of Empire* (Ithaca: Cornell University Press, 1991).

[5] East Asia's savings and investment rates are roughly 50 per cent higher than Europe's and, despite its recent economic troubles, its growth rate is expected to be more than twice that of Europe.

[6] Samuel Huntington, 'The Clash of Civilizations?' *Foreign Affairs* 72:4 (Summer 1993): 22-49.

[7] Robert Kaplan, 'The Coming Anarchy,' *Atlantic Monthly* 243:2 (February 1994): 44-76; Matthew Connelly and Paul Kennedy, 'Must It Be the Rest Against the West?' *Atlantic Monthly* 244:6 (December 1994): 76.

[8] For evidence that ideological factors are weak determinants of alliance formation, see Stephen Walt, *The Origins of Alliances* (Ithaca: Cornell University Press, 1987).

[9] In France, for example, a referendum held in September, 1992 approved the Maastricht Treaty by 51.05 per cent to 48.95 per cent. In Denmark, a referendum rejected the treaty in June 1992. In a second vote in May 1993, Danes approved the treaty by 56.8 per cent to 43.2 per cent.

[10] For an excellent discussion of European and American industrial structures and patterns of innovation, see David Soskice, 'Openness and Diversity: Thinking about Transatlantic Commercial Relations,' in *Transatlantic Economic Relations in the Post-Cold War Era*, ed. Barry Eichengreen (New York: Council on Foreign Relations, 1998).

[11] For a more detailed exposition of the dual character of contemporary power centers, the notion of self-binding, and the application of these ideas to the EU, NAFTA, and APEC, see Charles Kupchan, 'Regionalism and the Rise of Consensual Empire,' unpublished manuscript (New York: Council on Foreign Relations, 1996).

[12] See Erik Jones, 'Economic and Monetary Union: Playing with Money,' in *The Prospects for European Union: Deepening, Diversity and Democracy*, ed. Andy Moravcsik, (New York: Council on Foreign Relations, 1998); and Lloyd Gruber, 'Power Politics and the Transformation of European Monetary Relations,' presented at the annual meeting of the American Political Science Association, San Francisco, August 1996.

[13] *De jure* equality, by promoting a sense of collectivity, may enable members to be concerned more with the well-being of the EU as whole than with their own welfare. *De jure* differentiation, by eroding a sense of the collective, increases the likelihood that members will be more concerned about individual gain.

[14] Efforts to gain early entry into NATO have already triggered jockeying among the new democracies of Central Europe. Rather than cooperating with each other on security matters, states in the region have focused almost exclusively on attaining NATO membership, showing little concern for the strategic and political implications of their admission for neighboring countries.

[15] Martin Walker, 'Overstretching Teutonia,' *World Policy Journal* 12:1 (Spring 1995).

[16] *The Sunday Times,* January 16, 1996.

[17] Opinion polls show that some 62 per cent of the American public favours admitting 'some Eastern European countries such as Poland, Hungary, and the Czech Republic.' This figure drops to roughly 45 per cent when respondents are made aware of the costs and responsibilities associated with enlargement. See 'Americans on Expanding NATO,' Program on International Policy Attitudes, School of Public Affairs, University of Maryland, Steven Kull, Principal Investigator, October 1, 1996.

[18] On the general notion of establishing a union of Atlantic democracies, Deutsch, *Political Community and the North Atlantic Area*; and Clarence Streit, *Union Now: A Proposal for a Federal Union of the Democracies of the North Atlantic*, 8th ed. (New York: Harper, 1939).

[19] Clyde V. Prestowitz, Jr., Lawrence Chimerine, and Andrew Szamosszegi, 'The Case for a Transatlantic Free Trade Zone,' in *Open for Business: Creating a Transatlantic Marketplace* ed. Bruce Stokes (New York: Council on Foreign Relations Press, 1996): 22.

[20] I am not suggesting that an Atlantic single market should aspire toward the same degree of standardisation as a European single market, nor that the EU should relax its rules on standardisation in order to attain a better fit with the North American market. Rather, both sides should strive for as much convergence as possible, while recognising that incompatibilities will remain in certain sectors – such as electrical plugs and voltage.

[21] For discussion of the difference between collective security and collective defence see Arnold Wolfers, 'Collective Defence versus Collective Security,' in *Discord and Collaboration, ed.* Arnold Wolfers (Baltimore: Johns Hopkins University Press, 1962); and Inis Claude, *Power and International Relations* (New York: Random House, 1962). For different interpretations of the nature of commitments to joint action under collective security, see John Mearsheimer, 'The False Promise of International Institutions,' and Charles Kupchan and Clifford Kupchan, 'The Promise of Collective Security,' *International Security* 20:1 (Summer 1995): 52-61.

[22] For discussion of civic engagement within and among the members of the Atlantic community, see Josef Janning, Charles Kupchan, and Dirk Rumberg, eds., *Civic Engagement in the Atlantic Community* (New York: Council on Foreign Relations Press, forthcoming, 1998).

List of Contributors

Esther Barbé
Professor of International Relations, Universitat Autonoma in Barcelona

Jean-Marie Guéhenno
Chief of the International Service, Cour des Comptes, Paris

Christopher Hill
Montague Burton Professor of International Relations, London School of Economics and Political Science

Knud Erik Jørgenson
Associate Professor of Political Science, Aarhus University

Charles A. Kupchan
Senior Fellow, Council on Foreign Relations and Associate Professor, Georgetown University

Guido Lenzi
Director of the Institute for Security Studies, Western European Union, Paris

Yves Mény
Professor of Social and Political Science and Director of the Robert Schuman Centre, European University Institute, Florence

Richard Rosecrance
Professor of Political Science and Director of the Center for International Relations, University of California, Los Angeles

Reinhardt Rummel
Senior Research Fellow, Stiftung Wissenschaft und Politik, Ebenhausen

Karen Elizabeth Smith
Lecturer in International Relations, London School of Economics and Political Science

Jörg Wiedemann
Research Fellow, Stiftung Wissenschaft und Politik, Ebenhausen

Jan Zielonka
Professor of Social and Political Science, European University Institute, Florence

Index

acquis communautaire 136
acquis politique 37, 94
Afghanistan 84
Agenda 2000 38, 50, 133, 136, 140, 144
aid, humanitarian and development 3, 8, 72, 73, 74, 76, 83, 120, 123, 133-4, 144
Albania 44, 79, 85, 86, 134
Algeria 37, 76, 121, 125
Amsterdam Treaty 67, 70, 75, 78, 81
Arab-Israeli issue 42
Arab-Maghreb Union 125
arms embargoes 74, 84
Asia 148-9, 162
Asia-Pacific Economic Cooperation (APEC) 151
Asolo list 28
association agreements 69, 73, 76, 81, 83, 117, 133, 138, 139
Atlantic Union 9-10, 11, 148, 157-62
  commitments 158-9
  deepened civic engagement 10, 160-1
  and the global order 161-2
  initial members 158
  military component, downgrading of 9-10, 148, 158-9
  and regional integration 161
Austria 37, 48, 58, 138

Balance of Power concept 3, 16-19, 20, 26, 39
Belgium 47
bloc to bloc relations 38
Bosnia 37, 44, 46, 71, 143, 149, 154, 157
Brazil 19, 47
Britain 15, 18-19, 28, 37, 44, 47, 48, 57, 59, 75, 83, 95, 114, 123, 136, 155
Bulgaria 76, 140, 144
Burma 82, 83

Canada 44, 64
Chechnya 77, 134-5
China 16, 19, 20, 21, 22, 76, 82, 84, 85, 149
civilian power 6, 10, 67, 78-80, 93
Cold War 74, 106, 113, 141, 160

Combined Joint Task Forces (CJTF) 44, 59, 65, 75, 109
Common Agricultural Policy 140, 156
Common Commercial Policy (CCP) 38, 72
common European interests 28, 30, 32
Common Foreign and Security Policy (CFSP) 32, 35, 40, 42, 46-7, 53, 107, 108, 139, 140-1
  agenda 54, 57, 60, 64, 89, 124
  ambiguity and vagueness 1, 9, 15, 135-7
  balancing strategy 61-2, 124
  consistency problem 6, 15, 54-5, 60, 63, 68, 141
  decision-making process 10, 55, 56-7, 59, 63, 141
  degrees of cooperation with 36-7
  development strategy 30, 32
  EU institutions' evaluation of 88-9
  failure to develop 15, 154-5
  funding 56, 60, 68, 81
  institutional paradoxes 53-64
  instruments *see* foreign policy instruments
  inter-organisational links 57-60
  limited authority of foreign ministers 55
  link with outside instruments 53
  no direct say in UNSC decisions 59
  operational costs 56, 60
  passivity, periods of 40, 60
  potential sphere of activity 54
  reactive policy 56, 57
  solidarism/fragmentation dialectic 4, 5, 46-8, 60, 62-3, 64
  unanimity requirement 59, 60, 62, 63
  unique foreign policy strengths 15
  voting principles 62, 63, 81, 83
common positions and joint actions 5, 40, 55, 59, 60, 62, 63, 68-9, 70, 71, 81
Commonwealth of Independent States 21
competences, division of 55, 60, 65, 68, 70, 75, 80, 140
conditionality 6, 20, 73, 77, 84, 134
Conference on Security and Cooperation in Europe (CSCE) 70

168 Index

Conference on Security and Cooperation in the Mediterranean (CSCM) 120-1
'consistency problem' 6, 15, 54-5, 60, 63, 68, 141
convergence 37, 41, 42, 49
  criteria 136
  paths to 38-9
  of values 39
COREPER (Committee of Permanent Representatives) 56-7
Council of Ministers 48, 56-7, 61
Croatia 8, 15, 42, 71, 118, 132
Cuba 76, 77-8
Cyprus 37, 39, 71, 122
Czech Republic 41, 144, 157, 159

debt relief 72
declarations/statements 70, 71, 76, 82, 125
d,marches 70, 76, 82
democracy and foreign policy 32-4, 48, 142
Denmark 37, 48, 74, 109, 123, 162
development policy 64-5
diplomacy 6, 26, 27, 48, 68, 69-72
  coercive diplomacy 76-8, 80, 89
  declaratory diplomacy 88
  exchange of diplomats 40
  preventive diplomacy 72
diplomatic recognition 8, 42, 71, 118

East Timor 76, 77
Eastern Europe 8-9, 71, 131-42
  cooperation and partnership agreements 133, 143
  EU aid 8, 72, 73, 120, 123, 133-4, 138, 140, 144
  EU institutional involvement 8, 134
  EU lack of identifiable strategy 131, 132
  EU positive historical record 131, 132-5
  EU reactive policies 9, 142
  influence of EU parochial agenda 137-9
  relations with EU 119, 126-7
  Stability Pact 16, 72, 117, 121, 124, 134
  trade deficit 138, 145
  US influence 131-2
  see also enlargement
economic instruments 6, 68, 72-4
Economic and Monetary Union (EMU) 15-16, 22, 41, 103, 147, 152-4
  admission criteria 22
  disadvantages 9, 153
  political dimensions 31-2, 153
economic unity, external effects of 3, 18
election observers 72, 81, 124
encompassing coalition in world politics 21
enlargement 17, 38, 61-2, 71, 106, 147, 151, 155-6, 162
  admission criteria 3, 134, 135-6

cultural criteria 136
  Eastern Europe 3, 122, 123, 134, 136, 156
  economic aims and criteria 135-6, 137, 138
  macroeconomic criteria 136
  Mediterranean countries 122
  pre-accession strategy 81, 133, 136, 144
  and security policy 12, 111-13
  time frame 136-7
envoys 71, 82, 124
Estonia 106, 138, 144
Euro 16, 137-8, 152
Euro-Mediterranean Partnership 122, 123, 124, 125, 126, 127
euronationalism 34
European Economic Area (EEA) 61
European Parliament 33, 48, 56, 89, 154, 160
European Political Cooperation (EPC) 1, 35, 40, 41, 42, 47, 56, 57, 60, 70, 71-2, 81, 88, 90, 91, 118, 124
European polity 3, 4, 25, 28-9, 30, 31, 32, 33
European Union
  ambiguity of aims and functions 1, 9, 12, 132, 135-7, 141-2, 144
  borders 28-9
  budget 56, 73, 82, 140, 144
  competences 55, 60, 65, 68, 69, 70, 75, 80, 140
  contradictions and paradoxes 11-12
  deepening of the Union 12, 53-4, 155-6, 158
  economic power factors 2-3, 18
  economic problems 15-16
  enlargement *see* enlargement
  federalist agenda 9, 12, 142, 147, 151, 154, 156
  institutional change, need for 40-1, 106, 162
  institutional stagnation 54, 139-41
  intergovernmentalism 12, 41, 60, 141, 142, 154
  intervention capability 79
  lack of legal personality 53, 57, 63, 65, 69
  lack of a military capability 11, 57, 58-9, 74, 79
  normative power of attraction 11, 12, 16, 18, 22
  Ostpolitik 9, 138, 141, 142
  passivity 40, 90, 99
  performance in world politics, measuring 6-7, 87-99
  rewards and incentives, reliance on 3, 6, 19-20, 21-2, 71, 73, 76, 78
  Southern and Eastern dimension, balancing 8, 119-20, 122, 123, 126, 127, 156
  strategic and operational deficit 9, 11, 12, 141-2
  three-pillar institutional structure 5, 6, 55, 80
export credits 72, 82

federalism 9, 12, 142, 147, 151, 154, 156
Finland 37, 48, 58, 154
fishing rights 62, 64, 66
foreign policy
   ad hoc coordination 41, 44, 154-5
   common European interests 28, 30, 32
   convergence and divergence 35-9, 40, 42, 43
   democratic consensus and 32-4, 48, 142
   instruments of 6, 67-86
   multi-level and multi-actor system 4-5, 43-6, 48-9
   multilateralism 4, 37, 50
   multiple realities in European foreign affairs 7, 96-7, 98-9
   national interests and 2, 4, 5, 12, 26, 27, 28, 61-2
   nature of 2-6
   policy coordination 117-18
   policy-making process 4-5, 43-6, 56-7
   renationalisation 8, 36, 118-19
   see also Common Foreign and Security Policy (CFSP)
foreign policy instruments 67-86
   diplomacy 6, 26, 48, 68, 69-72, 71
   economic 6, 68, 72-4
   employment of 75-8
   military 6, 67-8, 74-5, 79
   propaganda 68, 69
France 8, 15, 28, 31, 37, 42, 43, 44, 47, 48, 57, 59, 62, 63, 64, 95, 114, 120, 121, 122, 123, 125, 126, 138, 152-3, 154, 155, 162
Franco-German coalition 152-3, 155
free trade zones 158, 161-2

General Agreement on Tariffs and Trade (GATT) 16, 38, 69, 133
Germany 8, 15, 18, 19, 28, 31, 36, 37, 41, 42, 47, 48, 62, 64, 71, 95, 106, 118, 119, 122, 123, 139, 149, 152, 153-4, 155
   Franco-German coalition 152-3, 155
   unification 143, 153
globalisation 18, 28, 41, 103, 151, 161-2
graduated reduction of international tensions (GRIT) 19
Great Lakes crisis 44
Greece 8, 15, 37, 39, 42, 48, 71, 74, 77, 122, 140, 143, 154
Gulf War 58, 74, 84, 121

Haiti 55, 60, 74, 76, 83
Hoffmann, Stanley 35-6
Hungary 41, 119, 132, 133, 144, 157

India 19, 71
Indonesia 76, 77
institutional paradoxes 53-64
institutional stagnation 54, 139-41

integration 27, 28, 29, 31, 32, 41, 53, 91, 105, 151
   competing national agendas 12, 142
   deepening vs widening 138
   functional scope 12, 142
   nature of 12, 142
intergovernmental organisations (IGOs) 43, 49
intergovernmentalism 12, 41, 60, 141, 142, 154
international economic clubs 3, 20, 21
International Monetary Fund 21-2
Iran 19, 20, 47, 76, 77, 78, 85
Iraq 74
Ireland 37, 58, 74
Israel 38, 42, 47, 82
Italy 8, 20, 36, 37, 47, 48, 95, 118, 120, 121, 138

Japan 16, 19, 38, 149, 161

Kissinger, Henry 26-7

Libya 55, 74, 82, 121, 125
lobbying 33
Lom, conventions 69, 83
Luxembourg 48

Maastricht Treaty 2, 56, 67, 69, 70, 74, 80, 81, 109, 136, 151, 154, 162
Macedonia 37, 42, 71
Maghreb 8, 29, 119, 127, 136, 144-5
Malawi 74, 84
Malta 122
Mediterranean countries 48, 117, 119-27
   EU aid to 8, 120, 123
   EU-Mediterranean partnership instruments 121, 122-3, 124, 125
   Euro-Mediterranean interdependence 120, 125-6, 127
   'parallel program' 119, 121
   security concerns 8, 121, 127, 144-5
Middle East peace process 124
military action: commitment and efficiency criteria 58
military instruments 6, 67-8, 74-5, 79
military integration 65
monetary union 16, 147, 151
   see also Economic and Monetary Union
multi-level governance 4-5, 43-6, 48-9

nation state, reassertion as an international actor 35-6
national foreign ministries 91
national interests
   CFSP as an instrument for achieving 61-2
   changing perception of 27-8
   EU foreign policy and 2, 4, 5, 12, 26, 27, 28, 61-2

interest and identity 39
'permanence' of 26-7, 28
'realist' notion of interest 3-4, 25
NATO 3, 5, 16, 20, 43, 49, 55, 74, 78, 96, 104, 107, 108, 143, 149
 and an Atlantic Union 9-10, 148, 158-9, 160
 conformity with UNSC policy 59
 enlargement 9, 23, 43, 107, 112, 143, 144, 147-8, 156-7, 159, 163
 missile deployment (1980s) 89-90
 NATO/WEU task-sharing 44, 58, 75, 115
 peacekeeping and intervention capabilities 79, 85
 responsibilities beyond territorial defence 108-9, 157
 US assistance and political backing 58
neo-mediaevalism 39
Netherlands 36, 47, 48, 123
neutrality 47
Nigeria 74, 76, 82
non-governmental organisations (NGOs) 33, 43, 44, 46
'norm of reciprocity' 19-20
North American Free Trade Agreement (NAFTA) 18, 151, 161
North Atlantic Cooperation Council (NACC) 43
Norway 44, 62, 106

Organisation for Security and Cooperation in Europe (OSCE) 44, 49, 96, 107, 108, 114, 160
Ostpolitik 9, 138, 141, 142
overpopulation and poverty 150-1

Partnership for Peace (PfP) 43, 117, 157, 159
peace corps 33
performance, measuring
 comparisons with other actors 94-6
 domestic challenges 90-1
 dynamic perspective 96-8
 EU declared aims and objectives 6-7, 89
 EU 'inaction' 40, 90, 99
 policy disasters 89-90
 standards of measurement 88-90
 time perspectives 91-4
PHARE 8, 46, 117, 119, 121, 124, 133, 134, 144
Poland 41, 77, 106, 119, 132, 133, 144, 157, 159
political communities, emergence of 30-2
political dialogues 71, 73, 82
political unity, external effects of 3, 18
politics of scale 38
Portugal 37, 47, 77, 140, 154
propaganda instruments 68, 69
protectionism 138, 151, 152

qualified majority voting (QMV) 81, 83, 140

regional political dialogue 68, 71, 82
religious diversity 29, 30-1
renationalisation of foreign policy 8, 36, 118-19
Romania 73, 76, 138, 140, 144
Russia 19, 20, 21, 22, 44, 77, 112-13, 133, 134, 143, 144, 154, 160
 and an Atlantic Union 145, 158, 159, 160
 attitude to NATO enlargement 23, 112, 156, 157
 involvement in European security framework 112
 partnership, cooperation and trade agreements 77, 133, 134-5
Rwanda 55, 81, 84

sanctions 60-1, 68, 71, 73, 74, 76, 77, 78, 81, 82, 84, 89, 110
security policy 7-8, 103-14, 154-5
 collective defence 106, 163
 conflict management 104, 110
 constructive abstention 112
 cooperative security 109, 111, 112, 113
 democratic involvement 104, 113
 and the enlargement process 111-13
 functional interlinkage of institutions 107-11
 humanitarian intervention 104, 110
 military division of labour, dangers of 118
 multilateral formulas 104-5
 new modalities of cooperation 8, 106
 new security agenda 113-14
 non Art. 5 cooperative security contingencies 106
 proactiveness and ad hoc coalitions 108, 109, 111, 112, 114, 118, 154-5
 Russian involvement 112
 tactical role-sharing 106-7
 'the rest against the West' fallacy 150-1
Serbia 74, 84, 89, 115
single market 151, 158, 162, 163
Slovenia 8, 42, 71, 118, 132, 138, 144
solidarism/fragmentation dialectic 4, 38, 46-8, 62-3, 64
South Africa 37, 38, 40, 60, 73, 76, 84
sovereignty 31, 37, 41, 106, 118, 147, 151, 152, 154, 156
Soviet Union 17, 19, 73, 77
 see also Russia
Spain 8, 37, 42, 47, 48, 62, 64, 66, 95, 118-19, 120, 121, 122, 123, 124, 125, 126, 140, 154
Stability Pact 16, 72, 117, 121, 124, 134
stability in world politics, creating 19-22
Sudan 74, 76, 84
supranationalism 41
Sweden 37, 48, 58, 106, 118
Syria 76, 82

TACIS 46, 133, 134

technocratic elitism 49
territorial scope, defining 30
Third World 3, 18, 44
trade embargoes and concessions 73
Trans-Atlantic Free Trade Area (TAFTA) 16, 18, 22
transgovernmental alliances 48
Treaty of Amsterdam 1, 44, 55, 139, 140
Treaty of the European Community (TEC) 56, 61, 64
Treaty of the European Union (TEU) 56, 62, 63, 64, 89, 110, 111
Turkey 15, 29, 33, 77, 136, 143

UN Security Council (UNSC) 21, 44, 59, 107
unilateralism 42, 47
United Nations 5, 20, 21, 79, 96
United Nations Charter 107
United States 19, 22, 30, 31, 40, 41, 42, 47, 75
    American polity 31
    and an Atlantic Union 158
    Asia-first strategy 148-9
    attitude to European integration 16, 17
    bilateral dialogue with 71
    coercive actions 77-8
    engagement in Europe 9, 10-11, 38-9, 44, 112, 131-2, 143, 149, 156-7
    'European power' 29, 30, 96
    historic Balance of Power effects 16-17
    role of facilitator and coalition-builder 112
universalism 30, 31

veto power 141

Western European Union (WEU) 5, 9, 49, 55, 57, 59, 104, 107, 108, 109, 113, 114
    in an Atlantic Union 160
    conformity with UNSC policy 59
    defence component of EU 58, 65, 67, 74-5, 84, 113, 143
    EU-WEU interlinkage 37, 43-4, 58, 75, 78, 110-11, 112
    NATO/WEU task-sharing 44, 58, 75, 115
    operational capabilities 75, 78, 110, 115, 154
World Trade Organization (WTO) 3, 21, 133

Yugoslav crisis 25, 28, 55, 57, 58, 70, 71-2, 74, 78, 95, 104, 132, 133, 134, 137, 143, 154
former Yugoslavia 89, 133, 134, 137

Zaire 74, 79, 84